A Training Course for Certification in the Oil Heat Industry
for the Advancement of Improved Efficiency,
Including Safety, Reliability and Repair of
Oil Heating Equipment

ADVANCED OIL HEAT

A Guide to Improved Efficiency

PETROLEUM
MARKETERS
ASSOCIATION OF
AMERICA

KENDALL/HUNT PUBLISHING COMPANY
4050 Westmark Drive Dubuque, Iowa 52002

Copyright © 1995 by Petroleum Marketers Association of America

Library of Congress Catalog Card Number: 94-73510

ISBN 0-7872-0395-5

Printed in the United States of America

10 9 8 7 6 5 4 3 2 1

Table of Contents

Foreword		**v**
1	**Introduction to Heating System Efficiency**	**1-1**
1.0	Purpose of This Manual	1-1
1.1	Parts of Oil Heating Systems	1-2
1.2	Equipment Heat Losses and System Efficiency	1-14
1.3	Important Heating Unit, Chimney, and House Interactions	1-33
1.4	Advantages of New Oil Heat Equipment and the Key Role of Service Technicians	1-37
2	**Oil Burner Efficiency Advances**	**2-1**
2.0	Introduction	2-1
2.1	Oil Combustion—What All Service Technicians Must Know	2-2
2.2	Oil Burner Parts and Their Functions	2-11
2.3	Fuel Nozzles and Conversion of Fuel Oil into a Vapor	2-13
2.4	Burner Air Supply and Fuel-Air Mixing	2-24
2.5	Smoke Production by Oil Burners	2-33
2.6	Smoke Has Its Functions	2-35
2.7	Excess Air, Smoke, Efficiency and Burner Adjustment	2-36
2.8	Advantages of New Burner Designs	2-40
2.9	Oil Burner Interactions with Other Heating System Parts	2-47
3	**High-Efficiency Boilers and Furnaces**	**3-1**
3.1	Boiler and Furnace Operation and Heat Losses	3-1
3.2	Efficiency Ratings of Boilers and Furnaces	3-14
3.3	Low-Mass Boilers	3-22
3.4	Expected Fuel Savings with New Boilers and Furnaces	3-26
3.5	Important Steps to Follow when Replacing Boilers or Furnaces	3-32
3.6	Summary of Recommendations	3-35
4	**Chimneys and System Efficiency**	**4-1**
4.1	How Chimney Venting Works	4-1
4.2	How Chimneys Affect Efficiency	4-29
4.3	What Actions Can Improve Chimney Venting and Efficiency?	4-38
5	**Alternative Venting of Oil Heating Equipment**	**5-1**
5.1	Sealed and Insulated Venting Systems with High Static Air Pressure Oil Burners	5-2
5.2	Power Side-Wall Venting	5-10

5.3   Vent Dampers for Heating Equipment with High Off-Cycle
      Heat Loss   5-23
5.4   Powered Chimney Venting   5-29
5.5   Outdoor Boiler Installation   5-32

6   Efficient Domestic Hot Water   **6-1**
6.1   Review of Oil-Powered Water Heating Equipment   6-1
6.2   Heat Losses and Efficiency of Domestic Hot Water
      Generation   6-10
6.3   Energy Conservation Options   6-16

7   Adjustment of Oil Heating Equipment for Maximum Efficiency **7-1**
7.1   Combustion Efficiency Testing Procedures   7-2
7.2   Understanding Combustion Efficiency Test Results   7-8
7.3   Oil Burner Efficiency Guidelines, Installation, and
      Adjustment   7-18
7.4   Reduced Fuel Nozzle Size—Selection Procedure   7-27
7.5   Boiler Water Temperature Reduction   7-35
7.6   Pipe and Duct Insulation   7-39
7.7   Automatic/Manual Thermostat Set-Back   7-45

8   Selecting Efficiency Improvement Options   **8-1**
8.1   Guidelines for Selecting Efficiency Improvements   8-2
8.2   Combining Efficiency Improvement Options   8-33
8.3   Summary—Putting It All Together for the Homeowners   8-36

9   Guidelines for Efficient Oil Heat in New Construction   **9-1**
9.1   Fuel Storage   9-2
9.2   Oil Burners   9-3
9.3   Boilers and Furnaces   9-5
9.4   Venting Equipment   9-6
9.5   Heat Distribution   9-10
9.6   Domestic Hot Water Source   9-12
9.7   Heating System Controls   9-14

**10 New Technology Research and Development—
     The Future of Oil-Heat**   **10-1**
10.1 Advanced Control Systems   10-2
10.2 New Oil Burner Advances   10-6
10.3 Advanced Oil Heat Systems   10-17
10.4 When Will It Happen?   10-22
10.5 The Oil Heat House of the Future   10-23

Answers

Foreword

This guide, published by the Petroleum Marketers Association of America, provides up to date information summarizing over fifteen years of research and development (R&D) effort to improve the energy efficiency of oil heat technology to better serve the twelve and a half million homeowners who choose to use oil to provide space heating comfort in their homes. It provides useful background information and guidance on how to incorporate energy efficient oil heat technology options into day to day customer service operations. This information explains the advantages of improving the energy efficiency of existing oil heating systems as well as the importance of installing new high efficiency systems, retrofitting old systems with energy efficient components, and/or performing modifications and adjustments to improve the performance of existing equipment.

This publication was prepared pursuant to funding provided to Brookhaven National Laboratory (BNL) by the United States Department of Energy (DOE).

John Batey, President of Energy Research Center, Inc., was the primary author of the text. John Batey was responsible for starting the BNL/DOE Oil Heat R&D Program (and research facility) while employed at Brookhaven National Laboratory during the late 1970's. John Batey is one of the industry's premier authorities on oil heat technology and efficiency and currently provides consulting services to BNL.

This book could not have been completed without the dedicated effort of the current BNL Oil Heat R&D Program Manager, Roger McDonald, who provided project planning, supervision, and management, and served as chief editor. Roger McDonald also contributed as a co-author of parts of the text and developed the graphics used throughout the document. Without his continued involvement, this book could not have been completed.

A special acknowledgement goes to John Andrews, Director, BNL Energy Efficiency and Conservation Division, for his assistance and contributions made during the final editing of the text. Thanks also goes to Arlene Waltz and Francine Donnelly at BNL who provided the word processing skills required to complete the project.

Thanks also goes to John Millhone, Deputy Assistant Secretary for the Office of Building Technologies, Theodore Kapus, Director, Office of

Building Energy Research, John Ryan, Director, Building Equipment Division, and Esher Kweller, Manager, Oil Heat R&D Program of the United States Department of Energy.

Credit is also extended to William Auer, Leonard Fisher, Gordon Barkell, John Nally, David Nelsen, Paul Heinrichs, Robert Boltz, Donald Allen, Bernard Smith, James Goins, Eugene Mangini, David Schmidt, and Clarence Heisey who all voluntarily served as proofreaders of this document.

Chapter 1—Introduction to Heating System Efficiency

1.0 Purpose of This Manual

The purpose of this manual is to give oil heat service technicians the information they need to convince home-owners to improve the efficiency of their existing heating systems.

It brings together in an easy-to-use format the latest information on all recent efficiency advances and equipment upgrades. It supplements existing oil heat technician manuals that focus on basic design, safety, reliable operation, and repair of oil heating equipment.

Figure 1-1 shows the steps needed to educate homeowners who heat with oil.

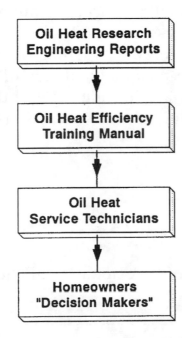

Oil Heat Research Engineering Reports

Oil Heat Efficiency Training Manual

Oil Heat Service Technicians

Homeowners "Decision Makers"

Information Transfer is the Purpose of the Oil Heat Efficiency Training Manual

Figure 1-1

Oil heat service technicians and companies gain many advantages by installing efficient oil heat equipment and upgrading existing units. These include:

- **Better equipment reliability** with fewer service call backs. This saves time and reduces service costs.
- **Improved customer satisfaction** with oil heat, which is important for your future.
- New oil heat equipment is **clean, efficient, safe, and the most economic fuel choice** for many homeowners. This allows oil to compete favorably against other home heating fuels.
- Customers who invest in oil heat equipment are **likely to stay** with oil heat, and this improves your future and the future of the industry.

This chapter gives an overview of oil heating system efficiency. It reviews all the parts of the heating system and discusses important efficiency factors for each of them. It explains the main heat losses and introduces the efficiency terms that are used throughout this manual. This chapter also discusses how the various parts of the heating system interact to affect overall system efficiency. Finally the many advantages of new efficient oil heating equipment are introduced and the important role of the service technician in "selling" efficiency to homeowners is discussed.

1.1 Parts of Oil Heating Systems

The main parts of a residential oil heating system are shown in Figure 1-2:

- Fuel storage tank,
- Oil burner,
- Boiler or furnace,
- Flue and draft control,

- Chimney,
- Distribution piping or ductwork,
- Domestic hot water coil (or separate hot water heater),
- Operating controls, and
- House.

Each of these has an important impact on the overall efficiency of the heating system as will be discussed in this section of the manual. The house is included because it has an impact on how effectively the oil heating system operates.

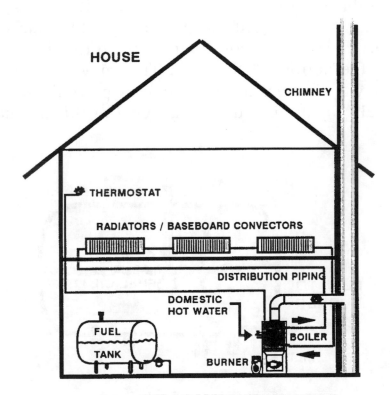

OIL HEATING SYSTEM

Figure 1-2

*Fuel
Storage
Tank*

The fuel storage tank gives homeowners the security of having a ready supply of home heating energy available at all times. The tank stores the fuel oil until it is needed to heat the home or provide domestic hot water. Two important factors that can affect efficiency should be considered. First, the **temperature of the fuel** (see Figure 1-3) can affect the burner's performance in two ways. Cold oil *increases* the oil flow to the burner and this can lower efficiency. Also, cold oil increases the size of fuel droplets produced by the nozzle. Both of these occurrences can lower the efficiency of the heating system unless corrective actions are taken. This is discussed in **Chapter 2** of this manual.

A second efficiency consideration is **fuel quality changes** during storage. In the vast majority of cases, the fuel remains unchanged during storage. In some cases, however, moisture can contribute to the formation of sediment at the bottom of the tank. This may lower system efficiency if the fuel nozzle becomes partially plugged. Fuel quality is discussed in **Chapter 7** of this manual.

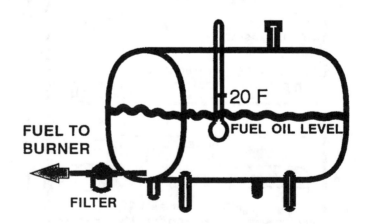

**Fuel Storage Tank Cold
Oil Can Affect Efficiency**

Figure 1-3

The oil burner can make or break the efficiency of oil heating systems. The burner receives fuel from the storage tank, atomizes it into a mist of fine droplets, combines it with a controlled amount of combustion air, and mixes the air and fuel for complete burning. Each of these steps has an important impact on efficiency. One thing that is not a problem is the actual conversion efficiency of No. 2 fuel oil to heat. Today's small residential oil burners release more than 99.9% of the fuel's stored energy into the hot combustion gases. The real problem is to capture this heat in the boiler or furnace and then transfer it to the living space in the house. Advances in oil burner designs over the past 20 years have significantly improved the efficiency of oil heat in homes (see Figure 1-4). Some of the key advances in oil burner designs are:

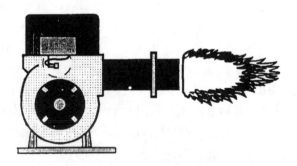

FLAME RETENTION HEAD BURNER

√ Low Excess Air

√ High Flame Temperature

√ Low Smoke and Soot

√ High Air Pressure For Stable Flame

Figure 1-4

- Low excess combustion air for high efficiency.
- Higher flame temperature for better heat transfer and high system efficiency.
- Reduced soot and smoke production for clean operation.
- Low air pollutant emissions.
- High static pressure for more stable operation (and side-wall venting).

These important advances make **burner replacement one of the best investments** for homeowners to improve the efficiency of their heating systems. Oil burner advances are the subject of **Chapter 2** of this manual.

Boiler or Furnace

The boiler or furnace includes a combustion chamber for the oil flame produced by the burner. Heat is then transferred from the flame and combustion gases, through the boiler or furnace walls, to the hot water or air that is used to heat the home (see Figure 1-5). The design of the boiler or furnace, its size (heating capacity) relative to the heating load, and other important installation factors determine its actual efficiency. The **Annual Fuel Utilization Efficiency (AFUE)** rates the efficiency of boilers and furnaces for "standard" operating conditions. The highest AFUE that is practical should always be selected. This will produce the highest system efficiency. The AFUE rates the boiler or furnace only and does not consider installation factors, oversizing, and other important variables that affect overall efficiency. The design of the oil burner and the boiler or furnace are the primary factors that determine heating system efficiency. Boiler and furnace efficiency ratings are discussed in **Chapter 3** of this manual.

High AFUE Ratings Are Important !

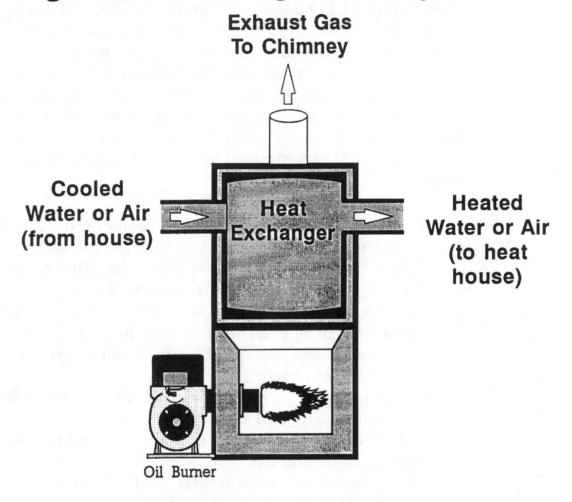

**Exhaust Gas
To Chimney**

**Cooled
Water or Air
(from house)**

**Heat
Exchanger**

**Heated
Water or Air
(to heat
house)**

Oil Burner

- **AFUE = Efficiency Rating**
- **New Higher Efficiency Units Are Available**
- **Homeowners and Fuel Oil Companies Benefit From Replacing Outdated Boilers and Furnaces**

Figure 1-5

Chimney

The operation of chimneys has a direct effect on the oil heating system efficiency. The chimney supplies a negative draft (suction) that helps remove the exhaust gas from the heater and helps pull combustion air into the burner. This was especially important for older burner designs that did not have powerful combustion air fans. Some modern oil burners do not require this chimney draft for efficient operation. They do require, however, that the exhaust gases be safely vented from the house (see Figure 1-6). The chimney can lower system efficiency in several ways:

> • Seasonal changes in outdoor air temperature cause the draft (suction) produced by the chimney to vary. This can change the amount of air supplied to the flame by the burner and lower the efficiency.
> • The chimney causes additional air flow through the barometric damper. This removes heated air from the house that is replaced by cold outdoor air. This increases fuel consumption.
> • The chimney remains hot during the burner off-cycle and causes cool air to flow through the heating unit. This removes heat from the boiler and furnace and increases fuel use.
> • The exhaust temperature from the heating unit cannot be too low or condensation can occur in the chimney. Some new, highly efficient oil boilers and furnaces operate with exhaust temperatures that are too low for chimney venting in some cases. Alternative methods such as side-wall venting are sometimes advisable for these high-efficiency heating units.

Proper design and adjustment of each component of the chimney venting system is important to reduce these unnecessary heat losses. This is discussed in **Chapter 4**.

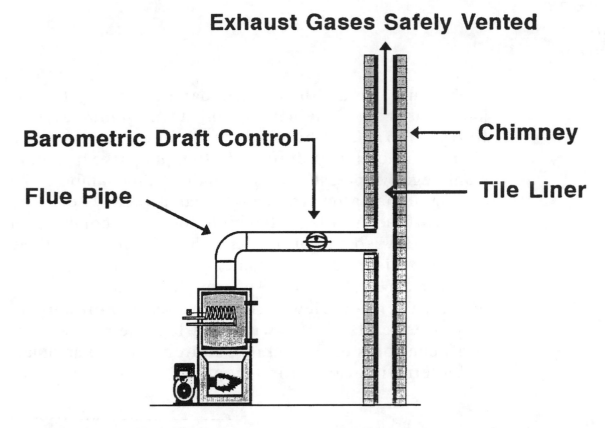

Exhaust Gases Safely Vented

Barometric Draft Control

Flue Pipe

Chimney

Tile Liner

Flue & Chimney Design Affects Efficiency:

- Draft setting affects efficiency
- Seasonal changes in draft can lower efficiency
- Barometric dampers needed to control draft, but they remove heated air from the house
- Off-cycle heat losses from the boiler or furnace are caused by the chimney draft
- Some new furnaces & boilers are designed to be side wall vented - not chimney vented

Figure 1-6

Flue and Draft Control

The flue pipe and barometric damper convey the exhaust gases from the heating unit to the chimney (see Figure 1-6). The barometric damper responds to changes in chimney draft and attempts to keep a constant negative pressure in the combustion chamber. The setting of the barometric damper can affect system efficiency. If the draft is set too high, too much combustion air can flow to the burner and the efficiency will be lowered. Also, settings resulting in excess draft will increase off-cycle heat losses from the boiler. This also lowers efficiency. New high-static-pressure oil burners may operate efficiently without a barometric damper. Draft control is discussed in **Chapter 4** of this manual, and alternative venting in **Chapter 5**.

Heat Distribution System

After the hot water or warm air is efficiently produced by the boiler or furnace, it must be delivered to the house. Hot-water or steam pipes are used to deliver heat from the boiler to the house, and warm-air ducts deliver heat from the furnace. Distribution heat losses are often overlooked, but they can drastically lower heating system efficiency (see Figure 1-7). Uninsulated hot-water pipes that pass through unheated spaces (such as basements, crawl spaces, and attics) can lose a large amount of heat before the hot water reaches the radiators. This loss increases during on-off operation. Similarly, warm air in ductwork loses heat before it reaches the air registers in the house. In addition, if the air ducts are not tightly sealed, air leakage into unheated spaces can cause another form of heat loss. Studies have found that these losses can range from only a few percent to more than 40% of the heat generated by the furnace. Simple improvements such as pipe or duct insulation and effective air duct sealing can

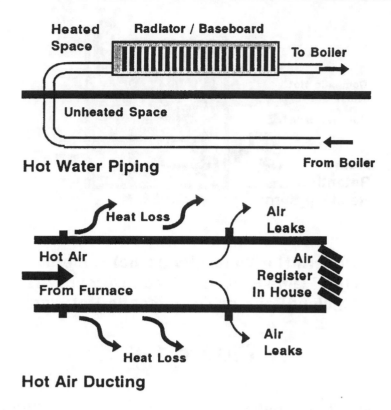

Distribution System Heat Losses Can Lower Efficiency Dramatically

Figure 1-7

reduce these unnecessary heat losses. These are discussed in **Chapter 7** of this manual and in **Chapter 9**.

Domestic Hot Water Generation

Domestic hot water production for showers, sinks, laundry and other purposes typically uses less fuel than space heating. Nevertheless, it can have an impact on oil heating system efficiency. Many oil boilers are equipped with tankless coils to produce domestic hot water from the space heating boiler (see Figure 1-8). These may include hot-water storage tanks that are heated by boiler water. An alternative method is a separate oil, gas or electric

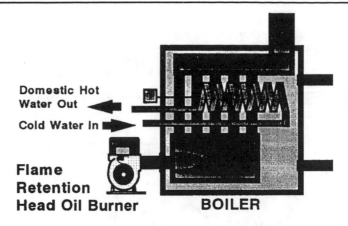

Domestic Hot Water Out

Cold Water In

Flame Retention Head Oil Burner

BOILER

**Modern Hot Water (Hydronic) Boilers
With Flame Retention Head Burners Are
Efficient Sources Of Domestic Hot Water**

Figure 1-8

water heater. Recent studies have shown that modern oil boilers with retention-head burners are very efficient sources of domestic hot water by using a tankless coil. **Chapter 6** of this manual presents information on the efficient production of domestic hot water.

Operating Controls

The operating controls for the heating system are the thermostat, which signals when the house needs heat, and the equipment controller, which tells the furnace or boiler when to turn on. The setpoints of these controls affect system efficiency (see Figure 1-9). For example, setting the boiler aquastat too high can increase fuel use by increasing off-cycle heat losses, especially for older burner-boilers. Similarly, longer on-times for fans on warm-air furnaces can lower off-cycle heat losses. Set-back thermostats, which deliver the minimum amount of heat needed at various times of the day based on setpoints selected by the homeowner, can also reduce fuel use. The setpoints of these operating controls for efficient operation are discussed in **Chapter 7** of this manual.

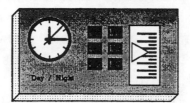

**SETBACK
THERMOSTAT**

**AQUASTAT CONTROL
FOR BOILERS**

**FAN CONTROLLER
FOR FURNACES**

SETBACK THERMOSTATS AND ADJUSTMENT OF
AQUASTATS AND FAN CONTROLS CAN AFFECT
EFFICIENCY AND FUEL USE

Figure 1-9

*House
Design*

The house itself is the last part of the heating system. The house design and construction determines the heat load that must be met by the heating unit. Several factors affecting overall system efficiency are:

- The various exhaust fans (attic, bath, and kitchen) and power-vented appliances can pull cold air into the house.
- Height of the house (number of floors) affects chimney height and draft.
- Wall and window areas and heat loss rates contribute to heating load.

- Air leakage rates into house around doors, windows, and into the basement affects that part of the air infiltration heat losses caused by the chimney and boiler or furnace.
- Ratio of space heating load to domestic hot water demand affects efficiency.
- Location of boiler room within the house affects boiler or furnace heat losses and the size of distribution heat losses. These and other house factors interact with the heating unit to produce an overall system efficiency for the house/chimney/ heating unit combination. While some of these interactions are beyond the control of the oil-heat service technician, the rest of this chapter will discuss the ones to be most aware of. This helps to decide on adjustments to the oil heating equipment to produce the maximum efficiency in all homes while maintaining customer comfort.

1.2 Equipment Heat Losses and System Efficiency

The purpose of an oil heating system is to convert energy contained in the fuel into useful heat in the home. No heating system can operate without some heat losses. Part of the fuel's energy is lost before it can be delivered as useful heat. The EFFICIENCY of the heating system is simply the percentage of the fuel's energy that is delivered to the living space of the house. The lower the heat losses, the higher the system efficiency (see Figure 1-10). This section of the manual describes heat losses that occur during the operation of the heating system. It then defines the various efficiency terms that are commonly used.

Many heat losses occur in a typical heating system, starting from the time the fuel is delivered to the burner up until the useful heat reaches the home. Some of these

SYSTEM HEAT LOSSES AND EFFICIENCIES

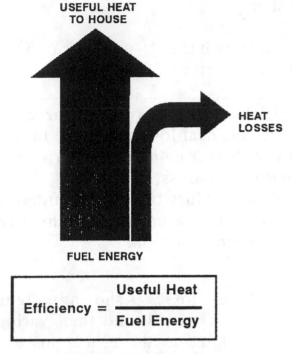

USEFUL HEAT
TO HOUSE

HEAT
LOSSES

FUEL ENERGY

$$\text{Efficiency} = \frac{\text{Useful Heat}}{\text{Fuel Energy}}$$

**Note: Heat Losses Must Be
Low To Produce High Efficiency**

Figure 1-10

depend on the design of the burner, furnace or boiler, draft damper, chimney and other system parts. The size of these losses also depends on how the system is installed and adjusted. The main installation factors are:

- House design,
- Chimney height and mass,
- Location of heating unit in the house,
- Distribution system details, and
- Boiler or furnace sizing.

After the system is installed, heating unit adjustment, periodic service, and maintenance are the major ongoing factors. We will see, for example, that burner adjustment plays an important role in how efficiently the heating system operates. Each of these factors can vary from one house to the next. It is important to recognize that each plays an important part in the overall efficiency of the oil heating system.

Heat losses from heating systems can be separated into five general categories as follows:

> - On-cycle flue heat loss (during burner operation),
> - Off-cycle flue heat loss (when the burner is off),
> - Jacket heat loss from the boiler or furnace casing,
> - Distribution heat loss, and
> - Infiltration heat loss from cold outdoor air flowing into the building, a portion of which results from heating system operation.

A diagram of these losses is shown in Figure 1-11. Each of these will be described, and then various efficiency terms that are related to these heat losses will be presented.

Flue Heat Loss During Burner Operation

One of the largest heat losses occurs through the flue while the burner is firing. The fuel oil flame produces hot gases that pass through the boiler or furnace. Only part of the heat contained in these gases is transferred to the hot water or warm air that is delivered to radiators or warm air registers in the home. The rest of this heat leaves the heating unit through the flue as the exhaust gases are vented from the house. This heat loss can be divided into two parts (see Figure 1-12):

> - Water Vapor heat loss.
> - Heat loss by hot exhaust gases.

The water vapor loss occurs because water is a product of fuel oil combustion. The exhaust gases are typically too hot for the water to be in liquid form, so it leaves the

HEAT LOSSES IN RESIDENTIAL HEATING SYSTEMS

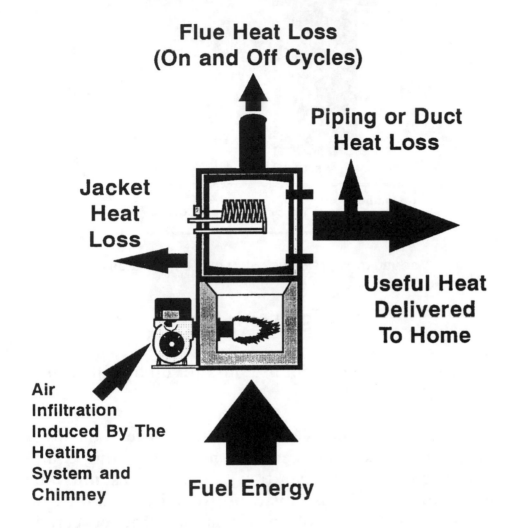

Flue Heat Loss (On and Off Cycles)

Piping or Duct Heat Loss

Jacket Heat Loss

Useful Heat Delivered To Home

Air Infiltration Induced By The Heating System and Chimney

Fuel Energy

Figure 1-11

heating unit as a vapor. This water vapor contains approximately 6.5 percent of the energy originally contained in the fuel oil. Part of this heat can be reclaimed in "condensing" furnaces or boilers that operate with exhaust temperatures that are so low that part of this water vapor is converted to liquid again. In these cases, part of this 6.5 percent water vapor heat loss is transferred through the heating unit to the house. For most cases, however, condensation of flue gas water vapor does not

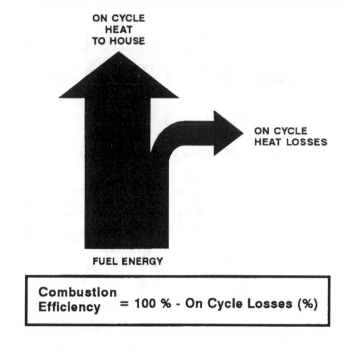

COMBUSTION EFFICIENCY & ON CYCLE HEAT LOSS

Figure 1-12

occur, and the water vapor heat loss for oil heating equipment is 6.5 percent.

The exhaust of hot flue gas from the house is the other form of heat loss that occurs from home heating equipment during burner operation. **These gases must be vented to avoid hazardous conditions in the home**. Incomplete combustion of any fuels can produce carbon monoxide, which is highly toxic and must be completely vented from the house. These hot exhaust gases usually exit from the heating system at a temperature between 350°F and 650°F because all of the oil flames's heat can not be transferred to the boiler or furnace. This hot exhaust gas carries heat away from the heating system. The size of this heat loss varies with burner and boiler/furnace design, burner adjustment, and other factors.

New efficient boilers and furnaces are now available that operate with on-cycle heat losses in the range of only 10 to 15 percent including the water vapor heat loss. This is lower than most older heating units. These new heating units are discussed in **Chapter 3**. New oil burners are also available that can operate with very low levels of excess combustion air **(see Chapter 2)** and very low on-cycle heat losses. Careful adjustment of these burners using combustion test equipment is important to produce the lowest possible on-cycle heat losses.

Figure 1-13 shows how low excess combustion air reduces on-cycle heat loss. The combustion air enters the burner at a temperature of about 70°F. This air is heated by the flame and most of the heat is extracted by the boiler or furnace. However, this air (now flue gas) leaves the system at a temperature of 350°F to 650°F which is much higher than its original temperature. Therefore, it is important to reduce excess air because each cubic foot of air carries useful heat away from the boiler or furnace. The use of new burners and proper burner adjustment for low excess air, without smoke, are both important steps for reducing on-cycle heat losses.

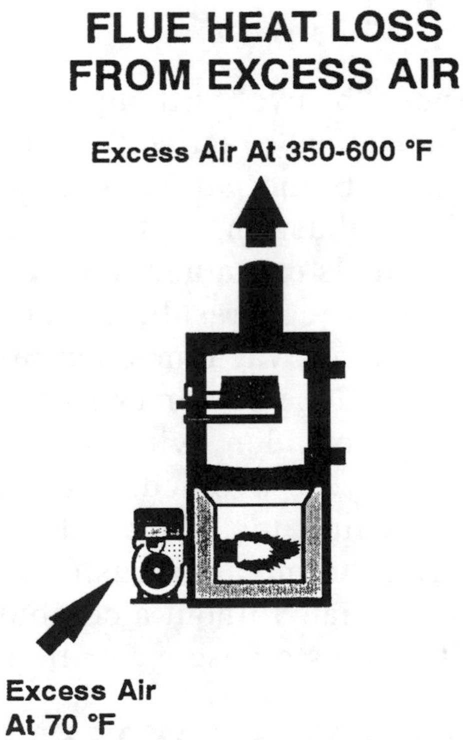

FLUE HEAT LOSS FROM EXCESS AIR

Excess Air At 350-600 °F

Excess Air At 70 °F

Figure 1-13

*On-Cycle
Flue Heat
Loss and
Combustion
Efficiency*

The efficiency term associated with on-cycle heat loss that is commonly used in the heating industry is "Combustion Efficiency." This name is misleading because it actually includes **combustion and heat transfer efficiency in the boiler or furnace**. The on-cycle heat loss is determined by measuring the exhaust gas temperature and the Carbon Dioxide (or Oxygen) levels of the flue gas. This indicates the amount of excess combustion air. Then the on-cycle flue heat loss and combustion efficiency are calculated (see Figure 1-14). Combustion test kits are available to evaluate on-cycle heat losses and "combustion efficiency." In fact, these test kits have been around almost as long as oil heat. These **combustion efficiency tests must be performed** whenever a burner is installed or tuned to be sure that minimum excess air and maximum efficiency is reached.

Adjusting burners "by eye" without test equipment is an unreliable and inefficient practice. A "number 1" smoke is not visible and the burner air damper can be set for too much or too little combustion air. In both cases efficiency will be lowered. This is explained in **Chapter 2**. In some cases soot production can result, which requires additional service calls for vacuum cleaning the heat exchanger. This will reduce customer satisfaction with oil heat and they may consider switching to other heating fuels. This can easily be avoided. Professional oil heat service practices which include combustion efficiency testing are important to maintain customer confidence in oil. A service technician without a combustion test kit is like a doctor without a stethoscope or thermometer.

**ALWAYS USE COMBUSTION TEST EQUIPMENT
TO ADJUST OIL BURNERS!**

Combustion Efficiency Is Highest For Low Flue Gas Temperature And Low Excess Combustion Air (High CO2)

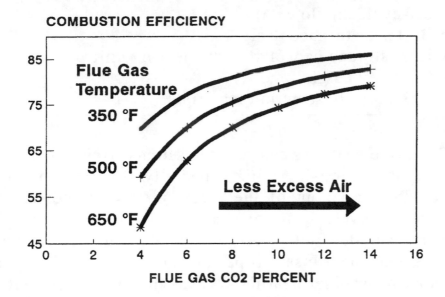

Figure 1-14

Off-Cycle Heat Losses and Annual Fuel Utilization Efficiency

Oil burners in homes do not operate continuously, but cycle on and off throughout the year. The typical burner operates between 15 and 20 percent of the time, or about 1,500 hours a year. A second important heat loss—**OFF-CYCLE HEAT LOSS**—occurs when the burner is not operating. The chimney produces draft during the off-cycle and cool room air enters the boiler or furnace through the burner air inlet and other openings. This air flows into the hot combustion chamber and across the inside surfaces of the boiler or furnace where it is absorbs heat and carries it away form the heating unit and up the chimney. These heat losses must be replaced during the next burner firing cycle. Off-cycle heat loss is shown in Figure 1-15.

The main factors contributing to off-cycle heat loss are:

> • Burner design (retention head burners allow less off-cycle air flow),
> • Boiler or furnace design,
> • Heat storage capacity of the heating unit,
> • Chimney height, and
> • Chimney construction materials.

Off-cycle heat loss can reduce system efficiency, and is an important consideration especially for older heating units. Proper sizing of the fuel nozzle is important to reduce off-cycle heat loss. Figure 1-16 shows that in general, smaller fuel nozzle shortens the burner off-cycle and reduces heat loss. Proper nozzle sizing is especially important for older heating systems that may have higher off-cycle heat losses than modern oil heat equipment. Detailed information on fuel nozzle sizing is included in **Chapter 7**. Reduction of off-cycle heat losses by new oil

OFF CYCLE HEAT LOSS

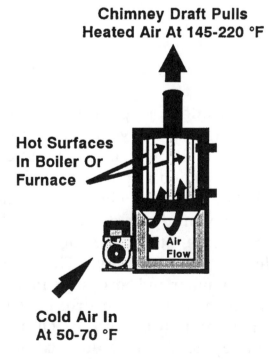

Chimney Draft Pulls Heated Air At 145-220 °F

Hot Surfaces In Boiler Or Furnace

Air Flow

Cold Air In At 50-70 °F

Figure 1-15

burners is also discussed in **Chapter 2**. These new oil burners have "tighter" burner heads that restrict off-cycle air flow more than older "open" burner head designs. This reduces off-cycle air flow and helps to lower off-cycle heat losses.

As we have seen, off-cycle heat loss depends on many factors that include burner head design, number and size of openings in the boiler or furnace (such as inspection doors), off-cycle chimney draft, adjustment of the barometric damper, and many other factors. Laboratory tests have found that off-cycle losses can vary from less than 5% to more than 10% of the fuel input to the heating unit. The Federal Efficiency Labeling program for oil heating equipment has determined that off-cycle losses (neglecting chimney draft, and other factors) is on the order of 3% to 4%. An estimate of on-cycle and off-cycle losses by this labeling program has established an Annual Fuel Utilization Efficiency (AFUE) that is used to rate the

Effect Of Burner Off Period On Heat Loss
(General Trend Indicated - For Illustrartion Only)

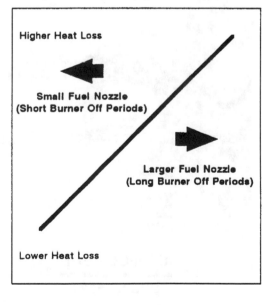

Off Cycle Heat Loss (%)

Higher Heat Loss

Small Fuel Nozzle
(Short Burner Off Periods)

Larger Fuel Nozzle
(Long Burner Off Periods)

Lower Heat Loss

Increasing Nozzle Size ▶

Figure 1-16

overall efficiency of new heating equipment over an average heating season for "typical" operating conditions (see Figure 1-17).

While this AFUE cannot take all factors that determine efficiency in a specific home into account, it does give a way to compare the relative efficiencies of new heating equipment. The AFUE can be represented by:

AFUE=100%-ON-CYCLE HEAT LOSS (%)-OFF-CYCLE HEAT LOSS (%)

More information on Annual Fuel Utilization Efficiency is included in **Chapter 3** of this manual.

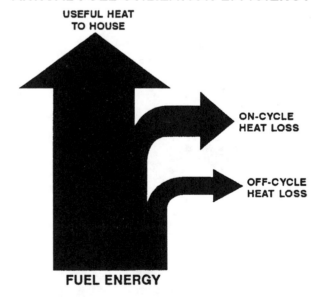

ANNUAL FUEL UTILIZATION EFFICIENCY

$$AFUE = \frac{USEFUL\ HEAT}{FUEL\ ENERGY}$$

AFUE = 100% - ON-CYCLE LOSS (%) - OFF-CYCLE LOSS (%)

Figure 1-17

*Jacket Heat
Loss*

Some of the heat from the oil flame is lost through the jacket or casing of the boiler while the burner is operating and also during the burner off-cycle. This is called JACKET HEAT LOSS (see Figure 1-18). It reduces the amount of heat delivered to the house and lowers system efficiency. This loss is not included in the Annual Fuel Utilization Efficiency (AFUE), where it is assumed to contribute to the heating load of the house. However, in many installations such as boilers in unheated basements, attics, crawl spaces and outdoor boiler installations, some or all of this heat is lost.

The size of jacket heat loss for hot water boilers varies from less than 1% to more than 10% based on laboratory testing. This loss is highest while the burner is firing and the combustion chamber contains the hot gases from the oil flame. Typical flame temperatures in the range of 2,000°F to 3,000°F drive heat through the chamber wall and then through the jacket of the boiler or furnace to its surroundings. Also, heat is lost from the water storage

**HEAT LOSS THROUGH THE BOILER
OR FURNACE JACKET**

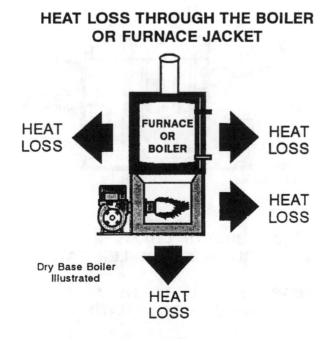

Figure 1-18

section of the boiler if it is not properly insulated. These losses occur during the burner on-cycle and off-cycle. This can lower system efficiency when the jacket losses are high.

Dry-base boilers that do not have boiler water around the combustion chamber tend to have higher jacket losses than "wet-base" boilers. Figure 1-18 is a schematic of a dry-base boiler, while Figure 1-19 shows a wet-base design. Some of the heat that escapes through the jacket of dry-base boilers is recovered in wet-base designs because boiler water surrounds the hot combustion chamber. This reduces jacket heat loss. The design of the boiler and its location should be considered when recommending a new efficient heating unit. If the jacket losses of the existing unit are high and it is located in an unheated space, then fuel savings may be higher than for the average boiler replacement. New wet-base oil boilers operate with low jacket loss and should be used to replace outdated heating units whenever possible. **Wet-base boilers are generally preferred over dry-base designs** for installations where

WET-BASE BOILER

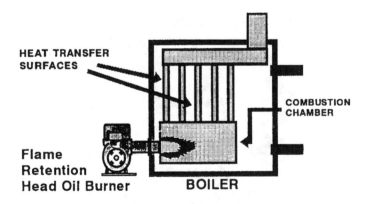

**THE COMBUSTION CHAMBER
IS SURROUNDED BY BOILER WATER**

**WET-BASE BOILERS GENERALLY
HAVE HIGH EFFICIENCY RATINGS**

Figure 1-19

the jacket losses do not produce useful heat. As always there are exceptions to the rule. One dry-base cast iron boiler manufacturer has designed a high efficiency system using a very well insulated combustion chamber base.

The AFUE efficiency rating *does not* take jacket heat loss into account because it assumes the boiler is located in the heated space. This is not always true. The probable jacket loss of the *existing* and new *replacement* boiler should always be considered whenever a boiler is located outdoors, in a garage, basement, attic or other unheated space.

Distribution System Heat Losses

Heat losses form the hot water piping or warm air ducts reduce the heat delivered to the house by the heating system and lowers system efficiency. This does not appear in the AFUE rating and varies from house to house. Figure 1-20 is a diagram of these heat losses. Properly installed and insulated piping and ductwork should operate with very low heat losses.

Hot water is usually delivered to radiators in the house at a temperature between 180^oF and 200^oF. If these pipes are not insulated and they pass through the basement, crawl space, attic and other non-heated spaces they can lose a part of their heat before they reach the heated space. This represents an unnecessary heat loss. Additional fuel must be consumed to make up for these losses and the overall **system** efficiency drops. For example, if 1-inch uninsulated hot water piping at 200^oF passes through an area at 50^oF, each foot of pipe loses 100 BTU per hour. This is equivalent to 10,000 BTU for 100 feet of uninsulated piping, and represents about 20% or more of the peak heating load of the house. The percentage heat loss becomes even higher for lower heat loads as the burner cycles on and off. Pipe insulation can eliminate most of this loss.

HEAT LOSS FROM DISTRIBUTION PIPES AND AIR DUCTS

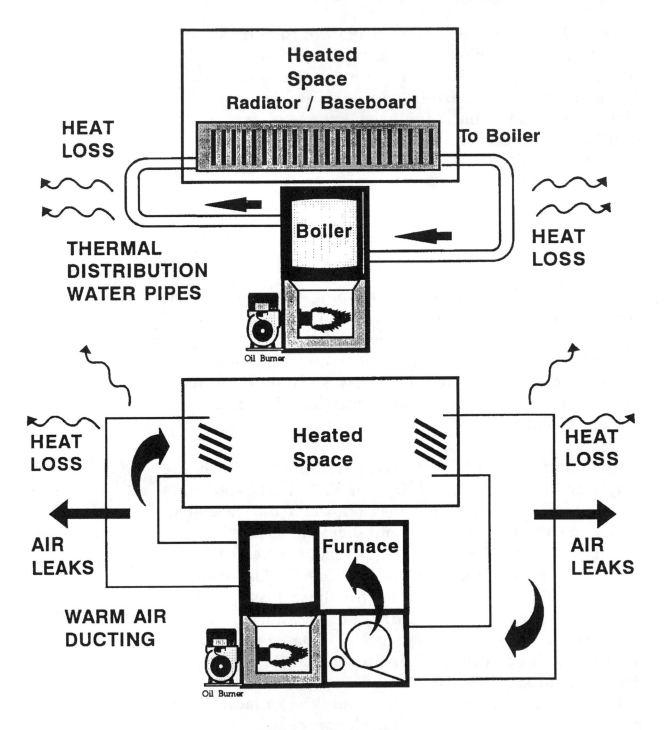

Figure 1-20

Similarly, heat loss from uninsulated warm air ducts can reduce the overall efficiency of the heating system. In addition the warm air ducts can lose heat in another way. If the duct joints are not completely sealed, some of the heated air can escape before it reaches the house. On leaky return duct runs cold air can be sucked into the system making things worse. This is especially troublesome for ducts that pass thorough unheated basements, crawl spaces and attics where this air does not produce any useful heating. Some studies have estimated that this heat loss can be as high as 40% of the energy delivered by the furnace.

THIS CAN BE THE LARGEST HEAT LOSS OF THE ENTIRE SYSTEM.

Distribution heat losses depend to a large degree on the way in which the heating system is installed. Careful attention must be directed to the piping and warm air ductwork to avoid these heat losses. More information is included in **Chapter 7** of this manual.

Outdoor Air Infiltration

Combustion systems require air for the burner and to control the chimney draft. This indoor air which is often heated must be replaced by cold outdoor air, which is heated to room temperature. This can increase the heating requirements of the house and is often referred to as outdoor air infiltration. The air infiltration induced by the operation of the heating system is another form of heat loss. Figure 1-21 is a diagram of cold air infiltration into the house that is caused by the heating system.

The size of this heat loss depends on many factors that vary widely from house to house which include:

- Oil Burner design and off-cycle air flow,
- House and Chimney height,
- Chimney construction material and insulation,

- Barometric damper setting,
- Air-tightness of the house,
- Location of heating unit in the house,
- Source of combustion and draft dilution air, and
- Size and location of leaks in a warm-air duct system.

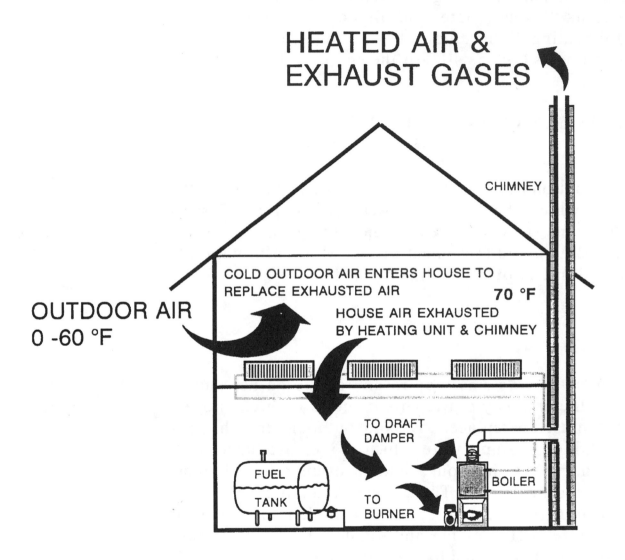

OUTDOOR AIR INFILTRATION CAUSED BY THE HEATING SYSTEM AND CHIMNEY

Figure 1-21

The Infiltration air heat loss can be separated into on-cycle and off-cycle air flows through the burner and through the barometric damper. Recent testing programs have shown that these losses can vary over a wide range depending on the many factors outlined above. The Annual Fuel Utilization Efficiency includes infiltration losses for oil heating equipment of 2 or 3 percent to represent the **average** case. However, more recent evaluations show that this heat loss can be more than 12% of the annual fuel use in extreme cases. Outdoor air infiltration should be considered whenever an older heating system is evaluated and new heating equipment is being considered. The source of combustion and draft control air should be carefully evaluated whenever oil heating equipment is installed in new homes. **Chapter 5** presents information on alternatives to chimney venting.

Summary of Heat Losses

Five important heat losses reduce the amount of useful heat delivered by a boiler or furnace and reduce the overall efficiency. These vary from house to house. Figure 1-22 shows ranges for these heat losses in "typical" and "high efficiency" oil heating systems. Proper installation and adjustment is important to minimize controllable heat losses such as on-cycle, distribution and air infiltration loss. Two important efficiencies are often referred to. Combustion Efficiency takes into account flue heat losses that occur during the burner on-cycle. This efficiency can be measured in the field using combustion test kits. It does not include off-cycle, jacket, distribution, or infiltration air heat losses. It is a measure of the fuel conversion efficiency (typically 99.8% or more) and the heat-transfer efficiency of the boiler or furnace. **Annual Fuel Utilization Efficiency (AFUE)** includes on-cycle and some off—cycle heat losses, but does not include jacket, distribution, and some of the infiltration air heat losses that can occur. The AFUE is an important guide for selecting new boilers or furnaces, but it does not give an accurate indication of how efficiently a particular heating system in the

TYPICAL HEAT LOSSES FOR OIL-FIRED HYDRONIC BOILERS
ACTUAL LOSSES VARY FROM SYSTEM TO SYSTEM

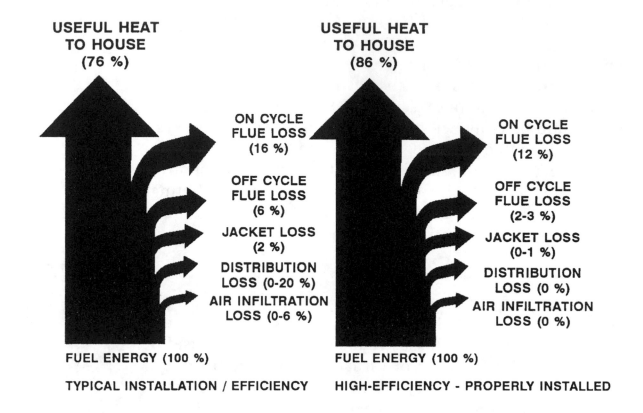

USEFUL HEAT TO HOUSE (76 %)

ON CYCLE FLUE LOSS (16 %)

OFF CYCLE FLUE LOSS (6 %)

JACKET LOSS (2 %)

DISTRIBUTION LOSS (0-20 %)

AIR INFILTRATION LOSS (0-6 %)

FUEL ENERGY (100 %)

TYPICAL INSTALLATION / EFFICIENCY

USEFUL HEAT TO HOUSE (86 %)

ON CYCLE FLUE LOSS (12 %)

OFF CYCLE FLUE LOSS (2-3 %)

JACKET LOSS (0-1 %)

DISTRIBUTION LOSS (0 %)

AIR INFILTRATION LOSS (0 %)

FUEL ENERGY (100 %)

HIGH-EFFICIENCY - PROPERLY INSTALLED

Figure 1-22a   Figure 1-22b

field is operating. Too many factors come into play in actual installations. Oil heat service technicians must be aware of all important heat losses so that heating systems can be installed and adjusted for the highest possible efficiency. Also, for older existing boilers, all heat losses must be considered so that accurate recommendations can be presented to the homeowner about fuel savings by installing new oil burners and new high-efficiency boilers and furnaces. The oil heat service technician has first-hand experience with each system and knows how they operate. This is important knowledge for helping home-owners make informed decisions about improving the efficiency of their heating system.

1.3 Important Heating Unit, Chimney, and House Interactions

We have seen that the heating system is made up of many parts that all interact together to produce a HEATING SYSTEM that operates with a number of heat losses that produce an overall system efficiency. This section describes some important interactions that take place and how they can change the overall efficiency.

The AFUE Rating Applies Only to the Boiler or Furnace

The AFUE is an important tool for selecting boilers or furnaces. However, it is calculated for all heating units based on a "STANDARD" set of operating conditions. The actual conditions vary from house to house, and the overall efficiency of the heating unit/chimney/house system can be very different form the predicted AFUE. The AFUE is similar to the EPA miles per gallon rating for automobiles. Fuel use by each home may vary depending on how the system parts are installed and adjusted.

House Design Affects Jacket Heat Loss

The location of the boiler or furnace in the house can affect jacket heat loss. If the jacket loss is small, then the location does not noticeably change the efficiency. However, a dry-base boiler with large jacket losses, located in a cold basement, crawl space, attic, or other unheated space, can lose a large amount of heat and the annual fuel use will be higher than predicted. These losses generally do not produce useful heat within the house. The same boiler located in a closet in the house may deliver some of the jacket heat loss to the house. However, it is important to remember that the air used by the burner and barometric draft damper comes from around the boiler. If this air is heated by jacket losses, some or most of this heat will be pulled from the house by the burner and chimney *before* it supplies useful heat to the house. **This effect is discussed further in Chapter 9.**

House Design and Chimney Height Affect Efficiency

If the house has a very tall chimney that produces a strong draft, both off-cycle and air infiltration heat losses may be much higher than the standard case. Tall chimneys produce more draft and more air will be drawn through the barometric damper. This increases the air infiltration induced by the heating system and lowers system efficiency as the incoming cold air must be heated. The "air-tightness" of the house, the location of the heating unit, and the places where the air infiltrates into the house all interact to determine the drop in efficiency. If the house is very tight, then less air infiltration will take place. Also, if a separate source of air is available for the heating system, then air infiltration into the house may be reduced. Many factors interact to determine the change in system efficiency for a specific house. **Further discussion is found in Chapter 4.**

Seasonal Changes in Chimney Draft can Lower Efficiency

The chimney draft is lowered as the outdoor air temperature rises. This can reduce the air that is supplied by the burner to the flame, especially for older burner designs. This can lower the combustion efficiency especially in the Spring and Fall when the outdoor temperature is highest. This is discussed in **Chapter 2**. The lower chimney draft can also lower air flow through the barometric damper, and this can reduce air infiltration heat loss. The net efficiency loss or gain will vary from system to system. This is another example of the many interactions that occur that affect overall efficiency. **This is discussed in Chapter 4.**

Heating Unit Sizing Relative to the House Heat Losses Affects Efficiency

The off-cycle heat losses depend on the length of the burner off-cycle. If a heating unit is oversized compared to the heat loss of the house, the burner off-cycle increases. This causes the off-cycle heat loss to increase and the system efficiency drops. Therefore, proper boiler or furnace (and fuel nozzle sizing) is an important factor that affects efficiency.

Barometric
Damper
Setting can
Change
Efficiency

If the barometric damper is set for too much over-fire draft in the combustion chamber, the on-cycle and off-cycle heat losses increase. The on-cycle loss rises because the excess air to the burner goes up which lowers the flame temperature. Also, during the burner off-cycle, the higher draft can cause more cold air to pass though the boiler or furnace producing higher off-cycle heat losses. On the other hand, if the draft is set too low, insufficient air may be supplied to the burner and efficiency will be reduced. This is discussed in **Chapter 2**, and it is especially important for older burner designs.

Summary of
Factors that
Influence
Heating
System
Efficiency

The SYSTEM EFFICIENCY, which includes boiler or furnace AFUE and all the other heat loses and system interactions, is difficult to determine and varies from house to house. Many of these interactions are important because they can substantially change system efficiency and fuel consumption. The SYSTEM that we are talking about is the HEATING UNIT/CHIMNEY/HOUSE combination and the five major heat losses that were discussed in this chapter. It is important to realize that the efficiency of a "burner" or a "boiler" or a "burner-boiler combination" cannot be determined independent of the other parts. It is the combination of the FUEL SUPPLY/ OIL BURNER/ BOILER/ VENT AND DRAFT CONTROL/ CHIMNEY/ PIPING OR DUCTING/ HOUSE that determines the overall efficiency and fuel use of the system. The heat flow diagrams in Figure 1-22 show the typical values for each of the heat losses discussed in this chapter. Figure 1-22a shows losses for typical oil heating systems installed over the past 10 to 15 years. The average AFUE for oil boilers and furnaces sold thirteen years ago was 76 percent. This has steadily risen to about 83 or 84 percent in 1990 according to data published by the Gas Appliance Manufacturers' Association. The overall system efficiency depends on how the system is installed and adjusted and other factors introduced in this chapter. Figure 1-22b shows the heat losses for a properly installed high efficiency oil heat system that is now available. The system efficiency can reach 90 percent or more if all other system heat losses are avoided.

1.4 Advantages of New Oil Heat Equipment and the Key Role of Service Technicians

Modern oil heating equipment including flame retention oil burners and high efficiency boilers and furnaces offer many important advantages over existing heating equipment. These include:

- **High Efficiency**—including combustion efficiency, Annual Fuel utilization Efficiency (AFUE), and overall system efficiency when properly installed and adjusted. Studies have shown that a homeowner who invests in new equipment is likely to remain an oil heat customer for many years. Therefore, installing new efficient oil heat equipment is also good for the future of the industry. In the long term this benefits consumers in many ways: they conserve energy, save money, and enjoy the higher reliability of a new system, reducing service requirements.

- **Clean Operation**—new burners operate with very low soot and smoke levels when they are properly adjusted. In fact, recent tests indicate that new oil burners can often operate as cleanly as natural gas burners. Replacing outdated oil burners with new models can improve the image of oil heat and disprove the myth that "oil heat is dirty." This will also improve the future of the oil heat industry and make oil more competitive against other home heating fuels. This is discussed in **Chapter 2**.

- **Low Air Pollution Emissions**—modern oil burners produce low levels of air pollutants including: particulate matter (soot and smoke), carbon monoxide, nitrogen oxides, sulfur oxides and other pollutants that are considered detrimental to the environment. In fact, it can be shown that residential oil heating equipment is as non-polluting as natural gas equipment. Homeowners must be informed of these findings to counteract the negative image that oil heat is damaging to the environment.

- **Improved Reliability**—new oil heating equipment will reduce the number of service calls required to keep the older, outdated equipment operating. This translates into less work for the service department and better profits for the company. The extra time available to service technicians can be spent on system installations and equipment tune-ups to keep all heating equipment operating efficiently which improves customer satisfaction and the image of the oil heat industry.

We have seen that the actual efficiency of an oil heating SYSTEM depends on all the heating system components and how they are installed and adjusted. This includes the oil burner, boiler or furnace, vent system, chimney, controls, and even the fuel storage system. The AFUE is an important measure for comparing the efficiency of boilers or furnaces for "standard" conditions. However, these standard conditions are seldom found in actual installations. The oil heat service technician must be familiar with ALL the heat losses and system installation factors that impact overall efficiency as introduced in this chapter and discussed throughout this manual. Each service technician serves a key role as a HEATING EQUIPMENT AND ENERGY EXPERT who understands how oil heat systems operate and how to adjust them for peak efficiency. Homeowners depend on oil heat service technicians to keep their systems operating reliably and economically, and to recommend equipment upgrades to improve performance when indicated by efficiency tests and inspections. This is vital to assure continued satisfaction with oil heat.

Here are some of the important roles of the oil heat service technician as an ENERGY EXPERT:

- **Informs homeowners of oil heat equipment advances**—the service technician is one of the main sources of information for homeowners on how their system operates and what can be done to upgrade the system and improve performance. Surveys prove that the oil heat service technician is trusted by homeowners because they keep their heating systems operating safely and reliably and make service calls whenever needed. Therefore, the service technician can supply valuable advice to the homeowner about upgrading their heating system.

- **Installs and adjusts oil heating equipment for peak efficiency**—which is an important part of delivering the oil heat product which is safe, reliable, economic, and comfortable space heating. The technician must be aware of all the factors that affect system efficiency so that they can do the best possible job for each homeowner.

- **Services the heating equipment**—oil heating equipment has an advantage over other home heating fuels because the systems are inspected and adjusted on a regular basis. The oil heat service technician is very familiar with the design, operation, and service history of each heating system in each home. This presents an important opportunity to recommend equipment upgrades to homeowners to improve the operation and economy of the heating system.

- **Keeps track of new equipment developments**—oil heating equipment is continually being improved and the service technician must be familiar with these new developments. For example, the new high static combustion air pressure flame retention burners can operate effectively in installations with poor chimney draft. Also, side-wall venting can be used in some installations that have inadequate chimney draft. The service technician must be familiar with these advances and be able to advise the homeowner on how they can improve their oil heating system.

- **Measures Combustion Efficiency**—as part of normal service, oil heat service technicians perform combustion efficiency tests and determine the on-cycle efficiency of oil boilers and furnaces. This enables burner adjustments and tune-ups for peak efficiency. It also helps the service technician to determine when energy conservation options (such as new flame retention oil burners) are needed. This is an important advantage for oil heat compared to other energy sources that do not regularly perform efficiency testing.

**ALWAYS USE COMBUSTION TEST EQUIPMENT
TO TUNE OIL HEATING EQUIPMENT**

The advantages for oil heat are worth restating:

- **Improves the efficiency** of all oil heating equipment—adjusting "by eye" is just not good enough;
- **Assures low smoke and soot** for fewer call-backs and less vacuum cleaning of boilers and furnaces;
- **Lowers air pollutant emissions** by assuring optimum combustion air supply;
- **Improves customer satisfaction** with oil heat.

THE OIL HEAT SERVICE TECHNICIAN CAN DISPROVE MANY OF THE MISCONCEPTIONS ABOUT OIL HEAT BY USING ALL THE TOOLS THAT ARE NOW AVAILABLE. BY INSTALLING NEW ENERGY-EFFICIENT OIL BURNERS, BOILERS AND FURNACES, AND BY ALWAYS USING COMBUSTION TEST EQUIPMENT YOU CAN PROVE THAT OIL HEAT IS CLEAN, SAFE, ECONOMICAL, AND NON-POLLUTING.

QUESTIONS

1-1.   Name four advantages to new oil heat equipment.

1-2.   Can you adjust oil burning equipment by eye? If not, why?

1-3.   What is included in the correct procedure for performing a combustion efficiency test?

1-4.   What is the required chimney height via N F P A?

1-5.   What is dew point?

1-6.   Cold oil is more beneficial to an efficient heating system than warm oil. True or false? Why?

1-7.   Too much chimney draft is not a factor in system efficiency? True or false?

1-8.   Heat losses from heating "systems" can be separated into five general categories. What are they?

1-9.   Proper burner adjustment for low excess air, without smoke are important for reducing on-cycle heat losses. True or false.

1-10. Proper nozzle sizing is an important factor in off-cycle heat loss. True or false.

1-11. Wet base boilers generally have less jacket heat loss than dry base boilers. True or false.

1-12. What does A F U E stand for?

1-13. Moisture can contribute to the formation of sediment at the bottom of the fuel storage tank. True or false?

1-14. What is the purpose of a chimney?

1-15. The barometric draft regulator responds to changes in chimney draft and attempts to keep a constant negative pressure in the combustion chamber. True or false?

1-16. Combustion efficiency test must be performed whenever the burner is _____.

1-17. How can the barometric control affect system efficiency?

Chapter 2—Oil Burner Efficiency Advances

**2.0
Introduction**

The oil burner is one of the important keys to efficient operation of oil heating equipment. This chapter will outline the basics of oil burning including burner design, adjustment and operation, and many variables that must be considered for clean and efficient oil burning. The advantages of flame retention oil burners will be discussed, and important installation guidelines are outlined. This information is useful for efficient operation of older burners in use for many years, and new models that are now available. This chapter discusses the following topics:

- An overview of **how oil burns**.
- A review of **oil burner parts** and their functions.
- Discussion of **fuel nozzle operation** and how it is a key to clean and efficient oil burning.
- The importance of **air supply** and **fuel-air mixing**.
- A Summary of the **important steps for oil burning, in theory and in practice**.
- **Smoke** from oil burners is shown to be unnecessary if the burner is properly adjusted. This includes a review of common causes of smoke, and ways to avoid it. The useful function of smoke is also explained.
- **Combustion efficiency** depends on burner adjustment:
  - Excess air supplied by the burner lowers combustion efficiency;
  - Some excess air is needed for clean burning;
  - New burners use minimal excess air for high efficiency;
  - Careful burner adjustment is important for all burners.

- **Efficiency advances** of new oil burners:
  - Combustion efficiency improvement by using less combustion air;
  - Higher Annual Efficiency from lower off-cycle heat loss;
  - Better flame stability with less variation as the chimney draft changes during the heating season.
- **Other advantages** of new oil burners:
  - More reliable operation with reduced service calls;
  - Better flame stability that does not depend on chimney draft;
  - Lower smoke production (near-zero) for clean operation;
  - Lower air pollution emissions that are less than most combustion sources.
- **Interaction** with other parts of the Heating System:
  - Boiler of furnace and air leakage affect fuel savings;
  - Combustion chambers affect burner operation and heat loss;
  - Venting system adjustment is important for good burner performance.

2.1 Oil Combustion— What All Service Technicians Must Know

Some of the information included here can also be found in other guides, but it is included because it is important for a complete understanding of oil-burner efficiency.

Fuel oil is a liquid that consists mostly of hydrogen (H) and carbon (C). Combustion is the process of combining these components of fuel oil with oxygen to produce a rapid chemical reaction. This reaction converts:

- The Hydrogen (H) to Water Vapor (H_2O)
- The Carbon (C) to Carbon Dioxide (CO_2).

These chemical reactions release large quantities of heat and the combustion product gases are raised to a very high temperature. These high-temperature gases form the oil flame that typically is between 2500 and 3500 degrees F. The heat contained in these hot combustion gases is used to heat water in a boiler or air in a furnace, which is then used to supply space heating in homes.

Figure 2-1 shows the components of fuel oil (carbon and hydrogen) combining with oxygen in the air to produce a flame that consists of carbon dioxide gas, water vapor, and nitrogen gas (from the air). All of these gases are at a very high temperature because of the heat released by the combustion process. Several features of the fuel oil combustion must be understood because they have an important effect on flame properties and combustion efficiency.

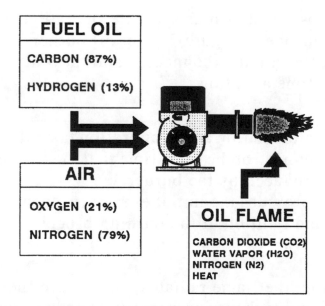

FUEL OIL BURNING PROCESS

Figure 2-1

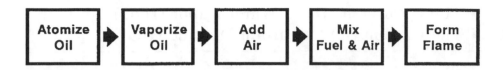

Steps In Combustion Process

Figure 2-2

Efficient combustion of fuel oil requires several important steps as shown in Figure 2-2:

> • Fuel atomization and evaporation to form a fuel vapor,
> • Supply of a precise amount of air to burn the fuel oil,
> • Thorough mixing of the fuel vapors and combustion air,
> • Ignition of the mixture to form a flame, and
> • Heat transfer from the flame helping to vaporize the fuel.

These steps are shown as separate operations that take place in sequence in Figure 2-2. In oil burners, however, these processes are interconnected and they all take place at the same time as follows:

> • Fuel oil atomization and evaporation take place near the burner head at the same time that the combustion air is introduced by the burner.
> • A spark provides the initial energy for local vaporization and ignition of the burning process.
> • The fuel vapors begin to mix with the air immediately.
> • Heat from the flame radiates back to the fuel droplets and helps them evaporate at the same time that the fuel and air are mixing.

- Recirculation of hot gases in the flame help to evaporate the oil and mix it with combustion air as part of a single step.
- Flames around individual fuel droplets combine the evaporation, fuel-air mixing, and burning processes into a single step.

Although the steps cannot be separated in an actual oil flame, each of them must be carried out completely to form an efficient and clean flame. Otherwise, incomplete combustion products including smoke and soot can be formed, and more combustion air must be added to clean up the fire. This lowers system efficiency. **IT CAN BE AVOIDED IN ALL CASES BY CAREFUL ATTENTION TO DETAIL**. All the burner parts including the fuel nozzle, air fan, fuel pump, air turbulators, end cones and all other parts must work as designed.

Fuel oil is a liquid and must be partially or completed vaporized before combustion can proceed and a flame can be formed. Many different vaporization methods have been used to burn fuel oil, and these will be discussed in this chapter. The most common method now used in modern oil burners is fuel **atomization** by a high-pressure nozzle that produces small fuel droplets that can vaporize quickly (see Figure 2-3).

Oxygen from the combustion air must be available for combustion reactions to occur. The quantity of combustion air that is supplied to the burner is also very important. Every gallon of oil contains 6.3 pounds of carbon and 0.9 pounds of hydrogen. A minimum of 1365 cubic feet of air is needed to completely burn one gallon of fuel oil. These reactions will produce:

- 23 pounds of carbon dioxide
- 8 pounds of water vapor
- 78 pounds of nitrogen (contained in the combustion air).

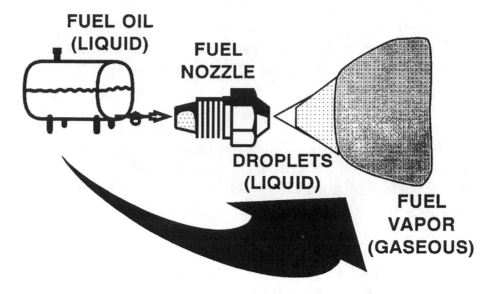

FUEL ATOMIZATION PROCESS

Figure 2-3

As a practical matter some excess combustion air is needed to prevent incomplete combustion which lowers efficiency and produces air pollution. Figure 2-4 shows that a fixed amount of air is needed to burn each gallon of fuel oil, and known quantities of flue gases are produced.

Fuel oil vapor and combustion air must be thoroughly mixed by the burner so that the combustion reactions can proceed to completion. Good fuel-air mixing is needed so that all of the fuel vapors can contact oxygen and the combustion reactions can be completed. Oil burners have air-handling parts that force the combustion air to mix with the vaporized fuel oil. The efficiency of the burner depends on the effectiveness of this mixing process (see Figure 2-5).

Too much combustion air lowers the efficiency of the heating unit. Excess combustion air does not increase the heat produced by the flame because all of the fuel is already burned. This extra air lowers efficiency because

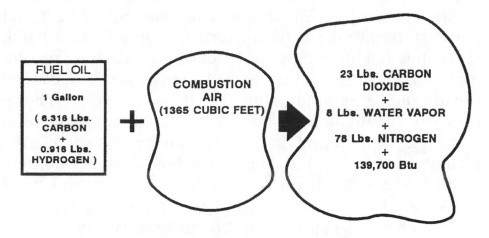

PERFECT COMBUSTION - NO EXCESS AIR

Figure 2-4

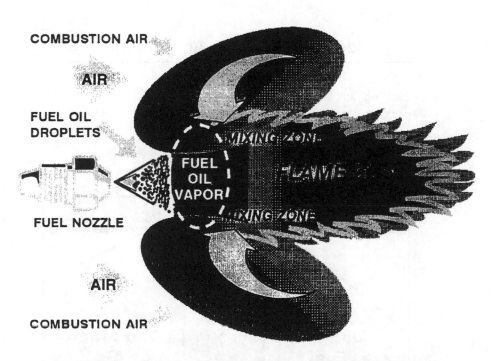

FUEL-AIR MIXING PROCESS

Figure 2-5

it takes heat away from the flame and lowers the peak flame temperature. This reduces the amount of heat that is transferred to the boiler or furnace. On the other hand, if combustion air supply to the burner is too low, incomplete combustion occurs, with decreased efficiency and greatly increased production of carbon monoxide. Therefore, careful attention to adjustment of burner combustion air intake is required for safety and peak system efficiency. In the past, installers have tended to set burners at high excess-air levels to minimize the possibility of smoke production, even though this reduced efficiency. Today's burners can be properly and safely set to lower levels of excess air. See Figure 2-6 which shows the "ideal" setting of the burner air damper for peak efficiency of a boiler or furnace.

The composition of the flue gases indicates the amount of excess combustion air and assists with burner adjustment. For every gallon of fuel oil consumed there are known quantities of combustion gases

Ideal Combustion Air Setting

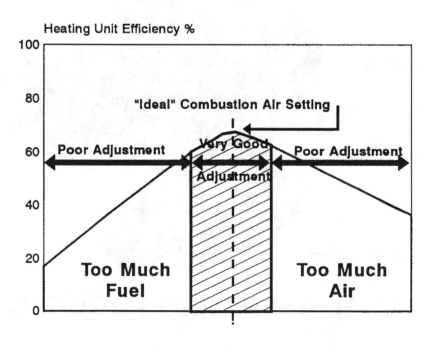

Figure 2-6

produced as shown in Figure 2-4. If excess combustion air is added, the total quantity of combustion gases increases and the percentage of carbon dioxide decreases. Therefore, it is possible to determine how much excess combustion air is in the flame by measuring the percentage of carbon dioxide in the exhaust gases (see Figure 2-7). Similarly, the percentage of oxygen (O_2) in the exhaust gases also indicates the amount of excess combustion air. The percentage of Oxygen rises as excess combustion air is added. Measuring flue gas composition is an important part of burner adjustment to assure peak system efficiency.

To summarize:

- The percent CO_2 or O_2 indicates the amount of excess air.
- CO_2 levels decrease as excess combustion air is added.
- O_2 levels increase as excess combustion air is added.

CO_2 In Flue Gas Changes With Burner Excess Combustion Air

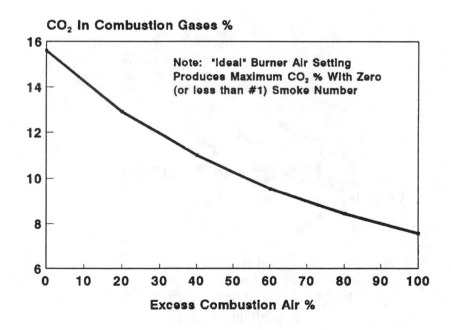

Figure 2-7

Heat from the flame helps vaporize the fuel for rapid intermixing with the combustion air and complete combustion. Combustion chambers radiate heat back to the fuel oil droplets, raises their temperature, and helps the droplets to vaporize quickly. This is especially important for older (non-flame-retention) burners. Most modern oil burners recirculate the hot gases within the flame, which also helps the fuel droplets to vaporize quickly. This allows all of the fuel to burn completely before leaving the flame. The volume of the combustion chamber must be large enough so that the reactions will have adequate time for completion before entering the heat-transfer section, where the flame gases are cooled and the burning process stops (see Figure 2-8).

Combustion of fuel oil requires several important steps:

- Break-up of the oil into droplets;
- A high voltage spark to initiate fuel vaporization and ignition;

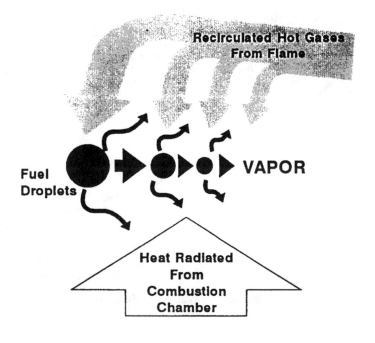

**Modern Oil-Burners Use Hot Gases
To Help Vaporize The Oil Drops**

Recirculated Hot Gases From Flame

Fuel Droplets

VAPOR

Heat Radiated From Combustion Chamber

Figure 2-8

- Heat transfer from the flame and from the chamber wall, to help the oil drops evaporate quickly and form a gas;
- Supply of the correct amount of combustion air;
- Effective mixing of the fuel vapors with the combustion air;
- A combustion chamber of sufficient volume that burning is complete before the gases leave the chamber.

2.2 Oil Burner Parts and Their Functions

Most oil burners in homes use high-pressure fuel nozzles to produce a spray of fuel droplets that are mixed with combustion air to produce a flame. The general operation of these pressure-atomizing burners is briefly reviewed here to show how oil burning takes place.

Figure 2-9 shows the key burner parts related to combustion performance:

1. An electric motor operates the fuel-oil pump and combustion-air fan.

2. The fuel pump pulls oil from the storage tank and sends out high—pressure oil at about 100 pounds per square inch to the nozzle.

3. The oil nozzle receives the pressurized oil and produces a spray of fine oil droplets at the head of the burner. The fuel begins to evaporate because the droplets have a large surface area. Heat from the flame and combustion chamber helps the fuel drops to evaporate rapidly.

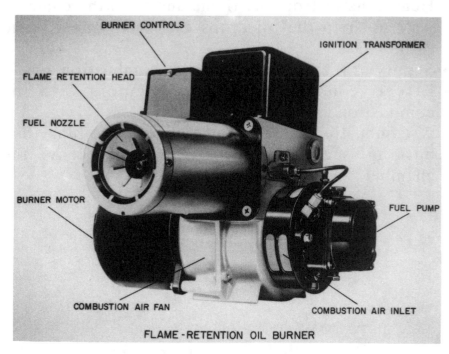

BURNER CONTROLS

IGNITION TRANSFORMER

FLAME RETENTION HEAD

FUEL NOZZLE

BURNER MOTOR

FUEL PUMP

COMBUSTION AIR FAN

COMBUSTION AIR INLET

FLAME-RETENTION OIL BURNER

Figure 2-9

4. The burner-air fan forces air into the burner, down the air tube, and out of the burner head. This air carries the oxygen needed to burn the fuel-oil vapor.

5. The burner head produces a swirling and recirculating air flow that mixes the fuel vapors with the oxygen in the air. Recirculation of the air carries hot flame gases back to the fuel droplets to speed up the rate of evaporation. This permits all the fuel to burn completely within the flame. The burner head is a key design feature that controls the amount of excess air needed to produce effective fuel and air mixing. As we have seen, this can strongly affect efficiency.

6. The amount of combustion air going to the flame is controlled by an air damper at the entry to the burner-air fan. Adjustment of this damper changes the volume of air supplied to the burner head. This allows only the exact amount of air needed for completely burning the fuel oil. Too little air produces, with smoke and CO, reduced efficiency. Too much air cools the flame and also lowers burner efficiency.

7. A combustion chamber of adequate size (with or without refractory) is needed so that the chemical reactions within the flame can be completed.

2.3 Fuel Nozzles and Conversion of Fuel Oil into a Vapor

The first step in fuel oil burning is changing the fuel oil from a liquid into a vapor that can mix easily with combustion air for rapid burning (oxidation) and formation of a flame. Many methods have been used in the past to vaporize fuel oil. The earliest burners heated a pot of oil to produce vapors. Later, atomizing nozzles using pressurized oil or air came into use. Most modern oil burners use pressurized fuel oil that is forced through a nozzle to produce a spray of small fuel oil droplets. These droplets then absorb heat and evaporate into fuel vapor. Good atomization is one key to clean and efficient oil burning.

Review of Fuel Nozzle Operation

A cross-sectional view of a typical high-pressure atomizing fuel nozzle is shown in Figure 2-10. Pressurized fuel oil enters the nozzle through an oil filter. The oil flows through the nozzle body to a distributor with slots that give it a rotational motion. The spinning oil enters a swirl chamber and the rotation increases as it approaches the nozzle orifice. The oil is now in the form of a hollow rotating cylinder around a core of air as it leaves the nozzle through the orifice. After leaving the nozzle the rotating oil forms a thin film of oil in the shape of a cone. As the cone travels away from the nozzle the oil film gets thinner until it ruptures into a mist of oil droplets.

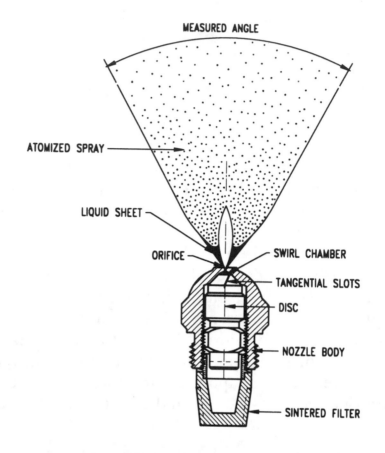

MEASURED ANGLE

ATOMIZED SPRAY

LIQUID SHEET

ORIFICE

SWIRL CHAMBER

TANGENTIAL SLOTS

DISC

NOZZLE BODY

SINTERED FILTER

Cutaway View Of A Fuel Oil Nozzle

(Graphics Courtesy Of Hago Manufacuring, Inc.)

Figure 2-10

- Flow rate of the oil,
- Angle of the oil spray,
- Pattern of the droplets (hollow, solid, or semi-solid fuel spray), and
- Droplet size distribution.

Each of these important nozzle functions can vary with fuel viscosity, temperature, and pressure as we will see later.

Fuel vapor is produced from the surface of the oil. By forming small fuel droplets the total surface area increases and the fuel can evaporate much more rapidly. That is the purpose of the atomizing fuel nozzle. A properly functioning fuel oil nozzle can produce more than 50,000,000,000 fuel droplets from one gallon of oil. This produces 4,000 times the surface area and allows the fuel to vaporize quickly and mix with the combustion air (see Figure 2-11).

Fuel Droplet Sprays Have Very Large Surface Area For Quick Vaporization And Burning

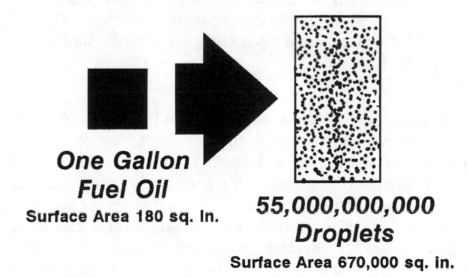

One Gallon Fuel Oil
Surface Area 180 sq. In.

55,000,000,000 Droplets
Surface Area 670,000 sq. in.

Figure 2-11

The fuel droplets that are produced vary in size from about .0002 to .0100 inches (5 to 250 microns). Droplet size is important to the oil burning process. The smaller droplets evaporate and burn quickly. However, larger droplets that may be produced by defective nozzles or cold oil may not completely evaporate and burn within the flame, which can produce incomplete combustion and smoke. The distribution of droplet sizes and the average droplet size both affect how much excess combustion air is needed, which in turn affects burner efficiency.

Large fuel droplets are difficult to burn completely and can lower system efficiency for several reasons:

- Large oil droplets may not vaporize completely within the flame and unburned fuel may escape (see Figure 2-12).
- Large fuel droplets produce soot that can deposit on heat—transfer surfaces and gradually lower heating system efficiency. As the large drops evaporate, the fuel composition within the droplet may change as the lighter fuel elements evaporate first. This leaves behind heavier parts of the fuel oil, which are harder to burn and can form soot and smoke.
- The larger droplets can form "droplet flames" (or fire-flies), which are small flames surrounding the larger droplets as they evaporate and burn. These droplet flames have been linked to smoke and soot production.

These undesired effects can be avoided by replacing worn fuel nozzles and supplying the oil at the recommended temperature and pressure. Recent tests show that modern flame-retention oil burners using pressure—atomizing nozzles produce very low levels of soot when properly adjusted. It is important to understand how the oil nozzle can affect combustion efficiency and completeness of combustion so that unnecessary problems can be avoided. If fuel nozzle problems are suspected, there are several options available to improve burner operation. Most oil heating systems can now operate cleanly and economically.

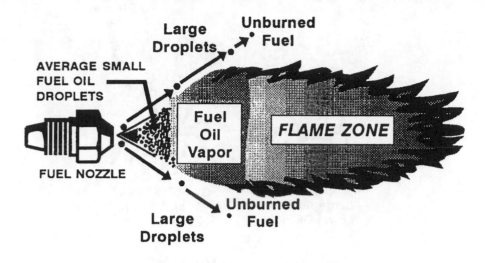

Large Fuel Droplets And Incomplete Combustion

Figure 2-12

Oil Temperature Affects the Nozzle Flow Rate and Droplet Sizes

More oil flows through the nozzle and the droplet sizes increase as the temperature of the oil drops. Both of these changes can degrade the flame quality and reduce the efficiency of the burner and boiler or furnace.

Changes in Oil Flow Rate. As the temperature of the fuel oil drops, its viscosity increases. Viscosity is the resistance to flow and colder oil does not flow as easily. You would think this would reduce the flow of oil through the nozzle, but in fact the opposite happens. The colder the oil, the greater the flow through the nozzle.

This is how it works. The higher viscosity slows down the speed of the oil rotating within the swirl chamber of the nozzle. The hollow cylinder of oil thickens and the

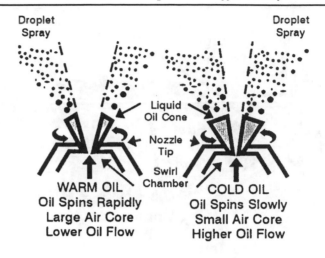

Colder Oil Causes More Oil To Flow
From The Tip Of The Nozzle

Figure 2-13

core of air gets smaller as the temperature of the oil drops. This means there is more oil at the nozzle tip being pushed out. So, more oil flows out of the nozzle through the orifice (see Figure 2-13). At 20°F the oil flow rate through a nozzle can be more than 15 percent higher than the oil flow at 80°F. This can increase smoke production in burners as the oil flow increases without a rise in burner air supply. The efficiency of operation drops lower.

Homes with above-ground outdoor fuel oil tanks can be seriously affected as the outdoor temperature drops. Consider the following example. A burner is set for near-zero smoke and optimum combustion air in the summer when the temperature is 80°F. When the outdoor temperature drops to 20 degrees the fuel in the above-ground tank is also at or near 20°F. The oil flow rate has now increased by more than 15 percent, but the air flow is about the same as in the summer. This can cause smoke levels to increase. It is important to be aware of this change in fuel oil delivery by a nozzle especially for homes with outdoor above-ground fuel oil storage tanks. Action can be taken to avoid this problem as discussed below.

Changes in Fuel Droplet Sizes. Lower fuel temperature also causes the fuel droplets to get larger. The average droplet size increases by more than 15 percent if the oil temperature drops from 80°F to 20°F (see Figure 2-14). The fuel spray will have a higher number of large fuel droplets, which can produce soot and smoke as discussed earlier. Additional excess combustion air may be needed to clean up the fire, which lowers the combustion efficiency of the burner. Therefore, low fuel temperatures should be avoided whenever practical. Indoor fuel tanks, tank insulation, fuel line heaters, nozzle pre-heaters, or other changes may be advisable for these cases. This will assure steady oil-flow rates and small fuel drops.

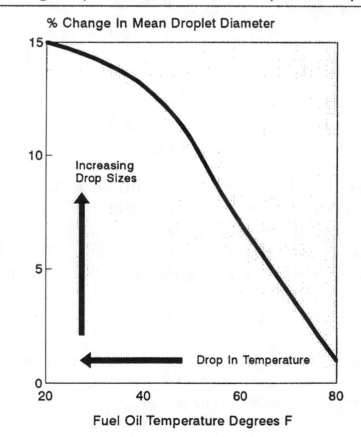

Average Droplet Size Increase As Oil Temperature Drops

Figure 2-14

To summarize, cold oil can lower burner and boiler or furnace performance by:

> • Increasing the oil flow rate from the nozzle, producing incomplete burning;
> • Producing large fuel drops that require added combustion air for a clean flame;
> • Causing poor combustion, resulting in soot deposits that can lower the efficiency of the boiler or furnace.
> • Be aware of these changes and take corrective action when needed.

Oil Pressure Also Affects Fuel Flow Rate and Droplet Sizes

Higher fuel oil pressure at the nozzle causes the oil flow to increase, and the average droplet size to decrease.

Changes in oil flow rate. As the oil pressure to a nozzle is increased the oil flow rises. The higher pressure pushes the oil to flow through the nozzle faster. The variation in fuel flow with pressure is shown in the table in Figure 2-15. Flow charts supplied by the fuel nozzle manufacturers or the equation in Figure 2-15 can be used to predict fuel flow as the oil pressure is varied.

It is possible to apply these known relationships to determine the fuel delivery from a pressure atomizing nozzle at various oil pressures.

Changes in fuel oil droplet size and efficiency. Higher fuel pressure also causes smaller fuel droplets to be formed. This can improve burner efficiency. Raising the pressure from 100 to 150 pounds per square inch (psi)

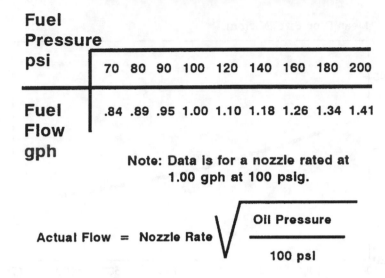

Typical Change In Oil Flow Rate As Oil Pressure Varies

Fuel Pressure psi	70	80	90	100	120	140	160	180	200
Fuel Flow gph	.84	.89	.95	1.00	1.10	1.18	1.26	1.34	1.41

Note: Data is for a nozzle rated at 1.00 gph at 100 psig.

$$\text{Actual Flow} = \text{Nozzle Rate} \sqrt{\frac{\text{Oil Pressure}}{100 \text{ psi}}}$$

Figure 2-15

causes the average droplet size to decrease by about 20 percent (see Figure 2-16). It also cuts down the number of large fuel droplets. This can be a useful method for improving the performance of oil burners where poor atomization is suspected.

For example, if colder oil is burned, the average droplet size rises. If the nozzle pressure is increased, the droplet size can be reduced and burner performance improved. However, the increase in fuel delivery rate must be considered, and a nozzle rated for less flow should be used. The smaller droplets produce less soot and smoke, and less combustion air is needed for a clean flame. This improves the efficiency of the burner. Many oil burners were designed for oil pressures of 100 psig. However, some new models recommend operating at 140 psig, to take advantage of the reduction in average droplet size. Check with the burner or fuel pump manufacturer about the highest oil pressures that are recommended for their equipment before changing the pressure.

Higher Fuel Pressure Lowers The Average Droplet Size

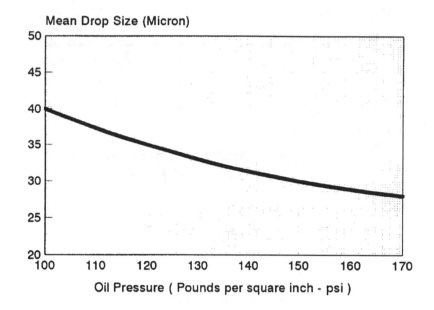

Figure 2-16

Combustion Chambers Help to Vaporize the Fuel

The heat radiated back to an oil flame from a hot combustion chamber also helps to evaporate the fuel droplets before they are mixed with air and burned. This was especially important for older oil burners prior to the development of flame-retention designs.

Lightweight combustion chambers are better than the massive firebrick versions because they heat up and cool down faster. This permits heat to be radiated back to the flame (and evaporate oil droplets) soon after burner start-up.

Another advantage of low-mass chambers is rapid cool-down after the burner firing cycle ends. This is important to reduce nozzle overheating during the burner off-cycle. When the burner is operating, the oil flow through the nozzle and the air flow around the nozzle help to remove the heat that is radiated from the hot chamber. When the burner firing cycle ends, this cooling effect stops. The combustion chamber is still hot, and this can heat the fuel nozzle. This causes oil and air trapped in the fuel line to expand, in some cases enough to force oil to drip out of the nozzle. This after-drip problem may produce odors and soot. The low-mass combustion chambers are preferred because they cool off faster and produce less nozzle overheating than the heavier chambers.

Some boilers do not have refractory-lined combustion chambers. Many only require a target-wall type refractory. High-speed retention-head burners can often produce a stable and clean flame without the help of a hot chamber. The reason for this is improved mixing of the fuel and air, which will be discussed in the next section of this chapter. Careful burner adjustment is important for these boilers to avoid smoke formation. These chamberless systems can operate efficiently and cleanly with modern oil burners. An advantage of firing without a chamber is increased heat transfer surfaces within the boiler. This helps to improve the overall efficiency of the heating unit.

Adequate combustion space must always be available whether or not a combustion chamber is used. The chemical reactions in all flames occur at very high temperatures, on the order of 3000°F, as discussed earlier. If the flame touches a cooler surface such as a chamber wall or boiler surface, then the flame gases are rapidly cooled and the combustion reactions stop immediately. This is referred to as "flame quenching". It produces smoke and soot as the fuel is not completely burned. The combustion space within the boiler or furnace must be large enough and properly shaped so that the flame does not touch any surfaces. This is especially important if no combustion chamber is used, because the inside surfaces are cool and can stop the combustion reactions if they come in contact with the flame.

2.4 Burner Air Supply and Fuel-Air Mixing

After the fuel oil is broken up into spray of droplets that begin to vaporize, the burner fan supplies combustion air that contains the oxygen needed for the oil vapors to burn. Several factors are important during this process of fuel oil and air intermixing so that the oil can burn cleanly and efficiently. The main ones are:

> • Controlling the quantity of air going to the flame,
> • Matching the air flow to oil spray pattern, and
> • Mixing of the combustion air with the fuel oil vapors.

Metering of the Air Flow

In order to have complete combustion, a minimum quantity of combustion air must be supplied by the burner. Review Figure 2-4. If not enough air is supplied by the burner to the flame, the oil cannot burn completely, the efficiency decreases and soot and smoke may be produced. If more air is supplied by the burner, the excess air lowers the flame temperature and efficiency drops. Combustion efficiency testing procedures are discussed in Chapter 5. Review Figure 2-6 for the effect of combustion air supply on efficiency. Air flow metering by the burner is an important part of burner operation.

Oil burners have an air shutter or damper at the inlet to the fan that is adjustable and controls the flow of combustion air into the burner by varying the size of the air inlet. This damper (see Figure 2-9) is adjusted in the field during burner installation and servicing. Opening this damper increases the air flow through the burner, while closing the damper reduces the flow of combustion air.

*Matching
the Air
Flow and
Fuel Spray
Patterns*

A second important function of the burner is to shape the combustion air flow so that it matches the oil spray pattern. More accurately, the burner must produce an air flow shape that is similar to the fuel spray available from fuel-oil nozzles. The oil spray pattern is described by the angle of the spray and the location of droplets within the spray. If most of the droplets are toward the outside of the spray, it is referred to as a "hollow" spray pattern. If the droplets are evenly distributed it is called a "solid" spray. An in-between pattern is referred to as "semi-solid."

The shape of the burner air flow depends on how long ago the burner was designed. Originally, oil burners used natural draft and did not have electric-powered blowers that could shape the combustion air. After power burners were introduced, devices were added to change and control the air flow pattern. The objective was to match the combustion air and fuel spray shapes so that good fuel-air mixing and complete combustion could occur with minimum excess air.

Some situations to avoid when matching the air flow and fuel spray patterns include those listed below. This is especially important for older non-flame retention burners:

- Air flow too wide for oil spray,
- Air flow too narrow for oil spray, and
- Air flow or oil spray imbalances or non-uniformities.

Air Flow Too Wide. This situation is illustrated in Figure 2-17. The air flow is much wider than the spray of oil droplets. This is not good because the droplets at the

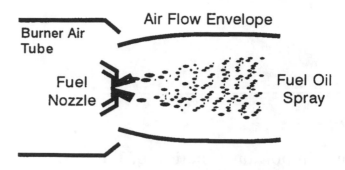

Air Flow Too Wide For Oil Spray Pattern

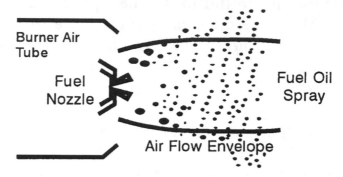

Air Flow Too Narrow For Oil Spray Pattern

Figure 2-17

center of the spray do not have enough air for complete combustion. The air at the outside of the pattern cannot easily reach the fuel droplets at the center of the flame. This can produce smoke, incomplete combustion, and loss of efficiency. More combustion air must be supplied to the burner so that all of the oil at the center of the flame can be burned. This excess combustion air lowers efficiency as discussed earlier. Whenever a fuel nozzle is replaced, the spray angle and pattern should be similar to the burner air flow. Consult and follow the recommendations of the burner manufacturer whenever possible. Also, for older burners, several nozzle patterns can be tested in the field, and the one that produces the **lowest excess air with a zero to number one smoke** should be used. A standard "Nozzle Application Procedure" such as one described in the **Oil Heat Technician's Manual** published by the Petroleum Marketers Association of America (former PMEF manual) should be used to save time.

Air Flow Too Narrow. This condition is also illustrated in Figure 2-17. The air flow envelope is too narrow for the oil spray pattern. Some of the fuel droplets escape from the air flow pattern and cannot mix with sufficient combustion air for complete burning. This is not good because it can produce incomplete combustion, smoke, and loss of efficiency as some of the fuel is unburned. The service technician can attempt to clean up the fire by opening up the burner air damper and increasing excess combustion air. This can lower efficiency of the burner.

Air Flow or Oil Spray Imbalances. If the air or oil flow patterns are not uniform, more fuel may be distributed to one part of the flame. Part of the flame has too much fuel while other parts have too little. This non-uniformity can produce incomplete combustion and smoke in the fuel-rich area of the flame. Excess combustion air must be added to clean up the fire and this lowers efficiency. Fuel nozzles should be replaced when fuel spray imbalances are observed. Also, the air fan, air-handling, and air-pattern forming parts of the burner should be inspected and cleaned or replaced as needed. This will help to maintain balanced air and fuel oil patterns for peak efficiency.

NOTE: The burner air flow can change the shape of the fuel droplet spray to improve fuel air mixing. This is especially true for newer oil burners including flame retention models with high-velocity air with recirculation. This high-velocity air flow can pull droplets into the flame and improve fuel and air mixing. This reduces the need for precise fuel and air pattern matching. However, careful attention to matching fuel and air patterns is always important whenever older burners are serviced. Always follow the recommendation of the burner manufacturer regarding nozzle spray angle and pattern. Use a systematic "Nozzle Application Procedure" for adjusting older burners in the field. Replacing older burners with newer flame-retention models is often advisable, especially if the expected remaining life of the boiler or furnace is more than three years. It improves efficiency, reduces the time required for future service calls, reduces emissions, improves burner reliability, and pays for itself in two to three years in many homes.

Fuel and Air Mixing

Complete and forceful intermixing of the fuel oil vapors with combustion air is necessary for efficient and clean burning. Oil burner design has evolved over the past 50 years. The method for mixing the fuel with the air is one of the areas that has received the most attention and development because it is a key to efficient oil burning.

Old vaporizing oil burners used heated pots to produce fuel vapors and relied on natural draft produced by a chimney to pull combustion air into the burner without the aid of a burner fan (see Figure 2-18). The negative pressure (draft) produced by a chimney is only about 0.05 (or 5/100) of an inch of water column. For comparison, it takes a negative pressure of 6 or 8 inches of water column to drink water from a glass through a straw. This is 100 times greater than chimney draft. This weak pressure from

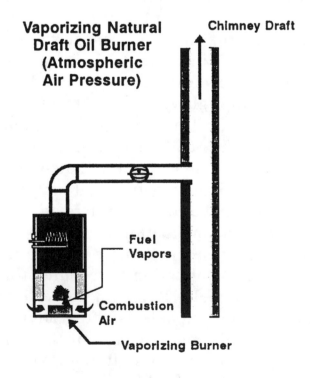

Vaporizing Natural Draft Oil Burner (Atmospheric Air Pressure)

Chimney Draft

Fuel Vapors

Combustion Air

Vaporizing Burner

Figure 2-18

Crossectional View Of An Early Powered Oil Burner

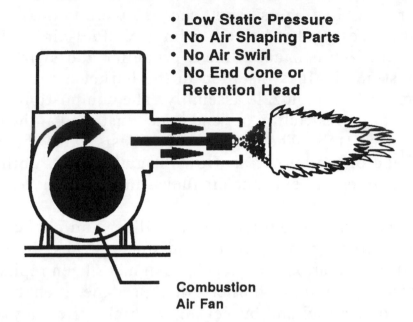

- Low Static Pressure
- No Air Shaping Parts
- No Air Swirl
- No End Cone or Retention Head

Combustion
Air Fan

Figure 2-19

the chimney produced low burner air velocities and prevented forceful intermixing of the fuel and air. This limited the efficiency of these early oil burners.

The introduction of forced-draft burners that incorporated an electric air fan for supplying the combustion air was an important advance in oil burner design. These early "gun-type" oil burners used pressure-atomizing nozzles and air fans to enhance fuel and air mixing. These fans produced air pressures of up to one inch of water column, 20 times greater than natural-draft burners. The air pressure supplied by the burner created more forceful mixing of the air and fuel and better control of the combustion air volume. Initially, the burner air tube was open at the end and no devices were installed to spin or "turbulate" the combustion air or to shape the air pattern that was produced. A diagram of an early "power" oil burner is shown in Figure 2-19. The powered air fan was a significant improvement in the ability to mix the combustion air with oil droplets for complete and efficient burning.

The next advance in burner fuel-air mixing was the introduction of devices in the burner air tube to shape and spin the air to improve mixing of the fuel vapors with the burner air. "Stabilizers" and "chokes" were two changes to burner design that helped to improve fuel-air mixing. The **stabilizer** is shaped like a propeller and swirls the combustion air. It is installed in the burner air tube upstream of the fuel nozzle assembly. The combustion head or **choke** is a restriction or "end cone" installed at the end of the burner tube. The choke size and design also changes the shape of the burner air flow. Together the stabilizer and choke tend to enhance air fuel—mixing.

The gun-type oil burner with stabilizer and choke was manufactured for many years, and some of these burners are still in operation today. This design has been replaced by "flame retention" burners that produce even better mixing of the fuel and burner air for high efficiency and improved performance. However, service technicians must be able to service the stabilizer-and-choke type burners and adjust them for peak efficiency.

The **flame retention oil burner** was the next advancement in burner design. It was primarily an improvement in burner end-cone design for better mixing of the burner air with the fuel oil droplets and vapor. The flame-retention design typically uses a high-speed motor to drive the burner air fan. This produces higher air pressure than older burners and pushes the air through the burner with more force. This allows the burner head to mix the air and fuel more intensely for complete combustion and reduced excess combustion air. The retention head of the burner is primarily a modified burner end cone that drastically changes the air flow produced by the burner. The retention head uses the high air pressure to produce a strong swirling motion and internal recirculation of hot gases within the flame. This is shown in Figure 2-20. The recirculation of hot gases by the flame retention-head design improves burner performance in the following ways:

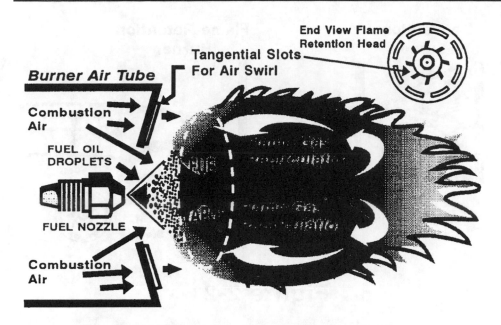

Oil Flame With Recirculation Produced By Flame Retention Burner

Figure 2-20

- The hot, recirculating flame gases come back to meet and help vaporize the fuel droplets. Even the large fuel droplets can be completely vaporized and burned within the flame. This produces very clean and efficient combustion.

- The recirculation and strong swirling motion of the burner air improves the mixing of the fuel vapors with the burner air, for more complete reaction of all the fuel-oil vapors and cleaner burning. This permits lower excess air and higher combustion efficiency.

- The intense swirling and recirculation flows produce a very stable flame that is located near the burner head. This is the reason for the name "flame-retention" burner. The strong mixing and air swirl produced by the high burner-air pressure is less sensitive to changes in chimney draft and other changing conditions. The flame is more stable than oil flames produced by older burner designs and is less affected by changes in chimney draft.

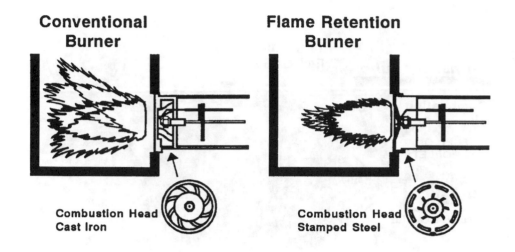

Figure 2-21

Figure 2-21 is a sketch of flames from flame-retention and older oil burner flames that demonstrates the difference in burning characteristics. The flame-retention model has a very intense and compact flame located near the burner head. The older oil burner produces a more diffuse, lazy flame that is characteristic of less intense fuel-air mixing.

A recent advance in fuel-air mixing is the high static air pressure flame retention oil burner. These burners produce about twice the air pressure of a conventional flame retention oil burner. This can produce even more intense fuel and air mixing than conventional flame retention burners and even better flame stability. Some of the performance advantages of these burners are discussed in a later section of this chapter.

Oil burner fuel-air mixing has evolved over the past 50 years to a point where near-perfect mixing of the burner air with the fuel droplets and vapors now takes place. Burner combustion air pressure has increased from about .05 inches to 3.0 inches of water column. This is an increase by a factor of 60. New oil burners have 60 times more force available for mixing the air and fuel for complete combustion. This is the primary reason for improved burner cleanliness and efficiency that has occurred over the past 50 years.

2.5 Smoke Production by Oil Burners

Smoke production by oil burners is unnecessary and causes undesired side effects. Smoke and soot deposit on the heat transfer surfaces of boilers and furnaces and this reduces efficiency. Smoke and soot deposits also increase the frequency of cleaning calls and increases the time required for oil equipment servicing. More important, soot production can be a nuisance to homeowners and can encourage customers to switch to other fuels. This is completely unnecessary, if the oil burner is properly adjusted and modern equipment is used to replace outdated burner models.

Some older oil burners could produce smoke as a result of changes in the air flow caused by changes in chimney draft. The draft produced by a chimney changes with the outdoor air temperature and wind, and this affects the volume of air flowing to these older oil burners. See Chapter 4 for more information. As discussed earlier, if the burner does not supply enough combustion air to burn all of the fuel, incomplete combustion products and smoke can form. This condition occurred with vaporizing pot burners and also to some degree with the early designs of gun-type burners that preceded flame—retention designs. Modern oil burners are, however, not strongly affected by changes in chimney draft, and can operate with zero smoke throughout the entire heating season when properly installed and adjusted.

All of the oil burning steps discussed earlier are necessary to avoid incomplete combustion and smoke.

Flame-retention burners are much less sensitive to chimney draft than older oil burners and can operate smoke-free without the assistance of strong chimney draft. The newer high static air pressure burners are even less sensitive to chimney draft variations and can operate without smoke over a wide range of operating conditions. This allows boiler and furnace manufacturers to design very high-efficiency heating appliances that take advantage of the superior characteristics of the high static air pressure flame—retention burners.

If an older oil burner is causing chronic smoke problems, the best thing to do is almost always to replace it with a modern flame-retention head burner. There are, however, some smoke conditions that simple burner replacement will not fix.

- **TOO MUCH COMBUSTION AIR** can cause smoke to form because the excess air lowers the temperature of the flame. If the temperature of the flame is too low, smoke can be formed. Therefore, it is also important to avoid too much excess air to prevent smoke production. Combustion test equipment should always be used to measure smoke and excess air levels whenever a burner is adjusted (see Chapter 7).
- Air leakage into the combustion chamber can also reduce the flame temperature and cause smoke to be formed in the same way that excess combustion air causes smoke. Boilers and furnaces should be sealed to prevent this unneeded air flow from reaching the flame.
- If the flame touches any surfaces inside the combustion chamber, boiler or furnace, the chemical reactions are immediately stopped because the temperature in this local region of the flame drops. This is referred to as "flame quenching". Always be sure to adjust the burner to avoid this condition.

Short burner cycling in heating units with heavy combustion chambers is another potential cause for smoke production if older oil burners are installed. The chambers require considerable time to heat up before they radiate heat back to the flame to help vaporize the fuel droplets. This is important for some older burners. If the burner operates with short on-cycles consider the following:

- Use a fuel nozzle rated for less flow, if practical,
- Readjust the setpoints to extend burner on times,
- Replace the chamber with a low-mass refractory that heats up quickly, and
- Install a flame-retention burner that does not depend on chamber radiation for clean burning.

2.6 Smoke Has Its Functions

The onset of smoke production by oil burners has two useful functions:

- Indicator for burner excess air adjustment.
- Safety indicator when combustion air drops too low.

Smoke measurement is an important part of combustion efficiency testing. It allows accurate adjustment of the burner air setting. The burner air damper is gradually closed until smoke just begins to form as indicated by a standard smoke tester. At this point the burner air is as low as possible while producing a clean flame. If the air damper is opened more, then too much air is admitted to the flame, the flame temperature decreases, and efficiency drops. If the air damper is closed more, then smoke production increases. Therefore, smoke serves as a primary indicator of proper burner air adjustment.

When the smoke produced by an oil burner is adjusted between zero and number 1 on the Bacharach scale (just barely above a zero reading of a "trace"), extremely light soot deposition is expected during the heating season. The boiler or furnace will operate with high thermal efficiency with very minor efficiency loss from soot build-up on heat transfer surfaces. Recent tests on oil burner soot production show that properly adjusted flame retention oil burners produce less than 6 ounces of soot and smoke over one year of operation.

Smoke also provides an important **warning signal** if an oil burner goes out of adjustment. Smoke is almost always produced **before** carbon monoxide and other dangerous combustion gases are formed by the flame. Smoke is a sign that burner adjustment is needed before hazardous levels of incomplete combustion gases are produced. This is not true of gaseous fuel burners, which produce hazardous levels of carbon monoxide (a toxic, odorless, colorless, and tasteless gas) without smoke or any other warning.

Under normal conditions, smoke production by oil burners is unnecessary and undesired. Careful attention to heating system and burner adjustment can reduce smoke levels significantly. If smoke is produced, then corrective action should be taken. Check all possible sources of smoke production and replace defective burner parts and readjust the burner air setting. If the existing oil burner is a continuing problem, replace it with a new flame-retention model or a high static pressure flame-retention burner. Remember, smoke is useful as an indicator for accurate burner air adjustment and as a "warning signal" of combustion problems before dangerous combustion gases are produced. Always use a smoke-spot test when adjusting or tuning-up oil burners.

2.7 Excess Air, Smoke, Efficiency and Burner Adjustment

Figure 2-22 shows how the flame temperature of an oil burner changes with excess combustion air. As the air flow to the burner increases, the flue gas CO_2 readings drop and the flame temperature is lowered. For example, at 12% CO_2 (25 percent excess air), the flame temperature is approximately 3,000 degrees F. If excess air is added and the CO_2 drops to 8% (85 percent excess air), the flame temperature is lowered to about 2,300 degrees F. The

Peak Flame Temperature (without heat losses)
As The Excess Combustion Air (CO2) Changes

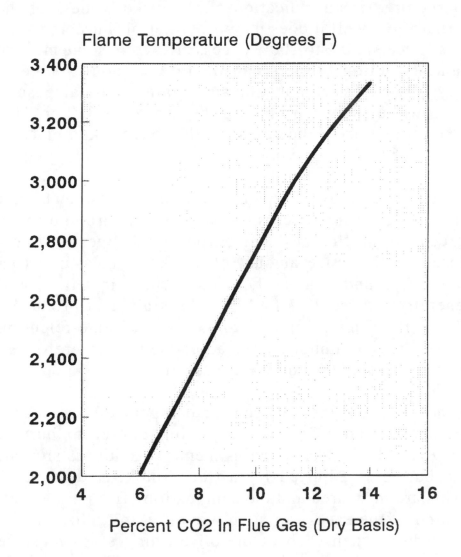

Figure 2-22

lower temperature flame transfers its heat more slowly to the boiler or furnace and the system efficiency drops.

All burners require some excess combustion air above the minimum amount needed to complete the chemical reactions. This is to compensate for the fuel-air mixing limitations of all burners. Figure 2-4 showed that each gallon of oil requires 1365 cubic feet of air for complete combustion. In practice, oil burners require excess combustion air above this amount for complete and smoke-free operation. The amount of excess combustion air required is an indication of the effectiveness of the burner (how well it does its job). Older oil burners sometimes needed 80% to 100% excess air, while some modern flame-retention burners can operate without smoke at only 10% excess combustion air. Again excess air results in a lower efficiency rating for the furnace or boiler. This is an indication of the advances that have taken place in oil burner fuel-air mixing.

Figure 2-23 shows a typical relationship between burner air damper setting, excess air, smoke and carbon dioxide percent in the flue gas. The burner air damper is slowly closed until a trace amount of smoke is measured (between zero and number 1). This burner air setting will generally require 20% to 40% excess air, and produce a CO_2 in the flue gas of 11% to 13% for a flame-retention burner. The optimum burner adjustment is, therefore in the range from 20% to 40% excess air.

The relationships between air-damper setting, excess air, smoke and CO_2 will vary from burner to burner. However, the burner air adjustment procedure is similar. The burner is adjusted for a trace smoke and the CO_2 levels are measured and the combustion efficiency is calculated. If the excess air supply required for a low smoke is too high, then each of the oil burning steps must be examined and corrective actions taken. These include many of the common oil burning problems discussed in this chapter. More information on combustion efficiency testing procedures, and interpreting test results is included in Chapter 7 of this manual.

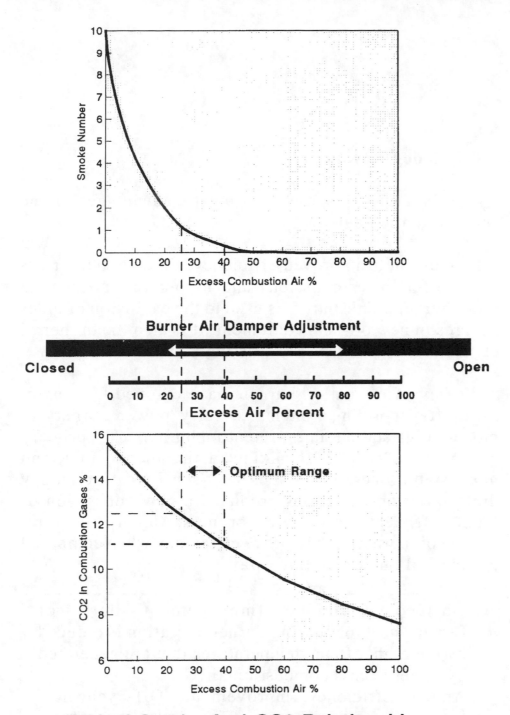

Typical Smoke And CO2 Relationship
For A Flame Retention Head Burner

Figure 2-23

2.8 Advantages of New Burner Designs

Efficiency Advances

This is a good place to sum up the advantages of the flame-retention burner.

In addition to improved efficiency, the new burner designs offer lower emissions and higher reliability than older burners. This burner is used to the exclusion of older designs in new oil-heat equipment. It is also the burner of choice for replacements in existing equipment.

We have seen that oil burners have evolved from natural-draft vaporizing systems to early power burners to modern high static flame—retention burners. The primary advances include better mixing of the air and fuel, and more stable operation that is less sensitive to chimney draft variations. This has produced a new generation of highly efficient and clean oil burners. Modern flame-retention oil burners can improve efficiency when compared to older oil burners in three ways.

- On-Cycle Efficiency Improvement—boiler or furnace heat loss during burner operation is reduced by the higher flame temperatures that are generated by lower excess combustion air.
- Annual Efficiency Improvement—Off-cycle heat losses are lowered because flame retention burners allow less off-cycle air flow through the burner, which reduces off-cycle heat losses from the heating unit.
- Better Flame Stability—The flame-retention burners are also more resistant to changes in chimney draft than older burners and operate with low smoke and high efficiency over the entire heating season.

These improvements reduce heat losses and increase the efficiency of the oil system by about 15 to 18 percent for the average installation. We will compare the efficiency of: older non-flame retention oil burners (A), flame-retention burners (B), and high static air pressure flame-retention burners (C).

Combustion (On-Cycle) Efficiency Improvement

Combustion Efficiency or "On-Cycle" Efficiency is improved by the lower excess combustion air that is needed by the newer oil burners to produce a clean flame with a smoke number of less than 1. Figure 2-24 shows the typical range of smoke versus excess air for the older and newer burners. The non-flame-retention burners need 50% to 100% excess air and produce smoke numbers between 1 and 3. The flame-retention burners typically need only 20% to 40% excess air to produce a smoke

Typical Ranges Of Smoke And Excess Air For Burner Operation

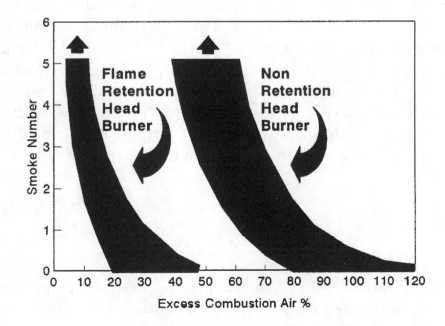

Figure 2-24

number between zero and 1. This is the result of better mixing of the air and fuel by the newer burners. The older non-flame-retention oil burners need more excess air and operate with flue heat losses in the range of 25% and combustion efficiencies of about 75%. In contrast, flame-retention burners require only 20 to 30% excess air and operate with average combustion efficiencies of 83%. The high static air pressure flame-retention burner is expected to operate with even higher combustion efficiencies and is a better choice in installations with poor chimney draft.

The combustion efficiency is determined by measurements in the stack, resulting in a net stack temperature and excess air indication (% CO_2 or % O_2). This information is used to look up the efficiency on a slide-rule type indicator or processed by an electronic efficiency measurement instrument that automatically indicates the efficiency level.

The flame-retention oil burners operate with on-cycle efficiencies that are about 8 percentage points or more higher than older burners. This produces annual fuel savings of more than 10 percent. Actual fuel savings by replacing older burners will depend on the efficiency of the existing burner, the nozzle size of the new burner, and the how the new burner is adjusted. Maximum savings are produced by reducing the nozzle size for the new burner and using combustion test equipment to carefully adjust the burner air supply for peak efficiency. A reduced-size fuel nozzle can be used to improve system efficiency in most cases without reducing heat output, because of the higher efficiency of the new burner.

Annual Efficiency Improvement

The improvement in annual efficiency by new oil burners includes the on-cycle improvement and also the effect of reduced off-cycle heat losses from the boiler or furnace. Off-cycle heat losses occur while the burner is idle and cool room air flows through the burner, across the warm heat exchanger and out of the chimney. This removes heat that is stored in boiler or furnace and lowers annual efficiency. Also, room air is removed from the house and is replaced by cold outdoor air that must be heated, which also lowers the annual system efficiency. Laboratory tests have shown that a flame-retention burner lowers off-cycle heat loss by about one-third because the burner head has a tighter design (see Figure 2-25). In total, the annual efficiency improvement is approximately 15 percent for flame-retention burners when they replace older burners. A slightly higher annual efficiency improvement is expected for the high static air pressure flame-retention burners because their air passages are even smaller.

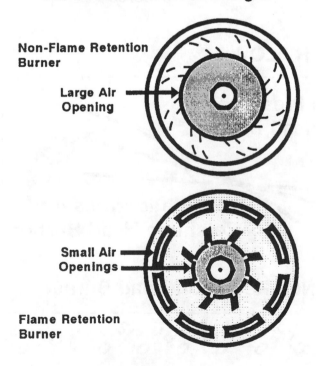

Comparison Of Air Flow Areas For Two Burner Head Designs

Non-Flame Retention Burner

Large Air Opening

Small Air Openings

Flame Retention Burner

Figure 2-25

Better
Flame
Stability

Another important advantage of modern burners is the stability of the flame that results form the higher static air pressures when compared to older non-flame retention models. This allows the newer burners to hold their air settings and maintain high efficiency and low smoke levels throughout the heating season as the chimney draft varies. This is discussed in Chapter 3.

Better flame stability is also produced by these new burners because of improved fuel-air mixing and higher static air pressure supplied by the combustion-air fan. Figure 2-26 shows that the new oil burners operate with higher air pressure and they are less sensitive to changes

EFFECT OF DRAFT ON BURNER EXCESS AIR

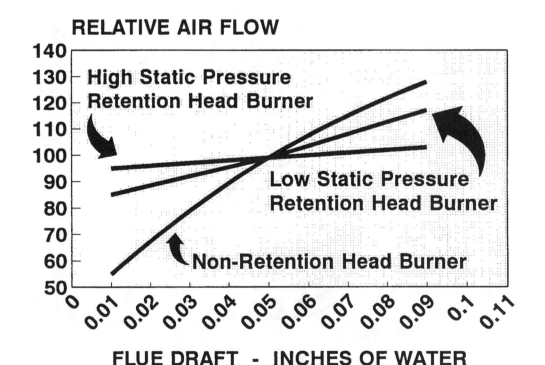

Figure 2-26

in chimney draft. As described earlier, the combustion air flow of the new burners remains constant throughout the heating season for high efficiency and low smoke and soot production when compared to older burner designs. Ignition is more reliable with reduced fouling of the ignition electrodes by the new burners. The more stable burners are less likely to produce "puff backs" because the higher pressure air fans can overcome chimney backdrafts, and this improves customer satisfaction. Improved flame stability also permits through-the-wall venting and other advanced system operations because the burner does not depend on chimney draft for good combustion as did older burners.

Smoke and Gaseous Pollutant Emissions

Reduced smoke production is another important advantage of modern flame-retention oil burners. Recent laboratory tests have demonstrated that flame-retention oil burners can operate with soot and smoke levels that are approaching near-zero levels. Oil burner smoke and soot production has decreased over the past thirty years to almost **zero** for **properly installed and adjusted flame-retention oil burners**. As the burner air pressure increased (and produced better fuel and air mixing) burner smoke and soot production decreased rapidly.

Modern oil burners can operate with particulate and soot levels of only 0.0027 pounds per million BTU. This is equal to natural—gas burners with an average particulate output of 0.003 pounds per million BTU. This is equivalent to about 0.3 pounds of soot produced each heating season. These reduced particulate levels are important for the following reasons:

> - Boilers and furnaces can operate over the entire heating season without the soot deposition that had reduced heating system efficiency when older oil burners were operated.
> - The service time and effort required for cleaning the inside surfaces of boilers and furnaces is reduced by the new oil burners that produce less soot.
> - Customer concerns about the cleanliness of oil heat can be corrected.
> - Outdated information used by competing fuel suppliers that "oil heat is dirty" can be refuted by the installation and operation of new oil burners.

Modern oil burners also emit very small amounts of gaseous pollutants. The formation of hydrocarbons, carbon monoxide, and nitrogen oxides are very low compared to other combustion equipment used in the U.S.

Hydrocarbons are unburned fuel elements that escape from the combustion process and can contribute to air pollution. Home oil burners produce on average only 0.00174 pounds per million BTU of fuel consumed, while the average for all types of combustion equipment in the U.S. is 100 times more. Therefore, residential oil burners are very clean burning and do not produce significant amounts of hydrocarbons.

Carbon monoxide (CO) is a colorless and odorless gas that can be lethal at very low concentrations. CO is formed by incomplete combustion of fuels, but is present at extremely low levels in the exhaust of properly adjusted oil burners. Typical residential oil burners produce only 0.026 pounds of carbon monoxide per million BTU of fuel burned. This is low compared to other combustion equipment used in the U.S., which, on average, generates more than 50 times more CO per million Btu. It is clear that residential oil burners are not a major source of Carbon monoxide.

Nitrogen oxide (NO) is an air pollutant that contributes to photochemical smog and is produced by most combustion systems. The average NO production by home oil burners is only about one-fourth of the average production of Nitrogen oxide by all types of combustion sources in the U.S.

Residential oil burners generate low levels of air pollutants and are not a major source of pollution in the U.S. In fact, smoke and soot emissions by modern oil burners are approaching zero and are as low as many natural gas burners. These advantages, combined with the increase in efficiency, make flame-retention oil burners an excellent option for improving the performance of home heating systems. Careful burner adjustment in the field is important so that these advances in oil burner design can be fully realized.

2.9 Oil Burner Interactions with Other Heating System Parts

We have seen that an oil burner is part of a "heating system" that includes a boiler or furnace, combustion chamber, vent connection, draft control and chimney. How well the burner operates depends on how these parts work together. Several important interactions are discussed here.

Interactions with Boiler or Furnace Design

If an older boiler or furnace has many air leaks into the combustion chamber or heating surfaces, the flame temperature will be lowered. This reduces combustion efficiency. A new burner cannot control this "secondary" air flow. Therefore, the fuel savings by installing a new oil burner may be less than expected. Sealing these air leaks is an important part of good burner installation. If sealing these air leaks is not practical, or the heating unit design is outdated, the homeowner should be advised that a new boiler or furnace is needed.

Interactions with Combustion-Chamber Design

We have seen that the combustion chamber is important for a clean and efficient oil flame, especially for older oil burners. The size and shape, weight, and temperature rating are all important factors that affect burner operation. The size and shape of the chamber must be large enough to prevent the flame from touching its surfaces to prevent smoke and incomplete combustion on burner startup. The weight of the chamber is also important. Lightweight chambers are better because they heat up and cool down faster. Rapid warmup allows the flame to reach its peak temperature sooner for more rapid evaporation of the fuel oil drops and clean burning. Low-mass chambers also cool down faster, which reduces overheating of the fuel nozzle during the off-cycle. This lowers fuel afterdrip and reduces nozzle caking. Also, low-mass chambers store less heat and this lowers off-cycle heat losses from the boiler or furnace. This can be especially important for warm-air furnaces, where a heavy combustion chamber can be a large part of the off-cycle heat losses. High temperature combustion-chamber materials are required for flame-retention oil burners because they operate with less excess air and higher flame temperature.

Interactions with Venting System Design

The venting system includes the flue pipe, barometric damper, and chimney. Each of these can affect burner performance. If the flue connections are not tight, secondary air can lower the chimney temperature, which lowers chimney draft. This can change the air flow through the burner and its operating efficiency. The barometric damper can also lower efficiency if it is not adjusted properly. If the damper is set for too high a draft, the efficiency of the burner can be lowered because too much excess air will be pulled into the burner. Also, off-cycle air flow through the burner can increase, which lowers system efficiency. This is especially important for older oil burners. We have seen that the new burners operate with much higher air pressure and they are less sensitive to draft changes. In some cases, the efficiency may be improved by using a high static-air-pressure oil burner without a barometric damper. This will be discussed more in a later section of this manual. The chimney design also can effect burner performance if insufficient draft is produced at some times during the heating season. Again, this is more important for older burner designs that need chimney draft to assist with the supply of burner air. If chimney draft problems are suspected, installing a new high static-air-pressure oil burner may correct the problem.

QUESTIONS

2-1. Droplet size decreases with oil atomization pump pressure increase.

2-2. Heat from the flame in the fire box helps to vaporize the oil.

2.3 A CO_2 of 11% to 13% is ideal for most burner settings.

2-4. Excess combustion air can be found by measuring CO_2 or O_2.

2-5. What are the two (2) things that must be mixed to have proper combustion?

2-6. What two major components make up fuel oil?

2-7. Incomplete combustion causes?

2-8. Pressure of the fuel oil affects flow rate of the oil going through the nozzle. True or false?

2-9. Flame-retention burners have a very intense and compact flame located near the burner head, while the older conventional burners produce a more diffuse, lazy flame that is characteristic of less intense fuel-air mixing. True or false?

2-10. Flame retention oil burners do not depend as much on chimney draft for good combustion as did older burners. True or false?

2-11. Breaking up oil into small droplets is called
1. Vaporization
2. Atomization
3. Liquidization
4. Minimization

2-12. Levels of CO_2 gas in the flue gas _____ as excess air is increased.
1. Remain the same
2. Decrease
3. Increase
4. None of the above

2-13. Too much excess air reduces efficiency by lowering flame temperature. True or false?

2-14. The two major advantages of using lightweight combustion chambers are:
1. Rapid heat up and rapid cool down
2. Slow heat up and slow cool down
3. Rapid heat up and slow cool down
4. Slow heat up and rapid cool down

2-15. Sealing air leaks into the combustion chamber areas is an important part of a good burner installation because:
1. Air leaks use up made-up air
2. Air leaks lower the flame temperature
3. Air leaks look unprofessional to the homeowner
4. None of the above

Chapter 3—High-Efficiency Boilers and Furnaces

New oil boilers and furnaces are now available that operate with low heat losses and very high-efficiency. When a heating unit needs to be replaced, always recommend one of the higher-efficiency models.

Replacing older, less efficient oil heating units with high-efficiency models is an important option for retaining satisfied oil heat customers. When adjusted properly, the new oil-fired boilers and furnaces offer many advantages over some older units:

> * **Economical operation** through improved efficiency;
> * **Improved reliability** for reduced service calls;
> * **Cleaner operation** with very low smoke and soot requiring less frequent cleaning;
> * **Customer satisfaction and retention** after their investment in new oil heat equipment.

3.1 Boiler and Furnace Operation and Heat Losses

General Operation of Oil Heating Units

The purpose of the boiler or furnace is to transfer heat from the oil flame to hot water (or steam) or warm air used to heat the house. Hot water or steam produced by boilers is sent to radiators in the house for space heating while furnaces produce warm air that is ducted into the house. Boilers and furnaces provide several important functions:

> - A **combustion chamber** for complete clean burning of the fuel oil for low air pollutant emissions.
> - **Containment** of the hot flue gases away from the warm air or water that is distributed to the house. This is especially important for warm-air furnaces because the gases produced by the flame may contain carbon monoxide and other hazardous products. These gases must not be allowed to mix with the circulating air that goes into the house.
> - **Large heat-exchange surfaces** so that the energy from the flame can be effectively transferred to the hot water or air that is used for heating.
> - **Good contact** between these heating surfaces and the hot combustion gases.
> - **Minimal heat losses** so that most of the heat from the oil flame can be transferred to the house for efficient and economical operation.

The overall operation of a boiler and furnace is shown schematically in Figure 3-1. Fuel oil and combustion air at or near room temperature are burned within the combustion chamber, producing the oil flame. Hot combustion gases are generated at a temperature of between 2,500°F to 3,200°F, depending on burner design and adjustment of the combustion air supply. The hot combustion gases pass over the heat-transfer surfaces of the boiler or furnace, and most of the energy in these gases is transferred through the heat-exchanger walls to the water or air. All of the heat cannot be extracted, however, and the exhaust gas leaves the heating unit at an elevated temperature that is typically between 350°F and 600°F. This can be higher or lower depending on heating unit and burner design and adjustment. On the other side of the heat-exchanger wall, water (at 160°F to 180°F) or air (at 70°F) receive the heat that flows through the wall from the combustion gases. This raises the temperature of the air to about 140°F and the water to about 180°F to 200°F. To summarize:

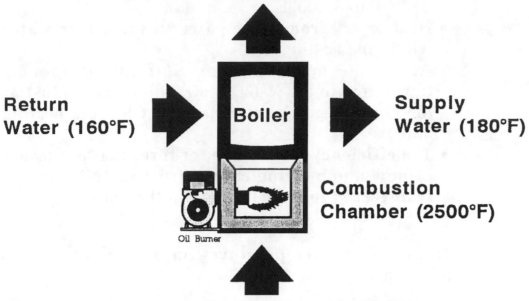

Exhaust Gases (350 - 650 °F)

Return Water (160°F)

Boiler

Supply Water (180°F)

Combustion Chamber (2500°F)

Oil Burner

Fuel And Combustion Air (70°F)

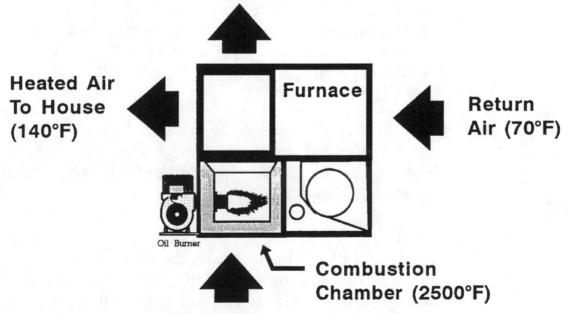

Exhaust Gases (350 - 650 °F)

Heated Air To House (140°F)

Furnace

Return Air (70°F)

Oil Burner

Combustion Chamber (2500°F)

Fuel And Combustion Air (70°F)

Typical Boiler or Furnace Operation (Note: Temperatures Can Vary)

Figure 3-1

- The oil flame **produces hot gases** on the order of 2500°F to 3,200°F.
- Heat passes **from these gases to the air or water** within the heating unit.
- All of the heat from the oil flame cannot be transferred to the water or air; **some heat is lost** as the hot flue gases are exhausted from the heating unit.
- The **efficiency** of the boiler or furnace is a measure of **how much of the energy** from the oil flame is **transferred into useful heat** in the home.

Higher Flame Temperatures Improve Heat-Transfer Rates

The **temperature of the flame** and the resulting combustion gases has a direct impact on:

- How fast the heat is transferred to the boiler or furnace
- The temperature of the exhaust gas and flue heat loss
- System efficiency.

Hotter flames transfer their heat faster and produce higher boiler or furnace efficiency. This was discussed in Chapter 2. A brief discussion of heat-transfer principles can explain this important fact.

Heat is always transferred from hotter bodies (or gases) to colder bodies. The heat from the oil flame is transferred in two ways: Radiation and Convection. **Radiation** is heat transfer **without direct contact** from a hot material to a colder material. This is how the sun heats the earth. Similarly, the hot oil flame can radiate heat to the boiler or furnace surfaces. The rate of heat-transfer varies rapidly as the temperature of the combustion gases increase. For example, as the temperature of a flame increases from 2,500°F to 3,000°F, the rate of radiative heat-transfer doubles. Convective heat transfer occurs with direct contact between the hot gases **and the** heat-transfer surfaces of the boiler or furnace. The rate of convective heat transfer also increases as the temperature of the hot gases rises. Therefore, it is important to produce the highest flame temperature that is practical so the both the radiation and convection heat-transfer rates increase. This reduces flue heat loss and improves heating system efficiency. Flame-retention oil burners operate with higher flame temperatures than older oil burners, and this contributes to the higher efficiency of these burners, and of new boilers and furnaces that use them. See Chapter 2.

Steel Firetube Boiler Designs

Oil-fired boilers can be separated into several general design categories based on materials of construction and configuration. Steel and cast iron are the two most common materials used for boilers. The most common configurations include vertical-firetube and horizontal-tube steel boilers, and sectional cast-iron boilers. These can be dry-based units in which the combustion chamber is separated from the boiler water, or wet-based (or partial wet-based) boilers in which the combustion chamber is enclosed by boiler water. These design features can effect heat losses, AFUE, and the overall system efficiency.

Steel boilers are fabricated from carbon steel. The hot gases pass through the inside of steel tubes that are surrounded by boiler water. That is where the name firetube is derived—the gases from the fire flow inside of these tubes.

Dry-base, single-pass, vertical-firetube boiler. One of the least expensive, and often lowest efficiency, oil boilers is shown schematically in Figure 3-2. The burner fires into a combustion chamber that is below the heat-transfer section of the boiler. The hot gases then flow up through the boiler tubes, which are immersed in boiler

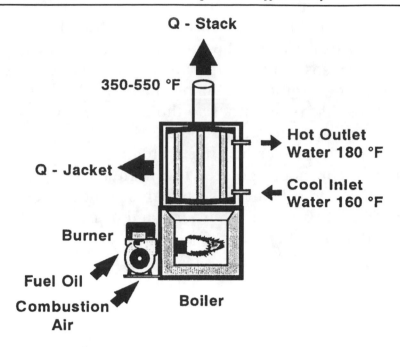

Dry Base Vertical Fire Tube Steel Boiler

Figure 3-2

water where heat is transferred. The unit is "dry-base" because the boiler water does not surround the combustion chamber, and this tends to increase the jacket heat losses from the boiler. Some of the heat from the combustion gases flows through the combustion chamber and is lost through the boiler jacket. Also, heat losses form the boiler casing which surrounds the water section of the boiler can lower system efficiency, especially during the burner off-cycle. The total jacket loss can be as high as 10% in some boilers of this design. This is an important heat loss to consider whenever boilers are installed in unheated or partially heated spaces because this can lower heating system efficiency. Dry-base boilers can often be identified in the field by looking at the return water piping. If the combustion chamber is below the return water, the boiler is usually a dry-base model. Single-pass refers to the fact that the hot gases flow up through the boiler tubes in only one direction, which tends to reduce the overall heat-transfer effectiveness. This design tends to increase on-cycle flue heat loss, which is reflected in the AFUE rating.

Wet-base, multi-pass steel boilers. A wet-base steel boiler is shown in Figure 3-3. This is a multi-pass horizontal firetube boiler. The burner fires into a combustion chamber that is surrounded by boiler water. Heat that passes through the combustion chamber walls is absorbed by the boiler. This reduces jacket heat loss to 1% or less in some boilers of this design. The hot gases then change direction and flow through horizontal firetubes, where heat is given up to the boiler water. This is considered a multi-pass boiler because the hot combustion gases first travel in one direction and then reverse direction and flow through the boiler tubes to the flue gas exit. Generally, the heat-transfer effectiveness of this multi-pass design is higher than the single-pass vertical tube configuration. This often produces a higher AFUE rating. Wet-base multi-pass steel boilers were among the highest efficiency boilers tested. In addition, the lower jacket heat losses produced by the wet-base configuration improves the system efficiency when boilers are located in unheated spaces. If the water return piping to the boiler is below the combustion chamber, the boiler is probably a wet-base (or partially wet-base) design.

Partial wet-base steel boilers. Some boilers cannot be classified as dry-base or wet-base because part of the

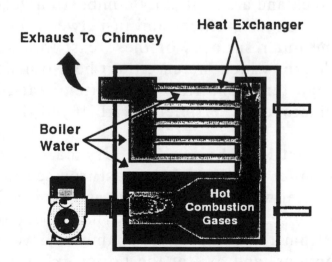

Wet Base Multipass Steel Boiler

Figure 3-3

combustion chamber is enclosed by boiler water. Typically the rear of the combustion chamber is water-backed, and radiant heat from the oil flame is transferred through this back wall. This is sometimes referred to as a "wet-leg" design. The hot combustion gases then reverse their direction of flow and pass through horizontal steel firetubes. However, the front and bottom (and in some cases, the sides) of the combustion chamber or not enclosed by boiler water, and jacket heat can be lost through these areas. Other steel boiler configurations are available where only part of the combustion chamber is backed by boiler water. It is expected that jacket losses for these boilers would fall between the wet-base and dry-base cases. The AFUE rating gives an indication heat-transfer effectiveness of this boiler design compared to other steel boilers. However, if the boilers are installed in unheated or partially heated spaces, the jacket losses may reduce **heating system efficiency.** Typical jacket losses may be in the 3% to 6% range for this type of boiler.

Cast Iron Boilers

These units are constructed of hollow cast iron sections that hold the boiler water. These are joined together in a horizontal stack and are heated by combustion gases that flow over the outside surfaces and in-between the joined sections. The outer surfaces of these cast-iron sections often include pins which increase their heat-transfer area and encourage turbulent flow for better heat-transfer rates. This improves the efficiency (AFUE) of the boiler.

Dry-base cast-iron boiler. The dry base cast iron boiler. This boiler is formed from cast iron sections that contain the boiler water. Below these castings is a firebox that is not enclosed by boiler water. The hot combustion gases flow from the combustion chamber, between the cast iron sections, and exit at the boiler exhaust outlet. Substantial heat loss can occur from the firebox and out through the casing of the boiler because it is not surrounded by boiler water. This is similar to the dry based vertical tube steel boiler except in this case the combustion gases flow on the outside of the cast-iron sections instead of inside of steel firetubes. There is at least one exception to the general rule that a dry-base design correlates with lower efficiency. One manufacturer of a dry-base cast iron boiler utilizes a very effective insulation system to surround the combustion chamber to prevent heat loss. The resulting high-efficiency boiler designs have very high AFUE ratings.

Wet-base cast-iron boiler. A wet-base cast iron boiler is again similar to the dry-base boiler except that the boiler sections that contain water surround the firebox. This produces more boiler surface for more heat transfer from the flame, and it reduces the heat loss from the firebox through the boiler casing. Most heat losses from the firebox are picked up by the boiler water surrounding the base of the heating unit. The added boiler surface area around the firebox also increases the rate of heat-transfer and improves boiler efficiency. Again, if the boiler is located in an unheated or partially heated space, the wet-base design is preferred because it offers the highest **heating system efficiency**.

Furnaces

The most common type of oil furnace is constructed from steel and is available in several configurations. Modern high-efficiency oil furnaces often include extra surface area and, in some cases, an additional heat exchanger to remove more of the heat from the combustion gases.

Oil-Furnace Operation. The typical heat-exchanger design for oil furnaces is shown in Figure 3-4. A complete unit is welded together from steel parts:

- A **lower chamber** that holds the firebox;
- A **primary heat exchanger**—which is the inner cylinder-shaped chamber above the firebox;

- A **secondary heat exchanger**—which is the outer round chamber that surrounds the primary heat exchanger;
- A **flue connection**—which transports the flue gases away from the furnace to the chimney or exhaust system.

The entire heat exchanger is enclosed in the furnace cabinet with an air blower that forces air over all of the heat exchanger surfaces. This warm air is sent through ducts to air registers in the home. The refractory firebox is needed to prevent overheating and failure of the lower chamber. The furnace cabinet is usually insulated to reduce heat jacket losses. Be sure that the insulation is in

Heat Exchanger
Typical Oil-Fired
Furnace

Figure 3-4

place after servicing the unit. Also, seal all air leaks in the furnace cabinet to reduce the loss of hot air before it can reach the house. This can improve overall heating system efficiency.

The general operation of the furnace is as follows. The oil burner fires into the refractory firebox within the lower chamber. Air flow around the outside of this chamber from the furnace air blower is necessary to prevent over-heating. The hot combustion gases rise out of the firebox and enter the inner drum (primary heat exchanger) where they are partially cooled. The combustion gases then pass through a connector to the outer drum (secondary heat exchanger) where they are cooled further. At the top of the outer drum is a flue connector that transports the exhaust gases away from the furnace.

To capture this heat, the furnace air blower draws air from the return ducts of the house and forces it around the lower chamber, up between the inner and outer drums, around the outer drum, and over the flue connector. The heated air is then ducted to the house for space heating. Air flow over each of these surfaces is needed to prevent overheating and to produce maximum thermal efficiency of the furnace. The Annual Fuel Utilization Efficiency (AFUE) is a measure of the effectiveness of this heat-transfer and is discussed later in this chapter.

Furnace configurations. Several different arrangements of furnaces are possible with the same type of heat exchanger, depending on the location of the furnace air blower. These include the following designs:

Upflow furnaces have the air blower located below the heat exchanger. The blower pulls air back from the house through the return air duct, across an air filter, over the heat exchanger in the furnace and out through the warm air outlet located at the top of the furnace. This is sometimes referred to as a "**highboy**" furnace.

Downflow furnaces have the blower located above the heat exchanger. The return air flows downward across the heat exchanger and out from the bottom of the furnace to the house. This is sometimes referred to as a "counter-flow" arrangement because the cool return air comes in contact with the cooler part of the heat exchanger first. As the air flows downward it warms up and comes in contact with the higher temperature parts of the heat exchanger. Counterflow heat-transfer is generally more efficient than other flow configurations.

Horizontal furnaces have the air blower located along-side the heat exchanger. This reduces the overall height of the unit. The return air enters one side of the furnace, flows horizontally across the heat exchanger and exits the other side of the furnace. These furnaces are used for low-headroom installations such as crawl spaces and attics.

Lowboy furnaces, like horizontal furnaces, have the air blower located alongside the heat exchanger to reduce the overall height of the unit. The inlet and outlet openings for house air are, however, located on the top and not the sides of the unit, so the air goes down and then up instead of from side to side. Return air from the house is pulled into the top of the unit, forced over the heat exchanger, and out of the top of the furnace.

High-efficiency oil furnaces. New highly efficient furnaces have appeared in recent years that can operate with Annual Fuel Utilization Efficiencies of 90%. One example of a high-efficiency model is shown in Figure 3-5. This unit has three heat-exchanger sections: a primary, a secondary, and a condensing heat exchanger. The added surface area reduces the flue gas temperature to very low levels (less than $120^{\circ}F$) so that a 3-inch PVC pipe can be used for venting the exhaust gases.

This unit operates as follows. The oil burner fires into the primary heat exchanger at the upper part of the furnace. The hot gases pass into the secondary heat exchanger located below the primary, flowing horizontally through heat-transfer tubes. The combustion gases then flow downward to the condensing heat exchanger and are

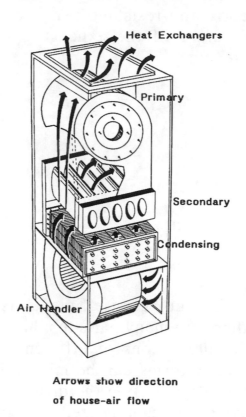

**High Efficiency
Heat Exchanger
Condensing
Furnace Design**

**Arrows show direction
of house-air flow**

Figure 3-5

then exhausted from the furnace with the help of an in-duced—draft fan. The return air from the house is forced by a blower over each of the heat exchangers in turn—first the condensing heat exchanger, then the secondary, and finally the primary. This counterflow arrangement, oppo-site to the direction the combustion gases flow, provides the most efficient heat exchange possible.

The third heat exchanger is called a "condensing" unit because the combustion gases are cooled so much that they can drop below their dewpoint, so that some of the water vapor generated by burning the oil is turned into liquid form. Special materials are used to handle the con-densate, to protect the heating system from corrosion damage. The main difference between these high-efficiency models and conventional furnaces is the added corrosion-resistant heat exchanger that reduces the temperature of the exhaust gases and raises furnace efficiency.

3.2 Efficiency Ratings of Boilers and Furnaces

Efficiency Definitions

The subject of efficiency is always confusing, because there are many parts to a heating system and many different definitions of efficiency. Also, some of these efficiency terms can be misleading. The first thing that we will do is define the different efficiencies that are used. These are summarized in Figure 3-6:

Fuel-Conversion Efficiency. This is the percentage of the fuel oil that is converted to heat in the oil flame. This efficiency is virtually 100%. All the fuel is consumed by the burner.

Combustion Efficiency. This is a confusing name because it sounds as if it should refer to the fuel-conversion efficiency as defined above, whereas in fact it also accounts for the heat-transfer efficiency of a particular burner-boiler or burner-furnace unit. This efficiency is determined by measuring the loss of heat out of the flue and subtracting it from 100%. It depends on the level of excess combustion air and the effectiveness of the boiler or furnace heat exchanger in extracting energy from the combustion gases. This efficiency does not include jacket heat losses, off-cycle heat losses, distribution-system (pipe or duct) losses, or outdoor-air infiltration heat losses. However, combustion efficiency is very important because it shows if the burner is properly adjusted, and if

Efficiency Category	Heat Losses Included					Comments
	On-Cycle Flue Loss	Off-Cycle Flue Loss	Jacket Heat Loss	Distribution Losses	Outdoor Air Infiltration	
Fuel Conversion						**Virtually 100% For Oil Heating Systems**
Combustion Efficiency	√					**Only Efficiency That Can Be Measured In The Field**
Steady State Efficiency	√		√			
AFUE	√	√ (1)			√ (2)	**(1) A Standard Factor Is Used For Off-Cycle Loss (2) Includes Values For A Standard Case (varies)**
Heating System Efficiency	√	√	√	√	√	**No Standard Method Exists For Accurately Evaluating This Efficiency**

Efficiency Definitions

Figure 3-6

the heat-transfer efficiency of the boiler or furnace is inadequate due to design limitations or fouling. **IT IS THE ONLY EFFICIENCY MEASUREMENT THAT CAN BE PERFORMED IN THE FIELD TO DIAGNOSE PROBLEMS FOR A PARTICULAR HEATING UNIT.**

Steady-State Efficiency. This efficiency is determined by measuring the on-cycle and jacket heat losses in a laboratory while the burner is operating continuously for an extended time period. The fuel consumption and heat output do not vary because they have reached a "steady state". This does not accurately represent actual operation in the field, where the burner cycles on and off at regular intervals. This measurement is important, however, because it can be combined with combustion efficiency tests to calculate jacket heat losses, and it represents the highest efficiency that the heating unit can reach.

Annual Fuel Utilization Efficiency (AFUE). This efficiency is based on standardized testing and calculation procedures that were developed by the U. S. Department of Energy in 1978. All residential heating units must have these tests performed. These AFUE efficiencies are shown on the boiler or furnace label and are listed in several heating equipment directories. The objective of this program is to supply consistent efficiency information to help homeowners select and install high-efficiency heating equipment. This information is the most reliable data available that service technicians can use to help homeowners install high-efficiency replacements for existing boilers and furnaces.

The AFUE values indicate the energy efficiency of burner-boilers and burner-furnaces for a standard set of operating conditions. It was not intended to measure heating system efficiency, which includes other heat losses that can vary from house to house. The test procedure measures on-cycle heat loss and cool-down characteristics, and then calculates off-cycle losses and infiltration-air heat losses for "standard" conditions. In some cases the off-cycle and infiltration losses may be higher (or lower) than predicted by AFUE. Jacket heat losses are generally not included, even though they can be significant in some installations such as unheated basements and attics. The AFUE listings are a useful tool for selecting boilers or furnaces by comparing their relative efficiency. This is why AFUE was developed. The service technician must be aware of its limitations, however, and be ready to use judgment when applying the AFUE values for particular installations.

Using AFUE data to select new, efficient oil equipment is the best insurance against a customer converting to another fuel source. If a homeowner has modern oil heating equipment, there is no advantage gained by switching fuels. In fact, it can easily be shown that conversion becomes a costly mistake for an oil heated home with a high AFUE boiler or furnace.

Heating System Efficiency. This efficiency includes the boiler and furnace and all other parts of the heating "system". This includes the chimney, the distribution system, and the many interactions that can occur between the parts. Chimney height, the location of the heating unit and its effect on jacket heat loss, and many other factors can affect heating system efficiency. The major losses include: on-cycle heat loss, off-cycle heat loss, jacket loss, distribution loss, and outdoor air infiltration. Each of these interacts with the others and can vary widely from house to house. At this time there is no standard method for determining heating system efficiency. The best option is to use AFUE values for each boiler or furnace and then adjust these values using the information in this manual and from other sources. Heating system efficiency is important because it determines the actual fuel use and resulting home heating costs. As their home energy expert, your customers arc counting on you to give them the best advise available on how to improve the operation of their heating equipment.

Directory of
AFUE
Ratings

The AFUE testing and calculation procedure was developed by the U.S Department of Energy in 1978, and it is now used to determine the efficiency of all residential heating units sold in the U.S. Equipment manufacturers are required to perform the standardized tests and the results are displayed on labels on each heating unit and on separate fact sheets. These test results are also listed in several directories. The most complete listing of AFUEs is published twice a year by ETL Testing Laboratory in Cortland, New York for the Gas Appliance Manufacturers' Association (GAMA). This directory includes AFUE values for natural gas, propane, fuel oil, and electric-powered boilers, furnaces and water heaters. Gas and oil furnaces with inputs less than 225,000 Btu per hour, and gas and oil boilers with input ratings of less than 300,000 Btu per hour are included in the program. The ETL/GAMA directory is titled:

CONSUMERS' DIRECTORY OF CERTIFIED EFFICIENCY RATINGS FOR RESIDENTIAL HEATING AND WATER HEATING EQUIPMENT

This directory is published twice a year—in April and in October—and it can be ordered from:

ETL Testing Laboratories, Inc.
Industrial Park, Route 11
Cortland, New York 13045
Tel: (607) 753-6711

Each section of the directory dealing with central heating equipment contains detailed information on various manufacturers and model numbers, and includes an AFUE rating for each of the models listed. This listing includes:

1. Type of fuel [Sections 2 and 4 are for oil heating units].

2. Name of manufacturing company.

3. Configuration of heating unit. For oil furnaces this includes: Upflow, Lowboy, Downflow (counterflow), and Horizontal.

4. Model numbers listed under the manufacturer's name for each model with an AFUE rating. Some model numbers with the same AFUE rating may be listed together.

5. Footnotes, for some models having specific design features (such as vent damper) or burner adjustment data such as carbon dioxide content of flue gas.

6. Input rating of the boiler or furnace in Mbtuh (thousands of Btu per hour) for steady-state or continuous operation. For example, a fuel nozzle rated for 0.75 gallons per hour would have an input of 104,000 Btuh based on a fuel oil heating value of 138,690 Btu per gallon.

7. Heating Capacity, in Mbtuh. This indicates the heat output of the heating unit when operated under steady-state conditions (continuous operation) for an extended time period.

8. PE, in watts. This is the electric energy consumption rate for the oil burner when operated continuously. This consumption is small and typically ranges from 100 to 300 watts. For an average burner, operating about 20% of the year, with an electric cost of $0.08 per Kwh, this equals approximately $28 per year.

9. EAE, in Kwh/yr (kilowatt hours per year). This is the auxiliary electric energy consumption by the boiler or furnace during a one-year period.

10. E_f, in MMBtu/yr (million Btu per year). This is the average fuel consumption for the oil boiler or furnace for a standard set of operating conditions based on the unit's AFUE rating.

11. AFUE %. This is the Annual Fuel Utilization Efficiency, which represents the expected efficiency of the burner-boiler or burner-furnace under a set of standard operating conditions. It is an important number because it can be used directly to compare the relative efficiency of all oil—and gas-fired boilers and furnaces. Comparing these AFUE values is an important part of selecting a new boiler or furnace.

12. Primary heat exchanger material (for boilers only)—steel or cast iron.

This directory provides valuable information on boiler and furnace efficiencies. It can help your customers select an efficient model that will increase their satisfaction with oil heat. This will discourage switching to other fuels by offering one of the most efficient heating systems now available for home heating.

*Ranges of
AFUEs for
Oil
Furnaces
and Boilers*

The Federal efficiency testing and labeling program requires each boiler or furnace to have a label that indicates the AFUE of the unit and the range of AFUEs available for all boiler or furnaces of the same heating capacity. Labels and equipment datasheets must include the following information:

1. Output capacity of the boiler or furnace in Btu per hour.

2. Model number.

3. Annual Fuel Utilization Efficiency (AFUE)

4. A bar chart showing the AFUE rating of the boiler or furnace and the range of AFUEs for all boilers or

furnaces with the same heating capacity. This appears as a high value, a low value and the AFUE of the model listed on the label.

The ETL/GAMA AFUE Directory also contains information on the ranges of AFUEs available for boilers and furnaces for a full range of heat input rates. These are located within the directory at the beginning of each section for oil boilers and oil furnaces. The furnace efficiency ranges are separated into the various furnace configurations discussed earlier.

As an example, the range of efficiencies for oil boilers published in the ETL/GAMA Directory in October 1991 (on page 90) is summarized in the table that follows.

| Heating Capacity | Ranges of AFUE Ratings (%) | |
Btu per Hour	LOW	HIGH
43,000 to 59,000	87.5	87.5
60,000 to 76,000	81.7	87.6
77,000 to 93,000	80.2	88.0
94,000 to 110,000	79.1	88.7
111,000 to 127,000	77.5	87.5
128,000 to 144,000	76.6	86.6
145,000 to 161,000	76.5	87.4
162,000 to 178,000	78.0	87.6
179,000 to 195,000	76.6	87.3

These ranges are important because they allow you to compare the AFUE of a particular heating unit with the range of efficiencies (AFUEs) that are available for all boilers of the same input rating. For example, if you need a new oil boiler rated at 135,000 Btu per hour, you see from the table that boilers of that size have AFUE ratings between 76.6% and 86.6%. If you are recommending a boiler with an AFUE of 85%, you are near the top of the range. However, if the boiler is closer to 76%, then a more efficient model is probably a better choice. Homeowners should be included in the boiler selection process, which is a balance between initial cost and annual heating costs. A less-efficient boiler is usually not the best choice, even though its first cost may be lower, and investment in conservation will improve customer satisfaction with oil heat.

Historic Efficiency Trends: Oil boilers and furnaces are among the most efficient heating systems now used in homes. In fact, the average efficiency of oil heating equipment sold each year for the past decade has been higher than the average gas unit. In 1980 the overage oil system had an AFUE rating of approximately 76% compared with gas equipment rated at 65%. The trend toward higher efficiency is continuing. The average AFUE for oil furnaces manufactured in 1990 was 83.7%, based on information published by GAMA. In contrast, the average gas furnace manufactured in 1990 had an AFUE that was more than 7 points lower, corresponding to increased fuel use of about 10 percent. Oil heat companies must continue to recommend and install high-efficiency oil boilers and furnaces, if this advantage is to continue. Starting in 1992, Federal regulations require all equipment manufacturers (gas and oil) to stop making units with less than a 78% AFUE rating (except for equipment installed in manufactured housing).

3.3 Low-Mass Boilers

Concept

One of the important heat losses identified by the Brookhaven National Laboratory efficiency testing program is the off-cycle losses that occur when the burner is idle. For older boilers and heating units without flame-retention head burners, this heat loss can be somewhat higher than for newer models. Also, if the heating unit is grossly oversized relative to the peak heating demand, this heat loss can be more significant than is indicated by the standardized AFUE calculations. This condition is aggravated when a home is weatherized and insulated, but the firing rate of the oil or gas boiler or furnace is not reduced. An important advancement in oil boiler designs are "low mass" boilers, which contain much smaller amounts of water than standard boilers, and therefore do not have much heat to lose during the burner off-cycle.

The concept for low-mass boilers was described in 1976 in an annual report by Brookhaven. The heating unit consists of two parts: a small combustion system containing a small quantity of water, and a separate well-insulated hot-water storage tank. The purpose of the design is to reduce the amount of heat stored in the combustion device so that off-cycle heat losses can be reduced. During burner operation, water flows through the combustion section and transfers heat to the home. When the burner on-cycle ends, water from the storage tank continues to flow to the combustion section and removes any residual heat. At the end of the firing cycle most of the heat has been removed from the combustion section and it is stored in the thermally insulated storage tank, which is not connected to a flue. Therefore, the off-cycle heat losses are reduced, and heating unit efficiency (AFUE) is increased. This also increases the efficiency of domestic hot-water generation, because the off-cycle or standby heat losses are often high for conventional heating units when supplying hot water during the non-heating season. The low-mass boiler with storage can operate with very low heat losses while producing domestic hot water.

Equipment Now Available

In recent years several boiler manufacturers have introduced low—mass boilers that operate with reduced water storage and the lower off-cycle heat losses. One of these systems is shown in Figure 3-7. It uses a low-mass combustion section and a water storage tank with an electronic control system that produces space heating and domestic hot water with very low off-cycle heat losses and high heating system efficiency.

Here is how this innovative heating system operates. When space heat or hot water is needed, the burner and circulator are energized, the boiler water is recirculated within the boiler for 1-1/2 minutes, and the water temperature rises to 130°F. The system contains multiple heating zones and the zone valve(s) opens to supply heat to the house. The burner operation continues until the thermostat is satisfied; then the burner goes off. The circulator continues to operate to remove any remaining heat from the boiler and sends it to the zone being heated. This is possible because of low mass of the boiler ensures that the residual heat will not overheat the space. This post-burner circulation is controlled by the electronic control system, and continues for ~20 minutes, cooling the boiler to about 105°F.

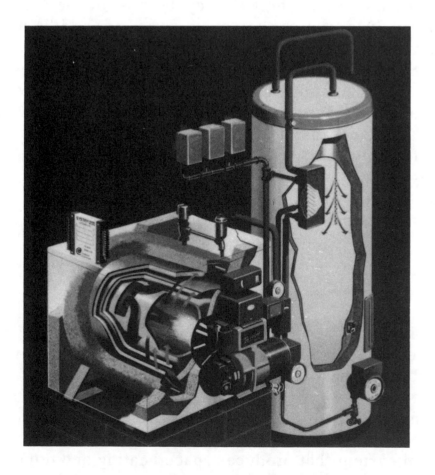

Figure 3-7

When domestic hot water is needed, the domestic-hot-water circulator (bronze) is energized, which forces water from the bottom of the hot water storage tank, through a plate-coil heat exchanger that is in turn heated by circulating boiler water. This 130°F to 140°F hot water is pumped back to the top of the storage tank, where it is then sent to satisfy the domestic hot water needs of the house. Burner operation continues until this hot water reaches within 12 inches of the bottom of the stratified storage tank. Then an aquastat operating through the system's control stops burner operation. The circulator continues pumping water through the boiler for 5 minutes and the remaining heat is transferred to the storage tank. The advantage of this heat-purging cycle is that most of the heat from the low-mass boiler is removed and off-cycle heat losses are very small compared to conventional boilers. This produces improved system efficiency for generating space heat and domestic hot water.

Efficiency tests conducted by Brookhaven National Laboratory with this heating system demonstrated the efficiency improvement available by using a low-mass boiler in a "heat purging" mode. The off-cycle heat losses were less than 1% of the fuel input, and seasonal efficiencies (AFUEs) could be very close to steady state efficiency.

These low-mass boiler designs can be combined with a hot-water storage tank to produce both space and domestic water heating very efficiently. Some of the advantages of these types of units are:

* High AFUE and heating system efficiency;
* High-pressure combustion for reduced draft fluctuations;
* High heat-transfer rates and a compact size (24 inch by 29 inch high);
* Simple design with easy access for cleaning;
* Faster warmup;
* Reduced sound levels due to firebox location and insulation.

These low-mass systems offer another important opportunity. Their relatively small size can make them good alternatives for new oil heat customers who currently heat with electricity. The energy and cost savings are usually excellent and offer reasonable payback to the homeowner. This is especially true if the unit can be directly exhausted without the need for a chimney. Annual heating costs for electric-to-oil heat conversions can often be reduced by 50% or more with high-efficiency models such as these low-mass boilers.

3.4 Expected Fuel Savings with New Boilers and Furnaces

Figure 3-6 summarized the important heat losses that occur in home heating systems and which of these the various efficiency definitions include. AFUE does not include all the off-cycle losses, jacket heat losses, distribution losses, and outdoor-air infiltration heat losses for all cases found in the field. A brief review of some of these and how they affect heating system efficiency and fuel use is included here. These are all discussed in appropriate chapters of this manual.

The following is a list of some of the system factors that can cause the heating system efficiency to vary from the AFUE value.

1. **Location** of heating unit (heated, unheated, or partially heated space).

2. **Chimney draft** (chimney height, materials of construction, temperature).

3. Source of combustion and draft **relief air**.

4. **Burner design** and operating air pressure.

5. Boiler or furnace **size and firing rate** relative to heating load.

6. **Zoning** of distribution system.

7. **Pipe or duct** design and insulation.

8. Source of **domestic hot water**.

9. **Low-mass** boiler design.

Some of these factors will affect both the existing and new boiler or furnace regardless of the type of fuel that is consumed. Other factors may give added advantage to the replacement unit because its AFUE is not decreased as much by these factors.

Location of the Heating Unit

If the boiler or furnace is located in an unheated or partially heated space, and the jacket heat losses of the new and old unit are the same, then both heating unit AFUEs will be reduced by the same amount. If the new boiler or furnace has lower jacket heat losses, then the heating system efficiency improvement may be greater than predicted by comparing the AFUE of the old and new unit. This is especially important for some older boilers that may have larger off-cycle heat losses. The annual energy savings may be higher than expected.

Chimney Draft

Some homes have very tall chimneys that produce very high chimney draft during system operation. This can have the following affects:

- **Reduced combustion efficiency** as excess air flow is higher;
- **Higher off-cycle heat losses** due to increased off-cycle air flow;
- **Higher air-infiltration heat loss** due to more draft control air.

The burner design is an important factor in controlling these efficiency losses. Flame-retention head burners and new high-static air pressure burners are more resistant to changes in chimney draft. They can maintain their excess-air setting even when the draft is high, so combustion efficiency is not adversely affected. They also restrict off-cycle air flow more than other burner designs, and this helps to prevent an increase in off-cycle heat losses when the chimney draft is high. If the system is converted to gas, the efficiency could drop, because the typical gas heater may produce much less resistance to off-cycle heat losses, and these losses can increase above the level of even the existing oil heating system.

Heating system exhaust temperature also affects draft. Systems with higher combustion efficiency and lower flue gas temperatures will produce less chimney draft, which can help to reduce the excess draft problem. The heat loss caused by draft control air flowing into the barometric damper attached to a system with a very tall chimney may not be significantly affected by the choice of burner, boiler, or furnace design. However, this heat loss may be higher than that predicted for "standard" conditions by the AFUE analysis. These important factors are not included in the AFUE calculations but can have an important effect on fuel savings. Chimney height is an important consideration when estimating efficiency improvement with a new heating unit.

Source of Combustion and Draft-Relief Air

Systems in which all of the air used for combustion and draft control come from the heated space are affected most by high chimney draft because more cold air is pulled into the house to replace the air exhausted by the chimney. If the new system is exhausted directly to the outside without using the chimney, then the improvement in heating system efficiency will be higher than predicted by simply comparing the AFUE of the old and new heating unit.

Burner Design and Static Pressure of Combustion Air

Boilers and furnaces with high static air pressure oil burners can operate with higher efficiency and reduced heat losses under various draft conditions. This may not be fully reflected in the AFUE analyses.

Boiler or Furnace Size and Firing Rate Relative to the Heating Load

The relative size of the boiler or furnace and its firing rate have a direct affect on the overall efficiency of the system. Extensive laboratory testing at Brookhaven has demonstrated the importance of proper sizing. If the heating unit is oversized, the burner operates for very brief periods followed by long off-cycles. This contributes to increased off-cycle heat loss and lower efficiency. The AFUE calculation is based on a specific heating unit input relative to the peak heating load. If the existing furnace or boiler is oversized, or if an oversized fuel nozzle has been installed, its actual efficiency will probably be less than the AFUE. This means that if an oversized heating unit is replaced by a properly sized model, the fuel savings produced can be higher than predicted by AFUE comparison, because the AFUE assumes that all units are optimally sized.

Zoning of Distribution Systems

If the boiler piping or furnace ducting can be separated in multiple zones, the heating system efficiency can be increased, because only part of the house is heated at various times of the day. This can reduce fuel use significantly compared to heating units that operate as a single zone. The AFUE calculations do not consider the effect of zoning on annual fuel use but some heating systems are compatible or even specifically designed with multi-zoning in mind.

Pipe or Duct Design and Insulation

If the hot water or steam pipes are uninsulated and travel through unheated parts of the house, then heating system efficiency will be much less than the AFUE rating. This will increase fuel use for the existing and new heating system regardless of the heating fuel that is used and this can impact fuel savings. See Section 7.6 for further information.

Source of Domestic Hot Water

If a boiler is used to produce both space heating and domestic hot water, its efficiency can be affected. Modern boilers with flame-retention oil burners are very efficient domestic hot water generators. This can reduce the fuel use of the system compared to operating a space heater and separate domestic hot water heater. See Chapter 6.

Low-Mass Boiler Design

Low-mass boilers can be more efficient for several reasons:

- Off-cycle heat losses tend to be much less than in higher-mass systems, because there is very little heat left in the boiler after it shuts down. For this reason also, the system is much less sensitive to oversizing.
- Domestic hot water can be produced very efficiently all year, because the hot water is stored in a separate tank without a flue.
- Chimney air flow is reduced during the off-cycle because the boiler-water and flue temperatures are lower.

In addition, some low-mass systems feature multiple zones that heat only part of the house at any time, and some are installed as direct-exhaust systems that do not require a chimney. Although these two features are not directly related to the low-mass design, the fact remains that they are not always available with high-mass boilers.

Careful review of the existing boiler and all the operating features of the new low-mass boiler is necessary to estimate savings. When all factors are combined, the low-mass system may reduce fuel use by 40% or more compared with an existing conventional boiler.

**3.5
Important
Steps to
Follow
when
Replacing
Boilers or
Furnaces**

Several steps most be included whenever a heating unit is replaced to assure high-efficiency. These are:

> - **Use AFUE ratings** to select a high-efficiency model.
> - **Size** the boiler or furnace **properly**.
> - Install the **optimum fuel nozzle size**.
> - Look at **other heating system factors** and minimize heat losses.
> - Always use **combustion test equipment** to adjust the burner.

*Use AFUE
Ratings.*

This chapter shows how to use available AFUE directories to identify the efficiency of particular boilers and furnaces and compare them with other models. Advise homeowners to install high-efficiency models. They will produce the lowest costs over the lifetime of the heating unit, and will maintain the efficiency advantage for oil heating equipment that currently exists.

*Size the
Boiler
Properly.*

The size of the new boiler or furnace can be selected by simply replacing the existing unit with one having the same output rating. This is not recommended. In many cases, the old boiler or furnace was oversized when it was installed. Also, any energy conservation efforts (such as new windows or attic insulation) that occurred after the unit was installed further aggravate the oversizing. A simple heat-loss calculation, such as the method recommended by the Hydronics Institute, should always be performed to determine the peak heating demand for the house. Avoid using oversizing factors such as piping losses and pick-up. These lead to boiler oversizing and are often unnecessary. If the piping losses are high, insulate the pipes to reduce this loss. Don't increase the output of the boiler. Also, pick-up factors are not always necessary for the lower-mass boilers now available, which heat up rapidly. Try to size the boiler or furnace accurately for each application without adding too much excess capacity. Remember, the off-cycle heat losses increase and efficiency drops if the heating unit is oversized for the load.

Install the Optimum Fuel Nozzle Size.

If the boiler or furnace is correctly sized, the system efficiency will decrease if an oversized fuel nozzle is installed. This lowers efficiency in two ways. First, the steady-state (combustion) efficiency is reduced because the flame is too large for the heat exchanger and more heat escapes up the chimney while the burner is firing. Second, the off-cycle heat losses can increase as the burner off-cycle increases. Both of these factors lower the efficiency of the heating unit. Chapter 7 has information on optimum fuel nozzle sizing.

Look at Other Heating System Factors.

Always review each installation for "heating system factors" that can affect overall efficiency that were described earlier. These include:

> • Location of the heating unit (especially for dry-based heating units)
> • Chimney draft
> • Source of combustion air
> • Burner design and static air pressure
> • Zoning of the distribution system
> • Pipe or duct insulation (and air duct leakage)
> • Source of domestic hot water.

Consider how the entire system is operating and make changes that minimize heat losses. For example, if a boiler is to be installed in an unheated basement, select a wet-base model with lower jacket heat losses.

Always Use Combustion Test Equipment.

Combustion test equipment must always be used when a new heating unit installed or whenever a burner is adjusted. It is the only reliable way to reach the highest operating efficiency. Even a highly efficient boiler or furnace cannot operate at peak efficiency and lowest soot levels, unless the burner is accurately adjusted. This requires combustion test equipment.

3.6 Summary of Recommendations

Many advantages can be gained for oil heat by installing and properly servicing high-efficiency boilers and furnaces. They will maintain the efficiency advantage of oil heat over other home heating fuels.

Boiler or furnace design has a direct impact on heat losses and system efficiency. Wet-based boilers generally have lower jacket heat losses than dry-based models, and are preferred for installations in unheated or partially heated spaces such as basements, attics, and crawl spaces. Many efficiency terms are used, and every service technician must know what each of them means. The Annual Fuel Utilization Efficiency (AFUE) is the most important value because it is used to compare boilers and furnaces. AFUE ratings for most heating units are available and should be used to select new heating equipment. It is the only means now available to compare all heating units on an equal basis.

High-efficiency boilers and furnaces are recommended to improve customer satisfaction with oil heat. Some of these units operate with efficiency near 90%, and special provisions for flue gas (and condensate) removal is required.

Low-mass boilers are now available and may produce excellent savings when used to replace older outdated equipment. "System" factors must be considered, because the savings from these low-mass boilers may be higher than what is predicted by simply comparing AFUE values.

AFUE ratings combined with combustion efficiency tests can be used to estimate fuel savings for replacing older boilers and furnace. "Heating System Factors" that go beyond the AFUE of the new boiler or furnace must also be considered.

Replacing outdated oil boilers and furnaces with new high-efficiency models is one of the best energy conservation options available to homeowners. It also helps oil heat companies by assuring continued fuel oil use for many years ahead.

QUESTIONS

3-1. What are the three types of heat transfer?

3-2. What happens when a boiler or furnace is oversized?

3-3. Name four advantages new properly adjusted oil fired boilers and furnaces offer over older units:

3-4. The larger the heat-exchange surface the more efficient the heating unit. True or false?

3-5. Which efficiency is most helpful when choosing a new heating unit?

Chapter 4—Chimneys and System Efficiency

Most oil heating equipment now in operation uses a masonry or metal chimney to remove the exhaust gases from the heating unit and safely transport these gases out of the home. Proper chimney venting is important to assure reliable and efficient operation of the heating equipment. It is also important because all combustion equipment can produce toxic gases if the burner is improperly adjusted. Combustion exhaust gases must always be removed from the building to prevent potential safety problems. Therefore, careful venting system design and operation are key elements to efficient and safe operation of all combustion heating systems. This chapter will include the following topics:

- How chimney venting works;
- How the venting system affects efficiency;
- What can be done to improve venting system performance and efficiency.

4.1 How Chimney Venting Works

What is Draft?

The force that removes the exhaust gases from the heating system is called draft. This is simply a pressure difference that pushes or pulls the hot exhaust gases out of the house through the vent or chimney. There are three common types of draft used by oil heating equipment. These are:

- Forced draft
- Chimney draft
- Induced draft

Forced draft is the air pressure created by the oil burner's air blower, which is used to push the hot exhaust gases out of the boiler or furnace. The new oil burners can produce positive air pressures of up to 3 inches water column. However, such positive pressures in the boiler or furnace (and hence in the flue pipe) could cause some of the exhaust gases to escape into the house. For this reason, most conventional home heating units are not designed for forced draft operation.

Chimney draft is the pressure difference created by the chimney that **pulls** the exhaust gases out of the heating unit and transports these gases from the house. Most conventional oil heating systems operate with a slight negative pressure in the combustion chamber (about 0.01 inches water column). The chimney causes this negative pressure that pulls the exhaust gases from the combustion chamber, through the boiler or furnace and flue connector, and out through the top of the chimney. This allows safe operation because most of the heating system is under negative pressure caused by the pulling action of the chimney, which reduces the escape of exhaust gases into the house.

Induced draft is a pulling action that is created by a draft fan or other mechanical device. For example, in installations where chimney draft is insufficient, a **draft booster** fan can be installed in the flue pipe before the chimney or at the top of the chimney to help pull the exhaust gases out of the heating system and up the chimney. This induced-draft fan adds to the negative pressure (suction) created by the chimney, and this helps remove the combustion exhaust gases. The pulling action of the induced draft fan also reduces the escape of combustion gases into the house.

Figure 4-1 shows how the pressure inside the heating system changes for forced-draft, chimney-draft and induced-draft operation. Forced-draft operation causes a positive pressure (above atmospheric) in most parts of the heating system including the boiler or furnace and flue connector. All of these parts must be air tight to prevent

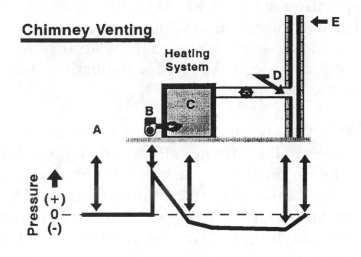

Chimney Venting

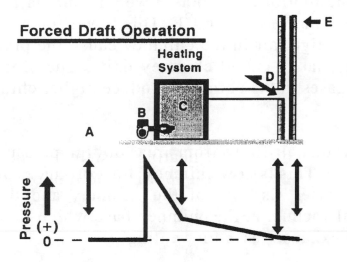

Forced Draft Operation

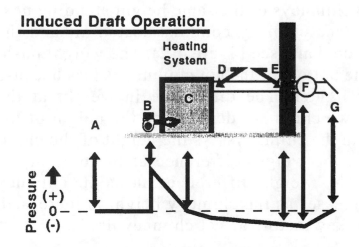

Induced Draft Operation

Pressure Profiles Within Heating Systems

Figure 4-1

escape of combustion gases whenever the pressure is above atmospheric. Chimney-draft and induced-draft operation cause a negative pressure (below atmospheric pressure) that reduces the leakage of combustion gases through most of the heating system.

Chimney draft is the pressure difference created by the heated exhaust gases in the chimney. Everyone knows that **hot air rises**. The air in the chimney is hotter than the outdoor air and this causes it to rise in the chimney. This is similar to a hot-air balloon that rises because it contains air that is hotter and lighter than the outdoor air. For example, a cubic foot of air at 600°F weighs one-half as much as a cubic foot of air at 60°F. This lower temperature and lower weight air in the chimney cause the pressure difference that is called chimney draft. Therefore, hotter exhaust gases in the chimney produce higher chimney draft.

We also know that air flows from areas of high pressure to lower pressure. This is how chimney draft produces air flow. The hot gases rise out of the chimney and this creates a partial vacuum at the chimney base which pulls in more heated exhaust gases for venting.

Imagine two chimneys of the same height standing next to each other. One chimney contains heated air and the other contains cold air (see Figure 4-2). The weight pushing down on the bottom of the hot chimney is less because the hot air is lighter. The difference in weight at the bottom of the two chimneys depends on the height of the column of air in the chimneys. As the height of the chimneys increases, the weight difference at the bottom becomes larger. This weight difference causes the chimney draft and it increases as the chimney height is increased. Therefore, two key factors affect chimney draft:

> - **Temperature difference** between the chimney gases and outdoor air;
> - **Height** of the chimney.

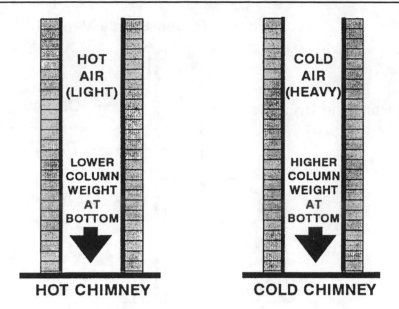

HOT AIR (LIGHT)

LOWER COLUMN WEIGHT AT BOTTOM

HOT CHIMNEY

COLD AIR (HEAVY)

HIGHER COLUMN WEIGHT AT BOTTOM

COLD CHIMNEY

**Hot Air Causes Lower Weight (Pressure)
At Bottom Of Chimney Than Cold Air**

Figure 4-2

*Chimney
Vent
Components
and
Operation*

The main parts of the chimney venting system used in oil heated houses include:

- **Chimney**
- **Flue connector**
- **Draft Control**—Barometric Damper.

Chimneys are often constructed from masonry materials such as brick or block that surrounds a ceramic-tile liner through which the exhaust gases flow (see Figure 4-3). In some cases a metal liner may be used inside of the masonry structure. Figure 4-4 shows two cross-sections of typical chimneys. Some chimneys are made from prefabricated metal sections that are joined together in the field

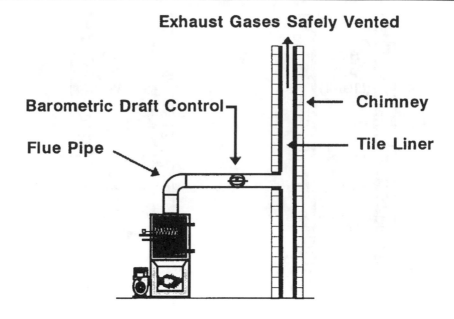

Flue & Chimney Design Affects Efficiency

Figure 4-3

and are often placed in an enclosure. These metal chimneys are usually double-walled and contain thermal insulation between the walls to reduce heat loss. In some cases the chimney passes through the inside of the house with only the upper portion exposed to outdoor air, and in other cases the entire chimney is installed on the outside of the building. As we will see, this has an important impact on chimney performance.

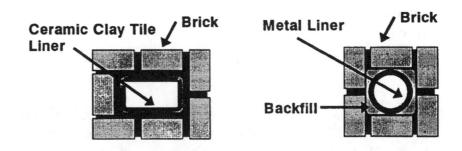

Typical Chimney Construction

Figure 4-4

An important function of the chimney is to keep the exhaust gases hot so that adequate draft is supplied to the heating unit and water condensation from the flue gases is avoided.

In the chimney-draft and induced-draft systems, the flue connector often consists of sections of sheet metal duct that are joined together and connect the flue-gas outlet of the boiler or furnace with the entrance to the chimney. In most cases, the flue is a single-walled pipe that is not insulated. Also, the flue connector is not air-tight. Leaks can enter sections of the flue pipe and at points where it connects to the heating unit and to the chimney. Remember, the chimney pulls a negative pressure on the system. These leaks can degrade chimney system performance. Also, the flue connector should be as short as possible and contain a minimum number of elbows to avoid excess pressure drop, because any pressure drop there just steals chimney draft that otherwise would be available to the heating unit.

A barometric damper is frequently installed in the flue connector between the boiler or furnace exit and the chimney. This damper helps to control the chimney draft to produce a nearly constant draft over the fire. This was very important for older oil burners, which could not tolerate large variations in draft. However, modern oil burners operate with much higher static air pressure and are not affected as much by change in chimney draft. This will be discussed more in this chapter and in the next chapter on alternative venting methods.

How Much Chimney Draft is Produced by Chimneys?

We have seen that the temperature of the chimney gases and the height of the chimney both affect the amount of chimney draft that is produced. The theoretical draft produced by a chimney can be calculated by using the following equation:

$$D = 0.255 \times H \times P_b [1/(T_o + 460) - 1/(T_c + 460)]$$

where:

D   is the chimney draft (inches of water column);

H   is the height of the chimney (feet);

P_b is the barometric pressure (inches of mercury);

T_o is the outdoor air temperature (degrees F);

T_c is the average temperature of the chimney gases (degrees F).

For standard atmospheric pressure of 29.92 inches of mercury, this equation becomes:

$$D = 7.63 \times H \times [1/(T_o + 460) - 1/(T_c + 460)]$$

The three important variables in this equation are the height of the chimney, the average temperature of the chimney gases, and the temperature of outdoor air. This equation can be used to show how chimney draft is affected by changes in these factors.

Chimney Height—The equation tells us that the draft produced by a chimney increases with chimney height. If we double the height of the chimney, then the draft doubles. For example, if the average chimney temperature is 200°F and the outdoor temperature is 40°F (an average winter temperature), the draft **increases** with chimney **height** as follows:

Chimney Height	Draft (Inches w.c.)
10 ft	-0.037
20 ft	-0.074
30 ft	-0.110

This information is shown on the graph in Figure 4-5. It is clear that the draft is stronger as the chimney gets taller. In houses with poor draft, a low chimney may be part of the problem.

Average Temperature of the Chimney Gases—also affects the amount of draft produced by a chimney. The equation shows that the draft decreases as the average chimney temperature drops. For example, if the chimney height is 20 feet, and the outdoor temperature is 40°F, the draft **increases** changes with average **chimney temperature** as follows:

Draft Increase With Chimney Height

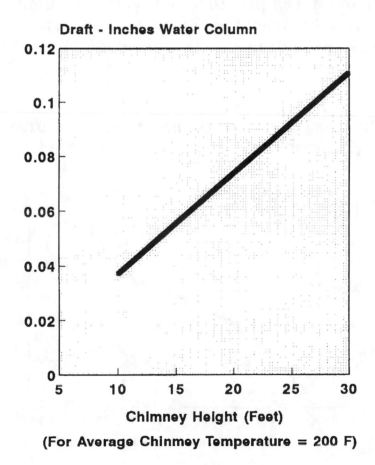

Draft - Inches Water Column

Chimney Height (Feet)

(For Average Chinmey Temperature = 200 F)

Figure 4-5

Average Chimney Temperature	Draft (Inches w.c.)
100°F	-0.033
150°F	-0.055
200°F	-0.074

This trend is illustrated in the graph in Figure 4-6. We see that the chimney draft more than doubles as the average chimney temperature increases from 100°F to 200°F. It is important to note that this temperature represents the average chimney gas temperature (T_{in} + T_{out} / 2), after the barometric draft damper. This damper mixes cooler boiler room air with the furnace or boiler exhaust gases and lowers the temperature of the gases that enter the base of the chimney. This lowers the average chimney temperature and reduces the draft.

Outdoor Air Temperature—also affects chimney draft and it varies throughout the heating season. The equation shows that the draft increases as the outdoor air temperature drops. For example, if the chimney height is 20 feet,

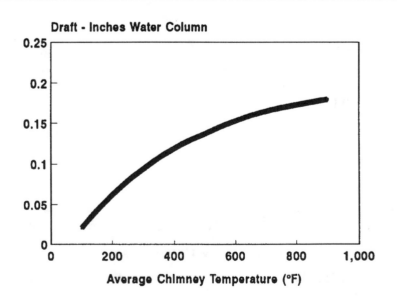

Chimney Draft For Different Temperatures
(Outdoor Temp. = 60°F, Height = 20 Ft.)

Figure 4-6

Draft Increase As Outdoor Temperature Drops

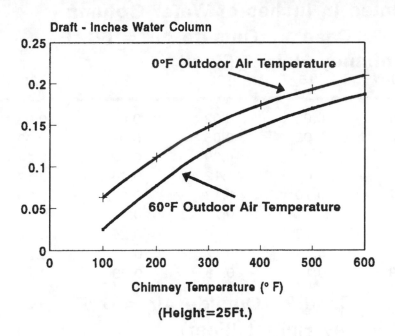

Draft - Inches Water Column

0°F Outdoor Air Temperature

60°F Outdoor Air Temperature

Chimney Temperature (° F)

(Height=25Ft.)

Figure 4-7

and the average chimney temperature is 150F, the draft increases as the outdoor air temperature falls as follows:

Outdoor Air Temperature	Draft (Inches w.c.)
60°F	-0.043
30°F	-0.062
0°F	-0.082

This trend is illustrated in the graph in Figure 4-7. The chimney draft increases by about a factor of 2 as the outdoor air temperature drops from 60°F to 0°F, which is typical during a heating season.

A chart of chimney draft based on the draft equation discussed above is included in Figure 4-8. This chart can be used in the field to check chimney performance and to diagnose chimney problems. The following procedure can determine if chimney repairs are needed.

Theoretic Chimney Draft For Various Conditions
Draft Indicated In Inches of Water Column

Average Chimney Temp. (F)	Case 1 Outside Air = 60 °F Chimney Height (Feet)				
	10	15	20	25	30
100	0.01	0.02	0.02	0.03	0.03
200	0.03	0.05	0.06	0.08	0.09
300	0.05	0.07	0.09	0.12	0.14
400	0.06	0.09	0.12	0.14	0.17
500	0.07	0.10	0.13	0.17	0.20
600	0.07	0.11	0.15	0.19	0.22
700	0.08	0.12	0.16	0.20	0.24
800	0.09	0.13	0.17	0.22	0.26
900	0.09	0.14	0.18	0.23	0.27

Average Chimney Temp. (F)	Case 2 Outside Air = 0 °F Chimney Height (Feet)				
	10	15	20	25	30
100	0.03	0.04	0.05	0.07	0.08
200	0.04	0.07	0.09	0.11	0.13
300	0.06	0.09	0.12	0.14	0.17
400	0.07	0.10	0.14	0.17	0.20
500	0.08	0.11	0.15	0.19	0.23
600	0.08	0.12	0.17	0.21	0.25
700	0.09	0.13	0.18	0.22	0.27
800	0.09	0.14	0.19	0.23	0.28
900	0.10	0.15	0.19	0.24	0.29

Draft = 0.01467 X Height X (1 - ([OAT + 460] / [TEMP + 460]))

Where:
Draft = Inches Water Column
OAT = Outdoor Air Temperature
TEMP = Average Chimney Temperature = (Tin - Tout)/2

Based On Information In The North American Combustion Handbook, Second Edition, 1978.

Figure 4-8

1. Measure the **chimney height**.

2. Measure the **inlet gas temperature** to the chimney.

3. Measure or calculate average **outlet gas temperature** leaving the chimney.

   NOTE: If the outlet gas temperature near the top of the chimney cannot be measured, estimate this temperature based on prior experience with chimneys of similar construction.

4. Use the theoretical draft chart to **find expected draft**.

5. If the measured draft at the base of the chimney is much less than the theoretical draft value, then **inspect the chimney** for air leakage, blockages, and other problems.

Other Important Draft Factors

In addition to the variables discussed above, several other important factors affect chimney performance:

> • Supply of air to the boiler room
> • Heat losses from the chimney
> • Heat losses from the flue-pipe
> • Temperature of gas entering the chimney
> • Condensation in the chimney or flue pipe
> • Burner firing rate
> • Cross-sectional area of the chimney
> • Wind effects
> • Air leakage into the chimney
> • Air flows caused by house exhaust fans and other devices.

Supply of Air to the Boiler Room. Various options for the supply of combustion air to the oil burner are illustrated in Figure 4-9. Tighter house construction practices have reduced the amount of air **leaking** into the structure from cracks around windows, doors, and walls. This has lowered the volume of outdoor air that is available in the boiler room for oil burner combustion air and draft control air. Therefore, all heating installations must be examined to be sure that adequate air is available for the heating unit. A chimney cannot produce draft strong enough to overcome a significant restriction on the air entering the boiler room. Therefore, the following steps are recommended:

1. Measure boiler-room depressurization (relative to outdoor air pressure) using a draft gauge. Be sure that all house exhaust fans are running when the test is performed. If the boiler room air pressure is less than the outdoor air, increase the supply of outdoor air to the room.

2. When installing a vent for outdoor, air follow the recommendations of the National Fire Protection Association (NFPA 31—Installation of Oil Burning Equipment), and all local codes. NFPA recommends an outdoor air opening of approximately one square inch for every 5,000 Btu per hour of fuel consumed (or about 28 square inches for every gallon per hour of fuel oil). Specific guidelines are included in NFPA 31.

3. Consider **sealed combustion** devices that directly duct outdoor air to the inlet of the burner. This can reduce the amount of heated air that is exhausted from the building and improve heating system efficiency. However, this should be used only with oil burners with low off-cycle air flows, such as high static air pressure flame-retention models. Otherwise, off-cycle heat loss from the boiler or furnace can increase and offset any efficiency gain.

Heat Losses from the Chimney. An important function of the chimney is to keep the flue gases warm so that sufficient draft is produced. After the flue gases enter at

Boiler/Furnace Combustion Air Source

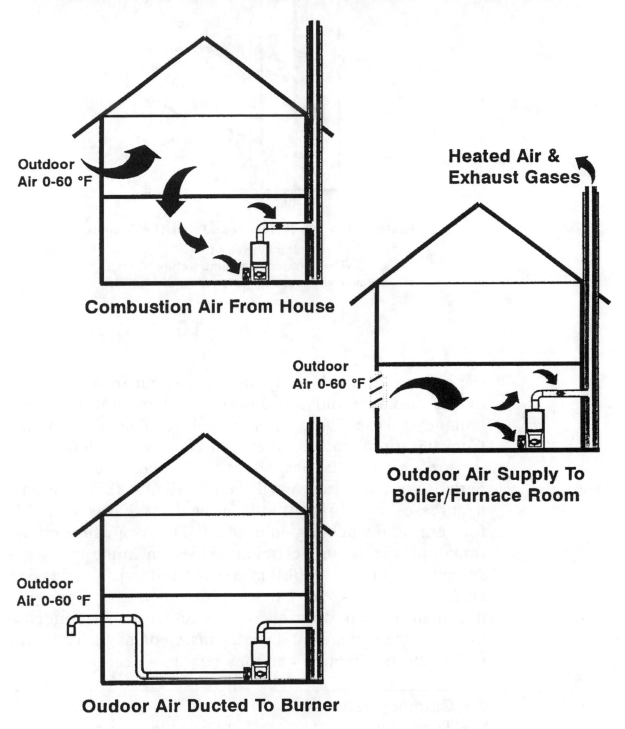

Outdoor Air 0-60 °F

Combustion Air From House

Heated Air & Exhaust Gases

Outdoor Air 0-60 °F

Outdoor Air Supply To Boiler/Furnace Room

Outdoor Air 0-60 °F

Oudoor Air Ducted To Burner

Figure 4-9

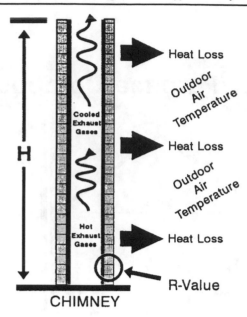

Factors That Affect Heat Loss From The Chimney

H = Chimney Height
OAT = Outdoor Air Temperature
R-Value = Insulating Properties Of Chimney

Figure 4-10

the bottom of the chimney, heat flows out from the walls of the chimney and this lowers the temperature of the chimney gases as shown in Figure 4-10. The gases exiting from the top of the chimney can be much cooler than at the breaching. This means that the average flue gas temperature in the chimney will be less than if there were no heat losses, and this will reduce the draft that is available for venting the heating equipment. That can cause operational problems and efficiency loss in some cases. A second important problem associated with excessive chimney heat loss is that some of the water vapor produced during combustion of the fuel oil can condense inside of the chimney and vent, causing damage. The three main factors affecting chimney heat loss are:

- Chimney height
- Temperature difference between the flue gases and the outdoor air.
- Insulating properties of the chimney design

The first two of these factors—chimney height and flue-gas/outdoor temperature difference—promote heat loss, but they also promote draft. So attacking a heat loss problem by manipulating these variables is unlikely to work. There are other reasons, of course, for avoiding too-tall chimneys and too-high flue gas temperatures, but chimney heat loss is not one of them.

Thermal insulating, however, can retard heat loss from the chimney without otherwise affecting draft. The design of the chimney affects its thermal insulating properties, and this affects the rate of heat loss. Conventional brick or block chimneys with a ceramic tile liner have typical heat loss rates of about 0.6 to 1.2 Btu per hour, per foot, per degree F. If the chimney is located outside of the house, it is totally exposed to outdoor air temperature, and large heat losses can occur during the cold winter months, which can adversely affect chimney operation. The worst offenders are uninsulated metal chimneys, which are not recommended at all because of very high heat loss rates and poor chimney performance.

Outdoor air temperature varies during the heating season, and the rate of heat loss form the chimney increases as the outdoor air temperature drops. Therefore, chimney problems caused by heat loss can increase as the outdoor temperature drops.

A properly-sized and well-insulated chimney is the best means for reducing chimney problems and efficiency loss caused by excessive heat loss.

Flue Pipe Heat Loss. Heat loss from the flue pipe connecting the boiler or furnace to the chimney can reduce chimney draft by lowering the temperature of the gases entering the chimney (see Figure 4-11). In many cases, these connectors are single-walled, uninsulated sheet metal, which offers very little resistance to heat loss. In addition, room air leakage through seams into these flue connectors can also lower the temperature of the chimney gases. Reducing these air leaks and insulating the flue pipe are especially important for installations where low chimney draft can be a problem.

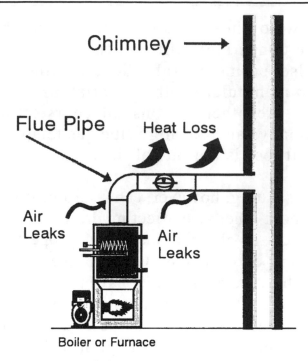

Flue Pipe Heat Loss

Figure 4-11

Temperature of Gases Entering Chimney. Highly efficient oil boilers and furnaces usually operate with reduced flue-gas temperatures. This lowers the draft available for venting the exhaust gases. Also, if the temperature is too low, water condensation can occur within the chimney, exhaust pipe, and heating unit, which can damage these parts of the heating system.

A second cause of low flue-gas temperature is air dilution from the barometric draft damper (see Figure 4-12). As discussed earlier, this device allows cool room air to enter the flue to reduce excessive chimney draft. However, this cools the flue gas from the boiler or furnace and reduces the temperature of the gases entering the chimney. Some recent studies have found that eliminating the barometric damper in some cases (when combined with high static air pressure flame—retention oil burners) can reduce chimney venting problems and improve heating system efficiency. This may be a good option for new high—efficiency heating units that use high air static oil

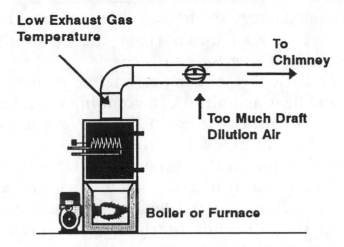

Causes Of Low Inlet Temperature At Chimney

Figure 4-12

burners. Always check local building codes before eliminating the barometric damper.

Condensation of Water Vapor. Chapter 2 showed that one of the primary products of combustion is water, which usually leaves the heating unit as a vapor. When the temperature of the chimney gases drops below their **dewpoint**, some of the water vapor condenses to liquid form. Problems associated with moisture condensation (see Figure 4-13) include:

- Ice build-up inside the chimney can occur during the burner off-cycle and can partially block the chimney and reduce the draft for venting the heating unit. This can lower burner efficiency. It can also become a safety issue as ice can dam up and block the chimney completely in very cold climates, especially if a cold snap lasts for a long period of time.
- Freeze-thaw damage occurs on the inside of chimneys as the water fills crevices and then expands on freezing. This could accelerate chimney aging and cause early chimney failure.

- Water can damage the house, flue pipe, and heating unit as it drains down from the chimney and accumulates on various surfaces.
- The condensed water can corrode the chimney, flue pipe, and heating unit. It can combine with the trace amounts of sulfur oxides in the flue gases to form an acid that can attack the chimney mortar, flue pipe and heating unit. If the chimney mortar is damaged, the chimney can leak and may collapse in extreme cases. The flue pipe and heating unit damage may shorten the lifetimes of these components and require early replacement. If the chimney flue liner is an acid-resistant ceramic material, then it is important to remove the condensate before it can enter the flue pipe or heating unit.

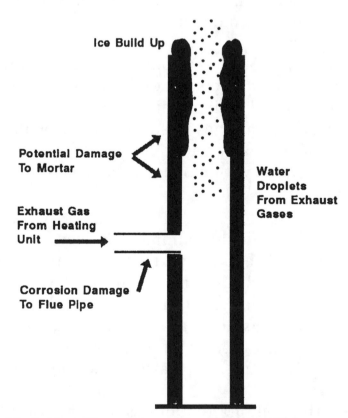

Ice Build Up

Potential Damage
To Mortar

Exhaust Gas
From Heating
Unit

Corrosion Damage
To Flue Pipe

Water
Droplets
From Exhaust
Gases

Moisture Condensation Within Chimney

Figure 4-13

The dewpoint for water is between 107°F and 119°F depending on the burner excess-air setting. However, in fuel oil that contains trace amounts of sulfur, acid can condense at higher temperatures. Acid condensation occurs whenever any part of the inside surface of the chimney is below the acid dewpoint temperature. According to the **Handbook of Oil Burning** (1951), the temperature of the exhaust gases leaving the chimney should be higher than 167°F. The temperature of the chimney gases near the wall can be 20°F or more lower than the average temperature. Therefore, a safety factor is recommended. If the temperature of the gases at the top of the chimney is above 200°F, then condensation problems should be avoided.

Burner Firing Rate. The burner firing rate has a direct effect on chimney draft because it changes the volume and heat content of the gases flowing up the chimney (see Figure 4-14). Recent trends toward lower firing rates for higher system efficiency tend to lower chimney draft. When the firing rate is reduced, the volume of gases is less, and the temperature of these gases drops faster for a given chimney heat loss rate. For example, if a heating

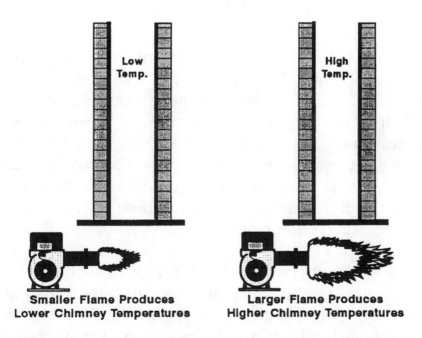

Burner Firing Rate Affects Chimney Temperature

Figure 4-14

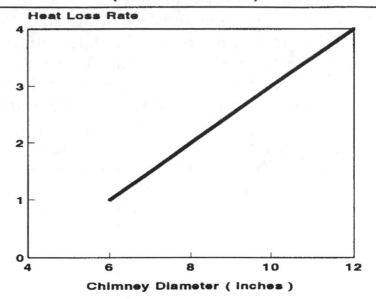

Heat Loss Rate = U x A x (Tgas-Tout)

Where:
U = Heat Transfer Coefficient Of Chimney Materials
A = Surface Area Of Chimney
Tgas = Temperature Of Chimney Gases
Tout = Outdoor Air Temperature

Figure 4-15

system is fired at 1.5 gallons per hour and the chimney temperature drops 50°F from inlet to outlet, the same system fired at 0.75 gallons per hour would have a nearly 100°F drop in chimney temperature, if all other factors were constant. This could produce inadequate draft or condensation problems in some installations. Reducing the firing rate is an important energy conservation option, but its impact on chimney venting must be considered so that corrective action can be taken if needed.

Cross-Sectional Area of Chimney. The diameter or inside area of the chimney also has an important impact on chimney performance (see Figure 4-15). It must be large enough to allow low pressure loss for unrestricted flow of the exhaust gas. On the other hand, large—diameter chimneys have large surface areas, which increases the rate of heat loss. The smallest inside area that permits proper venting is recommended to avoid excessive chimney cooling, loss of draft, and condensation problems. For modern, efficient heating units with reduced firing rates, inside diameters of 4 or 5 inches may be acceptable. The *Testing and Rating Standard for Heating Boilers—Sixth Edition, June 1989* published by the Hydronics Institute offers the following guidelines for mechanically vented systems:

GROSS OUTPUT -MBH	MINIMUM VENT DIA. (inches)
Up to 132	4
133 – 198	5
199 – 324	6
325 – 504	7

If a heating unit fired at 1.0 gallons per hour with a typical brick and ceramic lined chimney is reduced from 8 to 5 inches, the heat loss rate drops by about 30% and the chimney exit temperature rises from approximately 150°F to 200°F. Therefore, careful chimney sizing is an important factor for proper chimney venting.

Wind Effects. Wind can reduce chimney draft and even cause backdrafts when air flows down through the chimney (see Figure 4-16). The chimney should be higher than any surrounding roof or surface to reduce the chance of backdraft. In addition, chimney cap designs are available to reduce the effect of wind and to minimize backdrafting. Wind effects show up as a variable and unstable draft reading after steady-state operating conditions are established.

Air Leakage Into the Chimney. As discussed earlier, air dilution into the chimney lowers its temperature and reduces the draft produced. In some cases, air leakage can prevent the chimney from producing sufficient draft for operating the heating unit. Some common sources of air leakage (see Figure 4-17) are:

Wind Can Cause Backdrafting In Short Chimneys

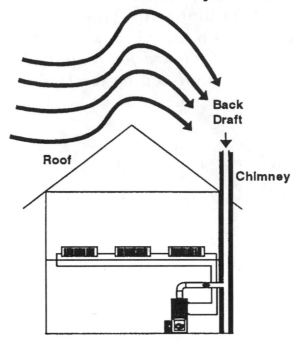

Figure 4-16

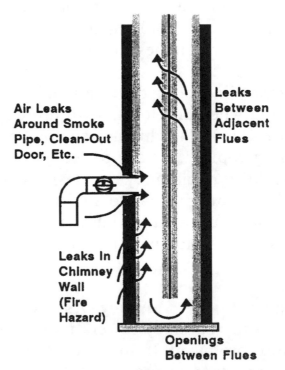

Air Leaks Into Chimney

Figure 4-17

- Loose-fitting clean-out door at base of chimney;
- Unsealed cracks around the flue pipe where it enters the chimney;
- Openings between adjacent flue passages in chimney;
- Cracks or openings in chimney wall;
- Other appliance or fireplaces connected to furnace flue;
- Furnace flue not extended to base of chimney.

A thorough inspection of the chimney, with draft testing and comparison to theoretical values, can identify these chimney problems so that corrective actions can be taken.

Air Flows Caused by House Exhaust Fans. If fans are used in the house and the supply of outdoor air is limited (tight house construction), a negative pressure can develop in the boiler room and chimney draft will be diminished (see Figure 4-18). Be sure that house fans are operating when investigating an installation where chimney problems are suspected. These fans include: bathroom exhausts, kitchen exhaust fans, whole-house exhaust fans (often in the attic), and air-to-air heat exchangers. If operation of these fans causes a draft problem for the heating unit, install a new source of combustion air and consider "sealed combustion," in which the outdoor air supply is directly ducted to the burner.

How Chimney Heat Loss Affects Draft and Condensation

If we look at example cases we can see how much heat losses can affect chimney performance. The temperature of the gases leaving the top of the chimney changes as the heat-loss rate varies for the two following sets of conditions:

House Depressurization By Exhaust Fans

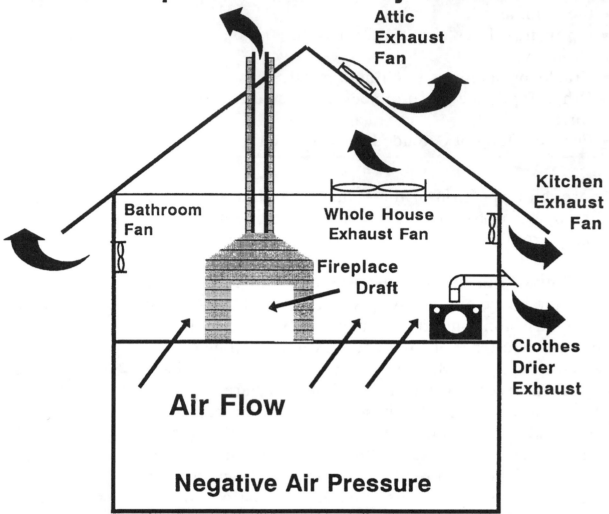

Figure 4-18

- Chimney height: 20 feet
- Chimney inlet temperature: 300°F (Case 1) and 200°F (Case 2) (after barometric damper)
- Outdoor air temperature: 20°F
- Burner firing rate: 1.0 gallons per hour
- Barometric air flow: 27 cfm (equal to combustion air flow)
- Chimney inner diameter: 7 inches.

Let us look first at Case 1, with an inlet temperature to the chimney (after the barometric damper) of 300°F. For low-heat-loss chimneys in the range of 0.25 to 0.50 Btu per hour per foot per degree F (Btuh/ft-F), the average exit temperature will be above 200°F and condensation problems are not expected. Typical chimney construction with an expected heat loss in the range of 0.6 to 1.0 Btuh/ft-F would have exit temperatures of about 170°F to 200°F and may experience some condensation problems on cold days (below 20°F), and at the inner wall of the chimney which is less than the average gas temperature. For chimneys with higher heat losses, the chimney exit temperature can fall below 120°F and may produce significant condensation on cold days.

The second case is for a chimney inlet temperature of 200°F with the other factors remaining the same. This would cause the temperature at the outlet of the chimney to fall below 200°F, even for low chimney heat-loss rates. For typical chimney loss rates of 0.6 to 1.0 Btuh/ft-F, the chimney gas exit temperature would be between 110°F and 140°F when the outdoor air temperature is 20°F. Flue-gas condensation would be expected for a significant part of the heating season. The high-heat-loss chimneys can produce exit temperatures of less than 75°F and severe condensation problems could occur.

While these two examples do not represent the full range of cases that are possible, they do illustrate the important effects of the inlet gas temperature on the chimney, and on the rate of heat loss from the chimney. Whenever possible, systems should be designed and operated to produce a sufficiently high inlet temperature and low chimney heat losses to avoid inadequate draft and condensation problems. Figure 4-19 shows the heat-loss rate for several example chimney designs.

Approximate Heat Loss Of Inside*
Type Masonry Chimney

Chimney Construction	Heat Loss **
Common Brick 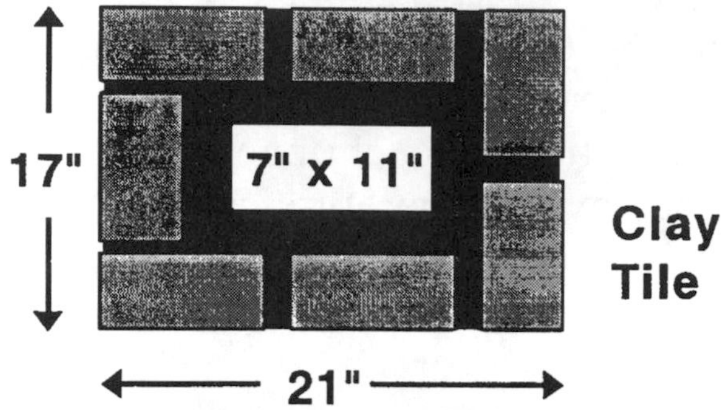 17" 7" x 11" 21" Clay Tile	**1.2**
Common Brick 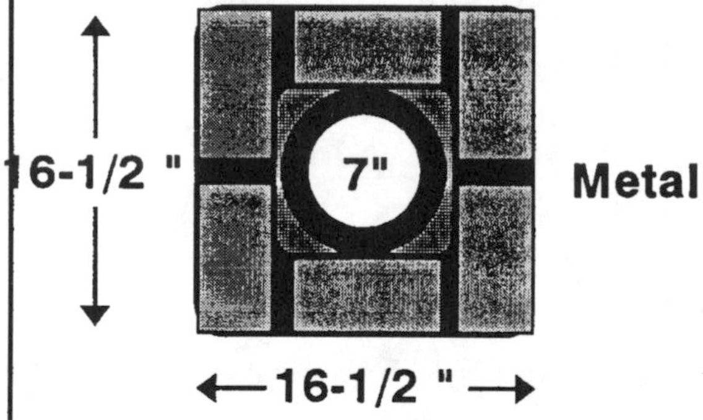 16-1/2 " 7" 16-1/2 " Metal	**0.7**

* Chimneys 15.5 Feet High With One-Third Of Height Exposed.

** Approximate Heat Loss In Btu Per Square Foot Per °F Per Hour. Factors Calculated From Tests at 200, 600, & 1000 °F Entering Temperature And At Gas Flow Rates Corresponding To 1/2, 1, & 1-1/2 Gallons Per Hour Corrected At 0 °F Outdoor Temperature.

Figure 4-19

4.2 How Chimneys Affect Efficiency

Chapter 1 summarized the five heat losses that occur in oil heating systems. Three of these losses are directly affected by chimney operation. These are:

- Burner On-cycle Flue Heat Loss
- Off-cycle Heat Loss
- Air Infiltration Heat Loss.

Chimney Draft Affects Burner On-Cycle Heat Loss

Chimney venting affects on-cycle efficiency in two ways, start-up transients and seasonal draft variations.

Start-Up Transients. If the chimney is cool when the burner starts, it must heat up before the draft is fully established. During the start-up period, the chimney draft is lower than normal and this can reduce the amount of combustion air delivered by the burner, especially for older oil burner designs with low static air pressure characteristics. How much this affects burner efficiency depends mainly on four factors:

- The length of the off-cycle
- The mass of the chimney
- Air leaks in the boiler or furnace
- Burner design.

The length of the burner off-cycle is important because the chimney will cool down more with longer burner off periods. A colder chimney will take longer to heat up to produce steady draft.

Chimney mass is important because high mass requires more time to heat up to steady operating conditions. This is especially important for low-firing-rate burners that generate less heat output. This can extend the time required to fully heat the chimney and establish a steady draft (see Figure 4-20).

Air leaks in the boiler or furnace can reduce system efficiency by increasing burner off-cycle heat losses. They do have a positive effect, however, because they keep the chimney warm during the off-cycle. However, these air leaks represent a net efficiency loss.

Burner design also is an important factor with respect to transient draft effects. Modern flame-retention and high-static air pressure oil burners are very stable and their combustion air flow rates do not change much when the chimney draft varies. They are, therefore, less sensi-

Chimney Start-Up Transients

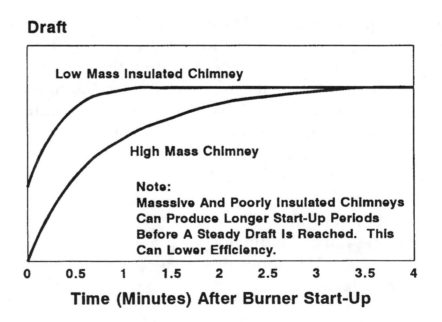

Draft

Low Mass Insulated Chimney

High Mass Chimney

Note:
Masssive And Poorly Insulated Chimneys
Can Produce Longer Start-Up Periods
Before A Steady Draft Is Reached. This
Can Lower Efficiency.

0   0.5   1   1.5   2   2.5   3   3.5   4

Time (Minutes) After Burner Start-Up

Figure 4-20

tive to draft changes are less affected by draft variations during the burner start-up.

The optimum design to overcome these transient effects is a low-mass, well-insulated chimney, which will produce minimal transients.

Seasonal Draft Variations. Chimney draft increases as the outdoor air temperature decreases. During a typical heating season the chimney draft can vary by as much as 6 to 1, and this can change the air flow to the burner. Burner air flow is produced by the **pushing** effect of the burner air fan and the **pulling** effect of the chimney. As the **pulling** action by the chimney increases, the air flow can increase, especially for older non-flame retention burners. Although some of this draft variation can be counteracted by the barometric draft regulator, draft changes can lower burner efficiency in two ways:

- If the chimney draft is too high, too much air is supplied by the burner, the flame temperature is lowered, and combustion efficiency drops.
- If the chimney draft is too low, not enough air is supplied by the burner, smoke can increase, and efficiency drops.

As the chimney draft varies during the heating season by a factor of six, both of these unwanted conditions can occur. The net change in air flow caused by chimney draft changes is determined by the oil burner design and, in particular, the burner static air pressure that is produced. Figure 2-26 shows how burner air flow is affected by changes in chimney draft for older non-flame retention burners, for flame-retention burners, and for high-static air pressure flame-retention burners.

The **older burners** are **strongly affected** by changes in chimney draft, and the air flow rate changes by 40% as the draft changes from 0.03 to 0.09 inches water column (a factor of 3). The air flow of the flame-retention burner is mildly affected by draft changes, and varies by only

20% as the flue draft changes by the same amount. In contrast, air flow to the high-static flame-retention burner is only weakly affected by changes in flue draft, and varies by less than 10 percent as the draft changes from -0.03 to -0.09 inches water column. This is represented by the flat horizontal line in the figure that shows very small changes in air flow as the flue draft varies. Therefore, the high-static pressure oil burner maintains a nearly constant air flow, with low smoke production and high efficiency over the entire heating season.

The examples that follow illustrate the changes in efficiency that occur in extreme cases (without a barometric draft damper) for older, outdated oil burners and high-static pressure burners. Four conditions will be examined to show the changes in chimney draft that can occur during a typical heating season for a 25 foot chimney without a barometric draft regulator, and neglecting flue and chimney heat losses.

Case 1. Burner start-up in the fall season

Outdoor air temperature: 60 degrees F
Flue gas temperature: 100 degrees F
Chimney draft: -0.03 inches water column

Case 2. Steady burner operation in the fall season

Outdoor air temperature: 60 degrees F
Flue gas temperature: 400 degrees F
Chimney draft: -0.14 inches water column

Case 3. Burner start-up in the winter season

Outdoor air temperature: 0 degrees F
Flue gas temperature: 100 degrees F
Chimney draft: -0.07 inches water column

Case 4. Steady burner operation in the winter season

Outdoor air temperature: 0 degrees F
Flue gas temperature: 400 degrees F
Chimney draft: -0.17 inches water column

We can see that the chimney draft could vary from a low of -0.03 to a high of -0.17 which could change the air flow supplied by the burner. The information in Figure 2-26 can be used to estimate the change in burner air flow and combustion efficiency for the full range of conditions that may be expected during a typical heating season. If an older (outdated) non-flame retention burner is adjusted for zero smoke and 9% carbon dioxide at a draft of -0.05 inches water column. The changes in burner air flow and efficiency for the cases shown above are estimated in the table that follows:

BURNER: OLD DESIGN (NON-FLAME RETEN-TION)

FLUE CO_2: 9%

FLUE GAS TEMP: 600°F

COMB. EFF: 76.5%

DRAFT CONTROL: NONE

FLUE DRAFT: -0.05 in. w.c.

	FLUE DRAFT	% EXCESS COMB. AIR	% DECREASE IN COMB EFFICIENCY
OPTIMUM	-0.05	70	0
CASE 1	-0.03	40	INSUFFICIENT COMB AIR
CASE 2	-0.14	145	10
CASE 3	-0.07	90	1
CASE 4	-0.17	160	11

When the older burner without a barometric draft regulator is adjusted for optimum operation with 70% excess combustion air (9% CO_2) at a flue draft of -0.05 inches water column, the efficiency can decrease by up to 11 percent due to seasonal chimney draft variations. In Case

1, insufficient combustion air can produce smoke and lower system efficiency. While this example is an extreme case and does not represent typical conditions because it is an obsolete burner without a barometric damper, it does indicate that variations in chimney draft can adversely affect system efficiency to a lesser degree for some older burners.

The same draft variations can be applied to a high-static pressure flame-retention burner to compare the change in efficiency from draft variation.

BURNER: FLAME RETENTION BURNER (HIGH STATIC AIR PRESSURE)

FLUE CO_2: 13%

FLUE GAS TEMP: 400°F

COMB. EFF: 84%

DRAFT CONTROL: NONE

FLUE DRAFT: -0.05 in. w.c.

	FLUE DRAFT	% EXCESS COMB. AIR	% DECREASE IN COMB EFFICIENCY
OPTIMUM	-0.05	15	0
CASE 1	-0.03	14.5	0
CASE 2	-0.14	15.6	0
CASE 3	-0.07	15.3	0
CASE 4	-0.17	16.2	less than 1

The table for the high-static burner indicates that near-zero changes in combustion efficiency occur as the chimney draft varies (even without a barometric draft regulator) for the high static air pressure oil burners. In fact, the older burner with a barometric damper had a larger variation in air flow than the high static pressure oil burner without draft control.

While some older oil burners may be adversely affected by changes in chimney draft, new flame-retention and high-static oil burners are much less sensitive to seasonal draft changes. In fact, no significant change in efficiency is expected for newer oil burners (with static air pressure of about 3 inches w.c.) even without a barometric damper. This is confirmed by on-going field testing programs in Canada that include high-static oil burners with sealed vents without barometric draft control dampers. The next chapter on alternative venting methods will discuss this subject in more detail.

Chimneys and Off-Cycle Heat Loss

The chimney is a primary cause of off-cycle heat loss from home heating equipment because it has thermal mass and remains warm during the off-cycle. This produces off-cycle draft. This draft pulls cool air into the burner and through the warm heating unit, and removes useful heat from the boiler or furnace (see Figure 4-21).

The exact level of off-cycle loss depends on many factors that include burner and heating unit design, size and thermal mass of the chimney, and all the other chimney draft factors discussed earlier. Heating unit installation factors are also important, and all leaks around the burner and heating unit should be sealed to reduce off-cycle air flow and heat loss. Oil heating equipment with modern oil burners have off-cycle heat losses in the 3% to 4% range as discussed in Chapter 1. Older equipment designs have much larger off-cycle losses (5–15%).

The preferred chimney design to minimize off-cycle loss is a low—mass chimney that cools down rapidly following the burner on cycle.

Chimneys and Air-Infiltration Heat Loss

Another heat loss that is caused by chimney operation is the infiltration of cold outdoor air into the house to replace the heated air that is exhausted by the chimney through the burner and barometric damper during both the burner on-cycle and off-cycle (see Figure 4-22). If all the air used for these purposes is heated air from the house, the total infiltration heat loss can reach 12% or more of the annual fuel use.

Factors that affect this loss include the following:

- Chimney height
- Location of heating unit
- Source of combustion and draft-control air.

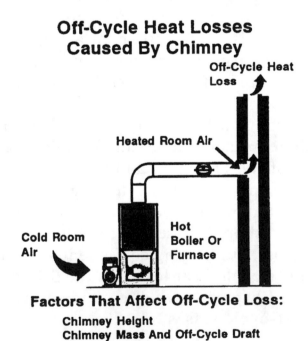

Off-Cycle Heat Losses Caused By Chimney

Off-Cycle Heat Loss

Heated Room Air

Cold Room Air

Hot Boiler Or Furnace

Factors That Affect Off-Cycle Loss:
Chimney Height
Chimney Mass And Off-Cycle Draft
Chimney Temperature
Wind Conditions

Figure 4-21

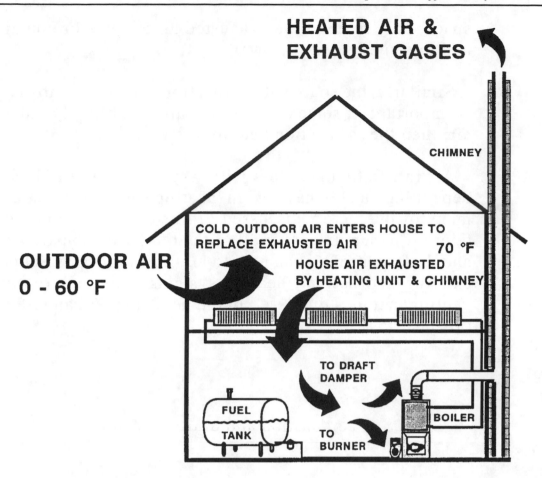

HEATED AIR &
EXHAUST GASES

CHIMNEY

COLD OUTDOOR AIR ENTERS HOUSE TO
REPLACE EXHAUSTED AIR   70 °F

OUTDOOR AIR
0 - 60 °F

HOUSE AIR EXHAUSTED
BY HEATING UNIT & CHIMNEY

TO DRAFT
DAMPER

FUEL
TANK

TO
BURNER

BOILER

OUTDOOR AIR INFILTRATION CAUSED BY THE HEATING SYSTEM AND CHIMNEY

Figure 4-22

Chimney height is important because, as we saw earlier, higher chimneys produce more draft. If more draft is produced than is needed by the oil burner, then the air flow through the barometric damper will increase. If heated room air is used, this will increase fuel use to heat the cold outdoor air that enters the building to replace the air flowing out the barometric damper.

The location of the heating unit is also an important factor. If the heating unit is located within the heated space, then all of the air exhausted by the heating unit will be heated air that must be replaced by cold outdoor air. If the heating unit is in an unheated, or partially heated space, only some of the exhausted air is heated room air, and this energy loss is lower.

Similarly, the source of combustion and draft control air is important. If some or all of this air is unheated outdoor air, then the infiltration heat loss is reduced.

Air infiltration heat loss will vary from house to house depending on chimney design, heating system design, and many of the factors discussed in this chapter. Using outdoor air to supply part or all of the burner combustion air and draft control air can help to minimize this loss in both existing and new oil heating systems. Also, alternative venting methods discussed in the next chapter can reduce this heat loss.

4.3 What Actions Can Improve Chimney Venting and Efficiency?

We have seen that many factors affect chimney draft, and changes in draft can affect the efficiency of the heating system. This section discusses practical measures that can reduce chimney problems and promote reliable and efficient operation of oil heating equipment.

1. Check to be sure that adequate combustion air is supplied to the boiler or furnace room. Follow the recommendations in NFPA 31.

2. Check for furnace room depressurization caused by house exhaust fans, clothes driers, fireplaces, or other equipment. Consider **sealed combustion** devices if the problem is difficult to correct. A retention-head burner or high-static air pressure burner is recom-

mended to avoid an increase in boiler or furnace off-cycle heat loss.

3. Always keep the chimney gases as hot as possible to produce sufficient draft and to avoid condensation. The temperature of gases leaving the chimney should be $200^{\circ}F$ or higher to prevent condensation. The following steps are recommended.

> - Use the minimum size chimney (see Hydronics Institute recommendations) that will meet the venting requirements. This will reduce chimney heat losses.
> - Avoid excessive chimney height because it allows the chimney gases to cool more than necessary and this can produce condensation in the chimney.
> - Use insulating materials within the chimney to reduce heat losses.
> - Locate the chimney within the house whenever possible to reduce heat loss. Avoid freestanding chimneys on the outside of the building because this arrangement exposes most of the chimney surfaces to cold outdoor temperatures and allows rapid cooling of the chimney gases.
> - If chimney temperatures are too low, insulate the flue pipe and seal flue pipe air leaks to increase temperature of flue gases entering the chimney. Also, seal air leaks between the flue pipe and chimney breaching.

4. Be careful that the chimney exit temperature is adequate to prevent condensation when the firing rate of a heating unit is reduced, or when installing new lower-input high-efficiency heating equipment designs. Measure or calculate the new temperature of chimney gases at the top of the chimney. If these gases are too cool, take corrective action.

5. Consider removing or sealing the barometric damper when new high-static air pressure flame-retention oil

burners are installed. Always check with all codes to be sure that this option is permitted.

6. Always seal air leaks around the burner flange, and boiler or furnace, to assure high chimney temperatures and to reduce off-cycle heat loss.

7. For high-efficiency heating equipment with low flue-gas temperatures, consider removing the barometric damper and insulating and sealing the flue pipe in order to increase the temperature of the chimney gases to improve draft and avoid condensation. A high-static air pressure burner is recommended.

8. If the chimney is oversized and has excessive heat loss, consider the following:

> • Relining with reduced-diameter metal liner and backfilling with an insulating material;
> • Installing a new smaller-sized, low-mass, thermally insulated chimney;
> • Installing power venting through the side wall, if permitted by code;
> • If the draft is adequate, and the chimney is lined with acid-resistant material, provide a means for collecting and disposing of condensate.

9. If the chimney is too short, or chimney draft cannot be raised to adequate levels, consider a powered draft inducer (draft booster fan) to increase the draft supplied to the heating equipment.

10. Adjust the barometric damper to produce low overfire draft (of about negative 0.01 or 0.02 inches water column, or as recommended by the equipment manufacturer).

11. Consider high-static air pressure burners (about 3 inches water column) for installations with low or variable chimney draft.

12. If chimney problems are suspected, measure the draft and compare it to theoretical draft values based on chimney design and operating conditions. If the actual draft is much less than the theoretical value, inspect the chimney and heating system for air leaks, blockages, excessive heat loss, and other problems. Take corrective action if needed.

CHIMNEY INSPECTION CHECKLIST:

Whenever the measured draft is lower than expected, thoroughly inspect the chimney for common problems that can reduce draft. These include the following:

Problem: Top of chimney lower than roof or nearby buildings or objects.
Found by: Visual inspection.
Action: Extend chimney or remove interfering object.

Problem: Chimney top or cap restricts flue area.
Found by: Visual inspection.
Action: Remove cap or enlarge opening.

Problem: Obstruction exists in chimney caused by broken tiles, bricks or other objects.
Found by: Visual inspection using a light and mirror.
Action: Remove obstruction.

Problem: Soot deposits have accumulated in chimney flue.
Found by: Visual inspection of chimney with light and mirror.
Action: Clean soot deposits.

Problem: Debris accumulate in chimney offset.
Found by: Visual inspection using a light and mirror, or lowering a light down the chimney from above.
Action: Remove debris.

Problem: Flue pipe projects into chimney flue.

Found by: Visual inspection with light and mirror.
Action: Position end of flue pipe flush with the inside of the chimney flue.

Problem: Chimney area is too small.
Found by: Measurement and comparison to vent sizing tables.
Action: Rebuild or replace chimney, or use an alternative venting method as described in the next chapter.

Problem: Chimney is too large.
Found by: Measurement and comparison to venting tables.
Action: See item 8 above.

Problem: Air leakage into chimney caused by:
Leaks in chimney wall;
Leaks between adjacent flues within the chimney;
Fireplaces or other appliances installed in the same flue;
Air leaks around flue pipe, cleanout doors, and other sources;
Furnace flue not fully extended to base of chimney.
Found by: Observations and smoke testing.
Actions: Repair leaks or have chimney repaired by masonry contractor.

QUESTIONS

4-1.   Name three types of draft.

4-2.   Name three (3) heat losses that are directly affected by chimney operation.

4-3.   As outdoor air temperature decreases, chimney draft increases: true or false?

4-4.   The draft produced by a chimney increases as the chimney height increases: true or false?

4-5.   What factors affect chimney performance:
1.   Wind
2.   Burner firing rate
3.   Air flows caused by house exhaust fan
4.   Supply of air to the burner
5.   All of the above

4-6.   The flue connection from the outlet of the boiler or furnace to the chimney should be as short as possible and contain a minimum number of elbows to avoid excess pressure drop, loss of draft. True or false?

4-7.   What does a barometric damper do?

4-8.   What are some common sources of air leakage into the chimney?

4-9.   What is the difference between forced draft and induced draft?

4-10.   What are the three main parts of the chimney venting system used in oil heated houses?

4-11.   When installing a vent for outdoor air, NFPA recommends an outdoor air opening of one square inch for every (5,000) BTU per hour of fuel consumed. True or false?

4-12.   Air flows caused by house exhaust fans. What effect does a whole house exhaust fan have on chimney draft?

Chapter 5—Alternative Venting of Oil Heating Equipment

The previous chapter discussed important factors that affect chimney venting and how they can change the efficiency of oil heating equipment. This chapter will present alternative methods for venting that can reduce heat losses and improve system efficiency. The specific options discussed are:

- Chimney lining and removal of barometric dampers;
- Power side-wall venting;
- Vent dampers recommended for some installations as a last resort;

The information presented for each of these alternative venting approaches will include:

- What it is?
- How to do it!
- Advantages and fuel savings.
- Key problem areas associated with each venting method.

In addition, shorter descriptions are given of two emerging venting options:

- Power venting through lined chimney;
- Outdoor boiler installation.

5.1 Sealed and Insulated Venting Systems with High Static Air Pressure Oil Burners

Chapter 4 on chimney venting showed that new flame-retention oil burners that operate with high-static air pressure (of about 3 inches of water column) are less sensitive to changes in chimney draft than older lower air pressure burners. In fact, the seasonal change in air flow caused by chimney draft variations with the new burners **without** a barometric damper can be **less than** older oil burners **with** a barometric damper. Also, the air dilution caused by the barometric lowers the flue-gas and chimney temperature, which can be a problem especially for the new high-efficiency boilers and furnaces. The barometric damper may not be needed for heating systems with new high-static air pressure oil burners. Smaller-diameter, insulated chimney liners with reduced amounts of dilution air can help to limit chimney problems including inadequate draft, flue-gas condensation, and chimney damage. They can also improve the efficiency of the heating system. Although we lack extensive field data on the long-term performance of sealed and insulated vent systems, they may offer a useful alternative to conventional chimney venting for some installations.

What Is It?

One alternative venting approach is under development in Canada, and initial tests have been favorable (see Figure 5-1). The three key parts of this system are:

- High-static air pressure oil burner;
- Reduced-diameter and insulated chimney vent;
- Sealed flue pipe (without a barometric damper).

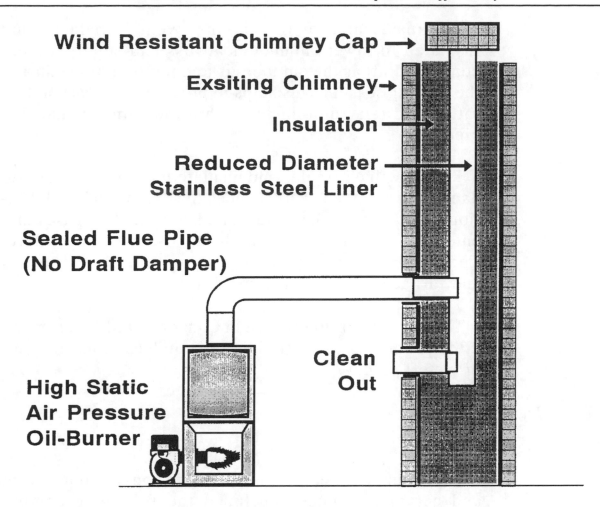

Wind Resistant Chimney Cap →

Exsiting Chimney→

Insulation →

**Reduced Diameter →
Stainless Steel Liner**

**Sealed Flue Pipe
(No Draft Damper)**

**High Static
Air Pressure
Oil-Burner**

**Clean
Out**

Sealed And Insulated Chimney System

- **High Static Air Pressure
  Burner ($\sim$3"w.c.)**

- **Sealed Flue Pipe (No Damper)**

- **Reduced Diameter Flue Insulated
  Chimney System**

Figure 5-1

High-static air pressure oil burners are required because they are less sensitive to changes in chimney draft and can operate efficiently without barometric draft dampers. (Building codes must be reviewed to be sure that removal of the barometric damper is permitted).

The inside area of the chimney vent is reduced and insulated to lower chimney heat loss and supply a more constant draft as the outdoor air temperature drops during the heating season. This helps to prevent flue-gas condensation and related problems within the chimney and flue pipe.

The flue pipe is sealed and insulated, and the barometric damper is removed. This reduces the amount of cold dilution air that enters the system and keeps the flue gases that enter the chimney at the highest possible temperature. This is particularly important for high-efficiency boilers and furnaces that produce low-temperature flue gas.

This venting option is used in Canada to reduce chimney draft problems, prevent flue-gas condensation, and improve efficiency.

How To Do It!

The Canadian venting upgrade for conventional brick and ceramic chimneys included the following components:

> • High-static air pressure oil burner;
> • Stainless-steel chimney liner;
> • Stainless Tee connector for base of chimney;
> • Insulation to backfill the chimney liner;
> • Removal or sealing of the barometric damper;
> • Wind-resistant chimney cap.

A high-static air pressure oil burner (at ~3 inches water column) is included in the package because it is less sensitive to changes in chimney draft as discussed in Chapter 4. This allows removal of the barometric damper (when permitted by building codes). These high-static pressure burners are now available from several manufacturers.

The flexible stainless steel chimney liner is used to reduce the diameter of the chimney flue and increase its resistance to condensate damage. The liner can be installed from the top of the chimney. Research in Canada has found that highly alloyed stainless steels that contain iron, chromium, nickel, copper and molybdenum are best suited for this use. A thin liner (0.125 mm) is used so that the liner will be flexible.

A stainless steel Tee connector is used at the base of the chimney to join the chimney liner with the flue pipe. A double or triple Tee is recommended to provide a cleanout at the base of the chimney.

An insulating material is used between the old chimney flue and the new liner to reduce chimney heat loss. This should be a water-resistant material, and some installers mix the insulating material with cement and water so that the insulation will be held in place if a hole forms in the liner. A water-resistant vermiculite fill is used by some installers as the insulating material.

The barometric damper is removed from the flue connector and the flue pipe is sealed. This reduces the amount of dilution air entering the chimney and increases the average chimney temperature. A reduced-size, insulated flue pipe may be advisable to reduce heat loss.

Chimney caps are installed to reduce the effects of wind on chimney draft. A cap that prevents back-drafts and minimizes the effect of high winds is recommended. This is important when the barometric draft damper is eliminated to reduce the impact of wind on chimney draft.

Important Note: This alternative venting approach has been used in Canada but limited information exists on its long-term performance. Also, code restrictions in the United States must be fully examined and more experience with this venting approach is needed before it can be recommended for widespread use.

Advantages and Fuel Savings

This alternative venting method offers a number of advantages over conventional chimney venting, especially for high-efficiency and reduced-input heating equipment, or homes with oversized chimneys. These include:

> • Reduced flue-gas condensation problems and damage;
> • Less combustion-gas spillage;
> • Improved efficiency.

Problems associated with lower chimney temperatures were described in Chapter 4. Condensation of flue gases was one of these. The sealed and insulated flue system helps to reduce condensation in several ways. The smaller diameter flue pipe operates with less heat loss, and this causes the average temperature of the chimney gases to rise above their dewpoint temperature. The added insulation between the chimney flue and the metal liner also reduces heat loss, and this also lessens condensation problems. These benefits can extend the lifetime of the chimney and the heating system.

Combustion spillage can also be reduced by the new venting system for three reasons. First, the higher on-cycle chimney temperature produces more draft. Second, the inside surface of the liner (which is low-mass and insulated) can heat up faster than a ceramic-lined brick chimney. This allows the chimney draft to reach its steady—state value more quickly. Third, after the barometric damper is removed, the chimney gases are hotter as the burner starts up and this can also reduce flue-gas spillage. All three of these effects tend to reduce combustion-gas spillage, especially on start-up. This is desired for all combustion heating equipment to reduce the amount of air pollution that enters the home.

Improved efficiency and reduced heat losses are important advantages of the sealed and insulated flue system. It improves efficiency in several ways (see Chapter 4, Section 4.2).

Reduced on-cycle heat loss—start up transients

In Chapter 4 we found that the burner fuel-air ratio can vary during start-up and this can reduce the combustion efficiency at the start of the burner cycle. The insulated, low-mass vent reduces these transients.

Reduced seasonal draft variations

The high-static air pressure burner is very stable. Its combustion air flow does not change with outdoor air temperature. This produces high combustion efficiency over the entire heating season, even when the barometric draft damper is removed.

Reduced off-cycle heat loss

The high static air pressure restricts air flow during the burner off-cycle, and this lowers heat loss from the heating unit. Furthermore, the lower-mass chimney liner cools down more rapidly than the heavier ceramic liners, and this can reduce the off-cycle draft that causes the air flow through the heating unit.

Lower Heating System Induced Air Infiltration

Reduced air infiltration occurs during both the burner on—and off-cycles because the barometric damper is removed. This reduces the amount of heated house air that is vented by the chimney, and this lowers annual heating costs.

Reduced Flue-Gas Condensation Problems

This system permits the use of new, highly efficient boilers and furnaces that operate with low flue-gas temperatures **without** running into flue-gas condensation problems.

Losses Due to System Over-Sizing (Firing Rate) Are Reduced

The firing rate can be reduced to match the heating load more closely. Reduced fuel firing rates can be employed without running into inadequate draft and condensation problems.

The Canadian savings experience with these sealed and insulated vent systems is very positive. The typical savings is expected to be about 20 percent, with some heating units as high as 40 percent. These savings are attributed to the entire package, which includes:

- New high-static air pressure flame-retention oil burner with higher on-cycle and off-cycle efficiency than older burners;
- Reduced fuel firing rate (up to 40% lower);
- Lower air flow through the vent system (no barometric damper) for reduced air infiltration induced by the heating equipment.

Problems and Limitations

The sealed and insulated vent system can be applied as a retrofit when combined with a high-static air pressure oil burner, or it can be used when a new high-efficiency heating unit is installed. Important considerations regarding the use of this venting method include:

Cost

The installed cost of the chimney liner and chimney modifications is relatively high and can be on the order of $1,000 or more, based on the Canadian experience. This option should be applied only after a careful analysis of other conservation options, to see which is most cost-effective.

Age of Equipment

In Canada, the retrofit of the sealed vent and high-static air pressure burner is not recommended for heating systems that are more than 15 years old.

Combustion Chamber Upgrade or Replacement

The flame-retention oil burners operate with a higher flame temperature, and the condition of the combustion chamber or chamber liner must be assessed. A new low-mass ceramic fiber chamber is recommended to handle the hotter combustion gases. This is especially important for older dry-based boilers, which can experience burn-out if the combustion chamber is not upgraded.

Application is Not Recommended for Furnaces

The Canadian experience is that the retrofit option is better suited for oil boilers, and its application to oil furnaces is not recommended.

Building Code Restrictions

Some features of the sealed and insulated vent system, including the removal of the barometric damper, may be prohibited by building codes. Be sure that this option is permitted before proceeding.

Limited Experience in U.S.

As mentioned earlier, this venting option has not been widely used in this country, and careful installation by experienced service technicians is needed to avoid potential vent problems.

5.2 Power Side-Wall Venting

We have seen that chimney venting causes heat losses that lower the overall efficiency of the heating system. One alternative to chimney venting is power side-wall venting, in which the exhaust gases are forced by a fan from the heating equipment and out of the house. Power side-wall venting offers many advantages over chimneys, including improved efficiency, but possible adverse affects must also be considered. The lower cost of the side-wall vent systems make them an attractive option for new homes and for conversion of electric heated home to oil heat.

What Is It?

Power side-wall venting systems use an electric-powered exhaust fan instead of natural chimney draft to force the exhaust gases from the house. A forced-draft system can be used where the oil burner develops enough air pressure to push the exhaust gases through the heating unit and out of the side-wall vent. In this case the heating unit, flue pipe, and all vent connections must be tightly sealed to prevent flue-gas leakage into the house, because the vent system is under a positive pressure. A more common side-wall venting arrangement uses an induced-draft fan to "pull" the exhaust gases out of the house. This produces a negative pressure in most of the vent system. Only that portion of the vent that is downstream of the fan needs to be carefully sealed because it has a positive pressure. The following discussions will focus on induced-draft side-wall venting systems.

Typical power side-wall venting systems are shown in Figures 5-2 and 5-3. The main parts include the flue connector, air-flow regulator, induced-draft fan, exit pipe, vent cap, and the controls.

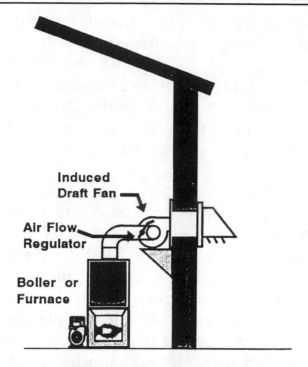

Power Side-Wall Venting

Figure 5-2

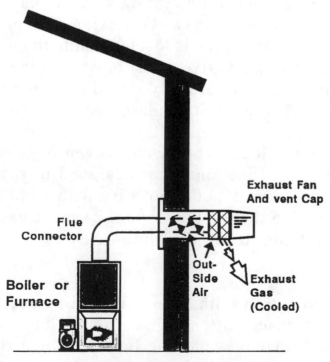

**Power Side-Wall Venting
(With Outdoor Fan)**

Figure 5-3

The flue connector joins the flue outlet of the boiler or furnace to the side-wall venting equipment.

The air-flow regulator is often a slide damper or similar device located before the inlet to the fan. It controls the air flow through the venting system and adjusts the draft supplied to the boiler or furnace (overfire draft).

The induced-draft fan, which is powered by an electric motor, produces the pressure required to move the flue-gas through the heating unit and out of the house. The draft produced is fairly constant, and does not vary with outdoor air temperature as it does with conventional chimney venting. Some manufacturers recommend the use of a barometric draft damper located before the draft fan, but this can increase energy use (through increased air infiltration into the house) and it may not be needed.

The exit pipe connects the outlet of the induced-draft fan to the terminal unit (end cap) on the outside wall of the house. Some side-wall venting systems have the fan located outside of the house and the exit pipe is eliminated (see Figure 5-3). If the fan is located inside the house, the exit pipe is under a positive pressure (it is at the outlet of the fan) and it must be carefully sealed to prevent exhaust gases from escaping into the house.

The vent cap is located at the end of venting system and serves important functions. It is designed to resist wind effects so that the draft does not vary with wind speed or direction. It also directs the flow of exhaust gases away from the building to avoid soiling or damage of outside walls.

The controls used with side-wall venting for oil-fired boilers and furnaces often include three elements. (1) A safety switch that prevents the burner from firing until required draft is proven, (2) A post-purge controller that operates the fan after the burner cycle ends to remove residual combustion fumes and to cool the fuel oil nozzle, and (3) A secondary safety switch that senses a backup of exhaust gases (spillage) and shuts down the burner. These devices are needed to assure safe and reliable operation of the side-wall venting systems. In fact, a side-wall vent system with these controls can be safer than an existing chimney vent system that cannot sense draft problems.

How To Do It!

Side-wall venting systems must be designed and installed to meet the following important objectives:

> - Always remove all combustion exhaust gases;
> - Produce a nearly constant draft for stable burner air-flow rates;
> - Operate under all outdoor air temperature conditions;
> - Resist wind effects;
> - Handle flue gases at temperatures up to 550F (see manufacturer specs);
> - Maintain flue-gas temperature above the dewpoint;
> - Resist acid attack (from condensed flue gases);
> - Survive for many years with minimal maintenance.

Side-wall venting systems are available from several manufacturers and are included with some new boilers and furnaces.

Careful attention to manufacturer recommendations concerning installation and adjustment is critical to assure safe and reliable operation.

Some general installation and adjustment recommendations and checkpoints are discussed in the following paragraphs.

Power side-wall systems should only be installed by qualified oil heat service technicians who are fully trained and experienced in the specific vent equipment that they are installing. **Follow the manufacturer's instructions!**

The air flow through the vent system must be measured and carefully adjusted using the **air flow adjustment damper** to produce safe operation with maximum efficiency. The overfire draft in the boiler or furnace should also be measured to be sure it is within manufacturer recommendations. Typically it should be about negative 0.01 inches water column. Too much air flow can lower boiler or furnace efficiency. Also, excessive air flow through a barometric damper (if included) can increase heat loss caused by outdoor air infiltration.

Wind pressure on the vent cap can change the vent pressure, combustion air flow rate, and efficiency. A 40 mile per hour wind can produce a static air pressure of 0.77 inches water column. Be certain that the venting system is designed to handle the expected variation in vent pressure caused by the wind, and install the system to minimize wind effects.

Adequate supply of combustion air is needed within the boiler or furnace room. Various options are illustrated in Figure 5-4. This topic is discussed in a more general sense in Chapter 4. Always follow the manufacturer's installation instructions regarding the combustion air supply when using a side-wall vent system.

The induced-draft fan should be installed close to the outside wall so that the length of exit pipe (at positive pressure) is minimized to reduce the chance of exhaust gas leakage.

A post-purge system is recommended to prevent fuel oil odors from escaping into the house during the burner off-cycle. However, this purge cycle should be short in duration to prevent excessive off-cycle heat loss from the boiler or furnace.

The side-wall vent system must be properly sized to minimize initial cost and to avoid excessive air flow and heat loss through the system. Follow the sizing recommendations supplied by the manufacturer.

Outdoor Air Supply Options

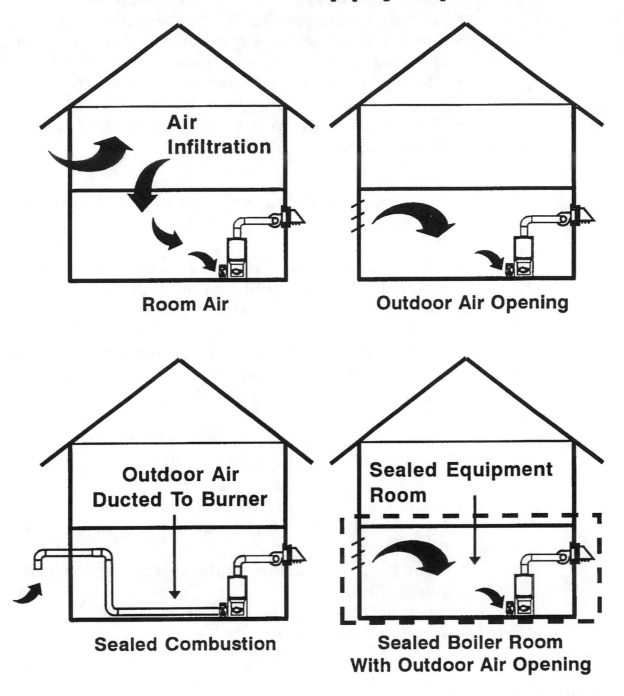

Room Air

Air Infiltration

Outdoor Air Opening

Outdoor Air Ducted To Burner

Sealed Combustion

Sealed Equipment Room

Sealed Boiler Room With Outdoor Air Opening

Figure 5-4

Location of the terminal point (vent end cap) must follow relevant codes for side-wall venting of combustion equipment. See manufacturer recommendations and codes. This may include for example:

- Not less that 7 feet above grade when located near public walkways;
- At least 3 feet above any forced-air intake;
- At least 4 feet below, 4 feet horizontal to, or 1 foot above any window, door, or natural draft air intake;
- At least 12 inches from any opening that would permit entry of exhaust gases into the house;
- The bottom of the vent must be at least 12 inches above grade.

For more specific information, refer to manufacturer recommendations and all relevant codes.

All other installation recommendations of the manufacturer must be carefully followed to assure safe and reliable operation.

The vent system and its operating and safety controls must be fully tested to assure proper vent system operation after the installation is completed.

Power side-wall venting systems should be inspected and maintained at least once a year to check:

- Motor condition and ease of rotation;
- Fan wheel condition, cleanliness and ease of rotation;
- Vent pipe connection tightness and evidence of flue-gas leakage;
- All other check points recommended by the vent system manufacturer.

Advantages and Fuel Savings

Power side-wall venting offers many advantages over conventional chimney venting:

- Reduction in vent-related heat losses for improved efficiency;
- Reduced installation costs compared to chimneys;
- More constant draft that does not vary with outdoor air temperature;
- High-efficiency oil heating equipment can be installed;
- Reduced service calls because chimney draft problems are eliminated;
- Lower smoke and air pollution emissions.

Reduced Vent Heat Loss

A primary advantage of power side-wall venting of oil heating equipment is reduced heat losses and improved system efficiency compared to chimney vented equipment. This occurs in several ways.

The power venting system can produce a more constant draft then chimneys, because it is not dependent on outdoor air temperature. This reduces seasonal changes in the air-flow rate through the burner, and this produces constantly higher combustion efficiency. With chimney venting, as the draft increases more combustion air is pulled into the burner, and this excess air can lower efficiency. Also, when the chimney draft drops, the burner air flow may be too low, and again the combustion efficiency is reduced. The more constant draft produced by the power venter can reduce these efficiency losses while the burner is firing. In some cases, fuel savings of 3% to 4% may be produced.

Burner off-cycle heat losses are also lower. Chapter 1 described losses that occur during the burner off-cycle when cool room air is pulled through the burner, heated by the boiler or furnace, and vented through the chimney. The heated chimney which produces off-cycle draft is the primary cause of this form of heat loss. Modern, high-efficiency oil heating equipment operate with off-cycle heat losses of 2% to 4%, while older equipment may have higher off-cycle losses. These could be substantially reduced if chimney venting is replaced by power side-wall venting.

Chimney draft is commonly controlled by a barometric damper, which allows additional air to enter the flue pipe when needed to produce a more steady draft. Some or all of this air is warm room air that is exhausted through the chimney and must be replaced by cold outdoor air. Heating this outdoor air to room temperature requires additional heating energy. Therefore, chimney operation increases fuel use by exhausting room air for draft control, which occurs during both the burner-on and burner-off cycle. This heat loss varies depending on the many chimney operating factors discussed earlier, but it can range from less than 2% to more than 12% of the annual fuel use. Taller chimneys with higher on-cycle and off-cycle drafts are expected to produce higher infiltration air flows and heat losses. Properly designed and operated power side-wall venting systems can eliminate or substantially reduce this heat loss.

Reduced Installation Costs Compared to Chimneys

The cost of power side-wall venting systems can be much less than a conventional brick or block chimney. This makes it a good choice for new construction and for conversion of electrically heated homes. In new construction the side-wall vent lowers the overall cost of the heating system and permits the installation of high-efficiency boilers and furnaces that operate with low flue-gas temperatures. The lower cost for the side-wall vent also makes conversion from electric heat to fuel oil more attractive. This is an excellent option for homeowners that heat with electricity because of the much higher efficiency and lower annual heating costs with oil. Removing the high cost of a chimney lowers the initial cost of conversion and offers a shorter payback period for homeowners who convert from electric to oil heat.

More Constant Draft

The draft produced by the electric-powered fan with the side-wall vent system is steady and does not vary as much with outdoor air temperature as does the draft provided by a chimney. The side-wall system, therefore, produces more consistent and reliable operation. This can reduce combustion-related problems, start-up smoke, and other chimney-related limitations.

Allows High-Efficiency Boilers and Furnaces to be Installed

The high-efficiency oil heating equipment now available often generates low flue-gas temperatures because most of the available heat from the combustion process is recovered. This is how these systems produce higher efficiency. Chapter 4 shows that chimney draft decreases as the flue-gas temperature drops, and that heat loss from the chimney can further lower draft and produce flue-gas condensation problems. The draft generated by power side-wall venting does not depend on the average flue-gas temperature. Therefore, the side-wall venting method allows the higher-efficiency boilers and furnaces to be installed where they could cause operating problems with conventional chimneys.

Reduced Service Calls

Problems related to chimney draft can be a major part of service calls that occur each year for oil heating equipment. Some of these problems are seasonal or transient and can be very difficult to diagnose and correct. A properly designed, installed, and maintained power venting system can reduce the number of venting-related service calls, produce more constant air flow for the burner, reduce smoke and soot generation (when adjusted properly). This can also improve homeowner satisfaction with oil heat. If these power-vent systems can eliminate or reduce backdraft (spillage), then the incidence of smoke production and consumer complaints can be reduced even more.

Lower Smoke and Air Pollutant Emissions

If the power side-wall venting system can produce more constant draft and reduce start-up transients, smoke and air pollutant emissions can be reduced. Modern oil burners, when properly adjusted, produce approximately the same amount of smoke (particulate matter) as gas burners, according to recent studies. Most of this is produced during burner start-up and shut-down transients. If these transients are reduced by power venting (by allowing the induced-draft fan to operate before the burner is started) some of these transient effects can be reduced. Lower levels of smoke, carbon monoxide, and unburned fuel (hydrocarbons) can be produced. **Clean combustion is vital with side-wall vents to prevent accumulation of smoke and other unburned materials on the side wall of the house.** Careful burner adjustment is a critical factor in the application of power side-wall venting to oil heating equipment, but it can produce reduced pollutant emissions as an important side effect. Modern oil burners are very clean burning, and this becomes a critical part of side-wall venting applications which can reduce emissions even further.

Problems and Limitations

Important considerations concerning the use of power side-wall venting for oil heating equipment include the following:

Reliability

Chimney vents are passive systems that rely on the heat contained in the flue gases to produce the forces needed to remove the combustion exhaust gases. The power vent system is an electrically powered mechanical system, and long-term reliability is an important issue. Some key issues include:

- How reliable are the safety controls?
- What happens if the flue-gas temperature rises and the vent system is overheated?
- What is the lifetime of the induced-draft fan?
- What is needed to prevent vent-system corrosion?
- What are the maintenance requirements?

Side-wall venting systems have been installed for several years and most of the results have been positive regarding their reliability.

Wind Effects

Wind can cause backdraft problems for all chimney-vented heating equipment and it can also adversely affect the performance of side-wall venting units. However, the power venting systems operate with higher static pressure and can be more resistant to wind effects if designed and installed properly. Overcoming wind effects is an important part of side-wall venting system design and operation. More research on the effects of wind on power venting performance is needed so that guidelines can be developed.

Combustion Odors

The chimney produces off-cycle draft because it stays warm after the burner firing cycle ends. This helps remove residual fumes and fuel oil odors. The power side-wall vent does not have this **built-in** off-cycle air flow, but a post-purge cycle is available to overcome this problem. Excessive oil or combustion odors indicates that other problems may exist in the burner or fuel system that are causing the problem.

Exhaust Gas Reentry Into House

The chimney exhausts the combustion gases at the top of the house and the hot gases rise above the building. The exhaust from power side-wall venting systems is at a lower level and there is a chance that some of these gases can re-enter the house. Building codes concerning side-wall venting of combustion equipment have been developed in recent years, and this helps minimize this problem. These codes must be carefully followed, and installers should use common sense when installing side-wall vents to keep exhaust gases from coming back into the house or fresh air intakes. Follow manufacturer's installation instructions.

House Discoloring

If the exhaust gases contain particulate matter or un-burned fuel, it can contact the side of the house and cause staining. Some ways to reduce this problems are:

> - Careful burner adjustment for complete combustion and no smoke;
> - Select a vent termination location to minimize staining problems;
> - Select a vent end cap that minimizes contact of exhaust gases with the side wall of the house;
> - Inform the homeowners that occasional washing of the sidewall with soap and water may be needed.

Training and Certification for Installers

All technicians who install power side-wall venting systems must be fully trained and experienced with the specific power venting systems that they are installing. These systems are much different from conventional chimneys, and a complete understanding of proper procedures for installing and maintaining this equipment is necessary for safe, efficient and reliable operation. Contact the vent equipment manufacturer for training manuals and courses.

Building Code Prohibitions

Many building codes exist that prevent the use of power side-wall venting equipment in oil-heated homes. Be sure that side-wall venting is permitted before proceeding with the installation.

Retrofit of Older Heating Equipment

Most of the power side-wall venting applications to date have involved new heating equipment installations. It is possible to retrofit power side-wall venting systems for existing oil heat equipment to reduce heat losses and improve efficiency. More information is needed, however, regarding retrofit applications before they can be recommended and guidelines developed.

5.3 Vent Dampers for Heating Equipment with High Off-Cycle Heat Loss

What Is It?

An automatic vent damper is a metal damper valve that is installed in the boiler or furnace flue to reduce off-cycle heat losses from the heating unit. The damper is **open** while the burner is firing, and then closes at the end of the burner operation to trap residual heat inside of the boiler or furnace. A diagram of vent damper operation is shown in Figure 5-5. The vent damper reduces off-cycle heat loss and increases the efficiency of the heating unit.

Vent dampers have been used in the past to reduce heat loss in oil heating equipment. **They are not needed today for most modern oil boilers that use flame-retention oil burners** because the off-cycle air flow through these burners is fairly low. However, vent dampers may be useful in some older heating systems where the building owner is unwilling to replace the entire unit and where, in addition, air leakage is so pervasive and general that replacing the burner with a flame-retention model and

Vent Damper Schematic

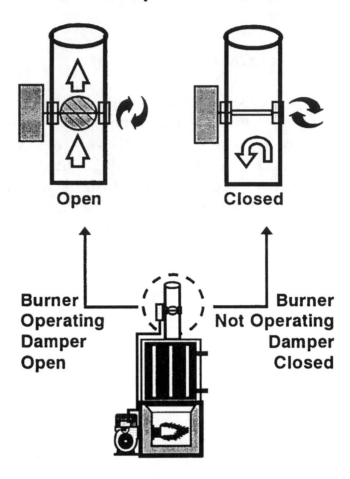

Open   **Closed**

Burner
Operating
Damper
Open

Burner
Not Operating
Damper
Closed

Figure 5-5

patching other leakage sites is unlikely to solve the problem. Examples would be old coal-conversion boilers and steam systems with excessive air leakage around the oil burner, into flame-inspection ports, between boiler sections, and elsewhere in the boiler. If in addition the system is vented by a very tall chimney, produces high flue-gas temperatures, has a massive firebrick chamber or massive heat exchangers, or maintains unusually high boiler-water temperatures, the vent damper becomes a very strong contender.

It should be emphasized again, however, that the vent damper is the **choice of last resort**. Usually it will be a better option either to install a retention-head burner, or, if the system is so decrepit that this won't help much, to replace the aging system that is the cause of all these problems. Nevertheless, you will come upon some situations where the building owner is unwilling to invest in a new heating plant despite its poor condition, and in these cases the vent damper should be considered.

How To Do It!

Vent dampers are self-contained units that include: the damper blade; the damper body that securely holds the damper within the flue pipe; an electric motor that opens and closes the damper; and controls that operate the damper and assure that it is in the fully open position before the oil burners is allowed to operate (see Figure 5-6).

Some vent dampers have cut-outs on the damper blade to reduce odors that may be produced at the end of the firing cycle. These units are not recommended because they reduce energy savings by up to 50%. A better solution is to find and correct the source of the odor problem (such as air leakage into the fuel line, or a malfunctioning oil pump cut-off). Be sure that the damper has a safety switch that prevents the burner from firing until the damper is fully opened. Also, carefully follow the installation recommendations of the damper manufacturer, and test the equipment after it is installed.

Vent Damper Design

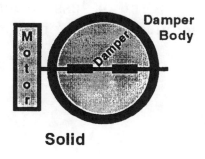 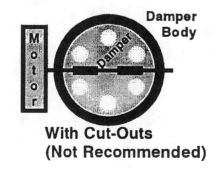

Figure 5-6

Advantages and Fuel Savings

The primary advantage of the vent damper is a reduction in off-cycle heat losses and annual fuel costs for heating units that use too much fuel. It is a relatively low-cost option (less costly than replacing the entire heating system). It may be useful in some installations with flame-retention oil burners if there are many air leaks around the boiler or furnace, or if a very tall chimney is in place. In these cases, the air-flow restriction offered by the burner may not prevent off-cycle heat losses.

Off-cycle heat losses cannot be easily measured in the field and they can vary over a wide range depending on many chimney venting factors as discussed in the previous chapter. Therefore, it is difficult to accurately predict fuel savings. Testing over the past 15 years has found that vent dampers can reduce energy use from 2% (when applied to high-efficiency units) to 14% depending on the heating equipment. Earlier we found that air infiltration can account for 12% or more of the annual fuel use in some installations. If an older heating unit has multiple factors that cause high off-cycle heat loss, then the damper may produce fuel savings of approximately 10 to 15 percent.

In contrast, when used with modern high-efficiency oil boilers and furnaces that are fired with flame-retention burners and that are attached to typical chimneys, vent dampers are expected to save 2 percent or less. Vent dampers are not generally recommended for these newer systems.

Problems and Limitations

Two unacceptable situations to be strictly avoided when using a vent damper are:

- Operating the burner while the damper is closed;
- Allowing fuel and combustion odors to enter the house.

Operating the burner with the damper closed is an obvious problem because it will produce incomplete combustion gases and prevent them from being vented from the house. Some of these gases are hazardous. If a vent damper is installed, the following steps must be followed:

- Carefully follow all the installation instructions of the manufacturer.
- Only trained and qualified service technicians should install vent dampers.
- Electrical wiring must follow manufacturer recommendations.
- The flue pipe and damper must be securely fastened so that damper movement is not restricted in any way.
- After installation, the operation of the damper (including the safety switch that prevents the burner form firing when the damper is closed) must be tested.
- The operation of the damper and safety switch must always be checked during burner service calls.

Vent dampers close off the flue during the burner off-cycle and this can permit fuel oil or combustion odors to be noticed within the house in some cases. Without the damper, the off-cycle chimney draft pulls air through the boiler or furnace and exhausts them up the chimney, which reduces the chance of odors from entering the house. The vent damper does not cause the odor problem but allows it to be noticed.

One source of unwanted odors can occur at the end of the burner firing cycle. The combustion chamber is hot, and some fuel oil may drip into the chamber and produce fuel oil vapors. The hot combustion chamber also heats the fuel nozzle during the off-cycle and any air trapped in the fuel line will expand and can force a small amount of fuel oil from the nozzle. This can occur more frequently with older heating units that have heavy combustion chambers which cool down slowly and heat the fuel nozzle more than modern low-mass chambers. Also, air leakage from loose fittings in the fuel line can add to the problem.

Actions to reduce odor problems after vent-damper installation include:

- Tighten all fuel pipe connections to reduce the amount of air trapped in the fuel line.
- Be sure that the low-pressure cut-off on the oil pump works properly.
- Install a fuel oil solenoid valve on the fuel line that closes as the burner firing cycle ends.
- Use low-mass ceramic fiber combustion chambers that cool down rapidly at the end of the burner firing cycle.
- Take other actions that can reduce air in the fuel line and over-heating of the fuel nozzle during the burner off-cycle.

Vent dampers with cut-outs in the damper blade are not recommended to reduce odor problems because they reduce fuel savings.

As noted above, vent dampers are not recommended for most oil burner installations, but they can be useful in certain cases. Some older heating equipment with high chimney draft and large air leaks can benefit from vent damper installation. **Careful installation and maintenance is required,** however, to avoid adverse affects.

5.4
Powered
Chimney
Venting

Given the drawbacks of conventional chimney venting, and the fact that power side-wall venting may not be feasible in some installations, it is reasonable to ask whether there are any other options. This section briefly describes a hybrid approach—powered chimney venting—that may enter the picture in the future, when adequate testing and evaluation have been done. Because we cannot recommend this alternative now, there is no **How To Do It!** section. It is included as something that you can watch for down the road.

The concept involves power venting through a lined chimney (See Figure 5-7). A power venting system would be used, but instead of ducting the exhaust gases through a side-wall, they would be exhausted through the chimney, which may need to be relined in some cases. The power venting supplies the pressure needed to remove the exhaust gases, the chimney provides the path, and the chimney liner prevents condensate damage. Provisions for condensate removal and disposal may be required.

What Is It?

The main parts of this system would be the existing chimney, chimney liner, power-vent fan, and the condensate collection and/or removal equipment.

The existing chimney would commonly be constructed of masonry materials and be located outside of the house where the heat-loss rate is too high for conventional venting of high-efficiency oil heating equipment. The existing chimney would not produce adequate draft (because of low flue-gas temperatures and high heat-loss rates) and could be damaged by flue-gas condensation if a high-efficiency heating unit is installed.

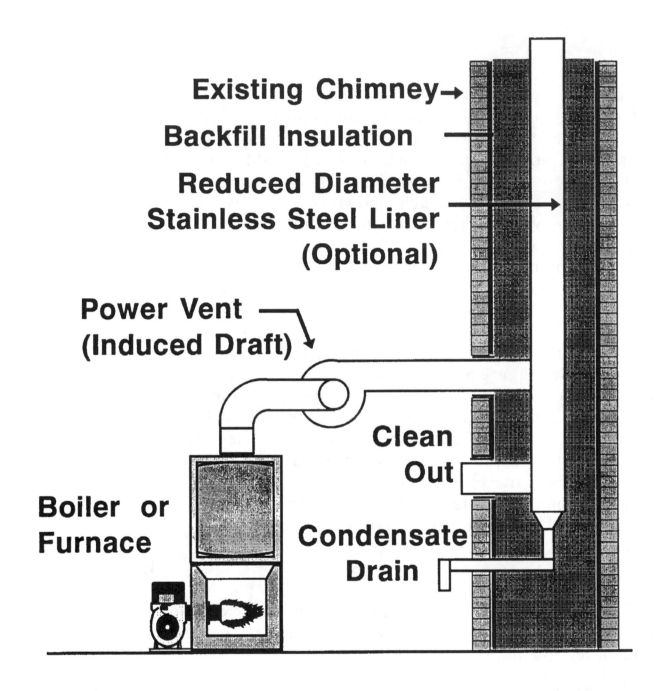

Existing Chimney→

Backfill Insulation

Reduced Diameter
Stainless Steel Liner
(Optional)

Power Vent
(Induced Draft)

Clean
Out

Boiler or
Furnace

Condensate
Drain

Power Chimney Venting

Figure 5-7

A reduced-diameter metal (or other acid-resistant material) chimney liner would be installed to prevent chimney damage and deterioration from flue-gas condensation. Insulation between the chimney flue and the liner may not be required. If the chimney is in good condition, and a condensate-resistant ceramic flue is in place, the liner may not be required.

A power-vent fan and ducting from the boiler or furnace to the chimney are needed to supply the draft required for venting. If the fan is before the chimney, the exhaust gases enter the chimney at a positive pressure. If the exhaust fan is at the top of the chimney, the entire vent system is under a negative pressure. Another alternative is to use a high-static air pressure oil burner and operate the entire heating system under a positive pressure. Special provisions are required, however, to prevent exhaust gases from leaking out of the boiler or furnace and flue pipe into the house.

Condensate collection and removal equipment may be needed if the flue-gas temperature drops very low and moisture condenses within the chimney. The rate of chimney heat loss must be considered. The condensate systems collects the water before it can damage the heating equipment or flue pipe, and transports it to a drain. Ice formation inside of the flue must be prevented to avoid blockage of the exhaust flue in the chimney.

Advantages and Fuel Savings

This system permits the use of highly efficient oil heating equipment when conventional chimney or power sidewall venting is not possible. Some key advantages include:

- Use of highly efficient boilers and furnaces;
- Lower off-cycle heat loss than conventional chimney venting;

- Reduced air infiltration heat loss (if no barometric damper is required);
- Safe venting through the existing chimney;
- Avoidance of some of the side-wall venting problems;
- Lower costs (in some cases) if the chimney liner is not required;
- Fewer building code restrictions.

Problems and Limitations

Powered chimney venting is a hybrid approach that uses parts of other venting systems. It has not been adequately studied and tested in the laboratory or in the field, and it cannot be recommended until more information is available. However, it may represent an acceptable option for some installations where other venting systems are not useful. Additional research is needed to fully evaluate this venting method and to compare it to the other options now in use.

5.5 Outdoor Boiler Installation

Another alternative to chimney venting is installing the boiler outdoors so that a venting system is not needed. Some boiler manufacturers have models available for this type of installation. Some of the benefits include:

- Lower cost (no vent system is needed);
- Safe operation (no combustion gases can escape into the house);
- Improved efficiency because chimney-induced air infiltration is eliminated.

It is important to consider several factors:

- The effect of outdoor installation on jacket, off-cycle and piping heat losses;
- The effect of cold outdoor air on combustion efficiency;
- More difficult servicing, especially in the colder months.

An outdoor boiler installation may be an efficient option in some cases (see Figure 5-8). More research and field experience is needed to fully evaluate this option.

Outdoor Boiler Installation

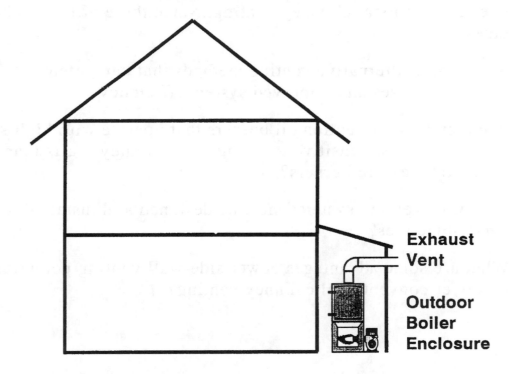

Exhaust Vent

Outdoor Boiler Enclosure

Advantages:

- **Lower Costs (No Chimney)**
- **Safe Operation - No Combustion Gases In House**
- **Improved Efficiency - No Chimney Induced Air Infiltration**

Figure 5-8

QUESTIONS

5-1.   The controls used with side wall venting often include 3 elements. Name them:

5-2.   Side wall venting systems must be designed and installed to meet the following objectives. Answer true or false.
1.   To always remove all combustion gases
2.   To produce a nearly constant draft for stable burner operation
3.   To operate under all outdoor air temperatures and conditions
4.   To handle flue gases at temperatures up to 550 deg. F or manufacturer specifications.
5.   To maintain flue gas temperature above the dew point

5-3.   Power side wall venting can potentially offer many advantages over conventional chimney venting. Name three of these advantages:

5-4.   Name three alternative venting methods that can potentially reduce heat losses and improved system efficiency.

5-5.   Are new flame-retention oil burners that operate with high-static air pressure less sensitive to changes in chimney drafts than old lower air pressure burners?

5-6.   Side-wall venting systems must be designed and installed to meet what objectives?

5-7.   What are some advantages power side-wall venting potentially offers over conventional chimney venting?

Chapter 6—Efficient Domestic Hot Water

Several alternatives are available for using home heating oil to produce domestic hot water for sinks, showers, tubs and other appliances in the home. These include separate **direct-fired** hot water heaters and **indirect** water heating methods. This chapter will review commonly used equipment and discuss the efficiency of each option. Methods for improving the efficiency of domestic hot water generation with heating oil will be outlined. Information on the proper installation, servicing, or safety considerations are not included in this manual. These can be found in other technical manuals such as the **Oil Heat Technician's Manual** published by the Petroleum Marketers Association of America (PMAA), and the National Association Of Oil Heat Service Managers (NAOHSM).

6.1 Review of Oil-Powered Water Heating Equipment

Direct-fired equipment uses a separate oil burner to produce hot combustion gases that heat water that is usually contained in a storage tank. **Indirect** heaters use a heat exchanger to transfer heat from hot water or steam produced by an oil-fired boiler to produce domestic hot water. The relative advantages of each general approach and the efficiency of hot water generation will be discussed in this chapter.

Direct-Fired Water Heaters

Direct-fired hot water heaters consist of an oil burner, combustion chamber, hot-water storage tank, and flue-gas passages. The oil burner fires into the combustion chamber located at the base of the hot-water tank. These hot gases then flow through flue passages where heat is transferred to the water in the tank; the exhaust gases are then collected at the top of the water heater and exit through the venting system. The hot-water tank varies in size, usually from 30 gallons to 50 gallons. The water heater storage should be carefully sized for the peak needs of the people living in the house to avoid unnecessary heat losses that can occur with larger water heaters.

Two types of direct-fired storage water heaters are commonly used. These are the center flue and the rear flue. In the center flue, the hot combustion gases flow through a heat-transfer pipe that runs through the center of the water tank. One example of this design is shown in Figure 6-1. The rear-flue water heater configuration has the flue passage surrounding the outside of the water storage tank, which increases the surface area for heat transfer. However, the hot gases are close to the outer jacket of the water heater, and added thermal insulation is needed to

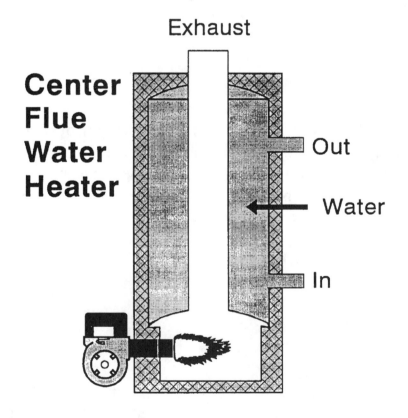

Figure 6-1

avoid excessive heat loss from the water—heater casing. Figure 6-2 is an example of a rear-flue water heater.

The primary heat losses that are associated with direct-fired water heaters are: on-cycle losses, off-cycle heat losses through the flue, and jacket or casing heat losses.

Indirect Water Heaters

Indirect water heaters use some type of heat exchanger to transfer heat from boiler water to the domestic hot water supply. The advantages of indirect heaters are:

- Elimination of exhaust flue (and reduced off-cycle heat losses);
- A separate oil burner is not needed;
- Longer lifetimes than direct-fired equipment;
- Higher efficiency (when installed with an efficient oil boiler).

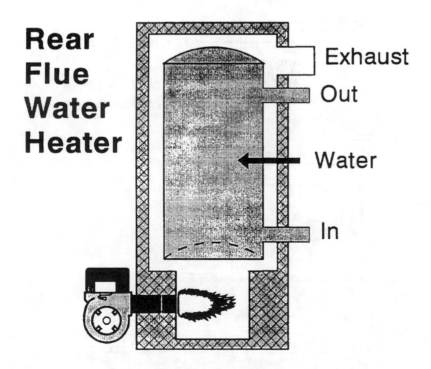

Rear Flue Water Heater

Exhaust Out

Water

In

Figure 6-2

Many types of indirect water heaters are available. The following are the ones most often seen:

Internal Tankless Coil. One of the most common indirect water heaters in use today is the tankless coil, which is a heat-transfer coil that is immersed within the hot water stored in an oil-fired boiler. Cold domestic hot water flows through the inside of this coil, it is heated by the hot boiler water, and then it goes directly to the taps and appliances in the home that use hot water. A schematic diagram of a tankless coil is shown in Figure 6-3. If the tankless coil is sized properly, it can provide an almost endless supply of hot water without the need to **recharge** a storage tank.

External Tankless Coil. One older variation of the tankless coil is the **external** configuration where the tankless coil is installed in a small tank that is outside of the boiler (see Figure 6-4). This **side-arm** arrangement permits a larger coil to be installed that can supply more domestic hot water than an internal coil. The tank contains

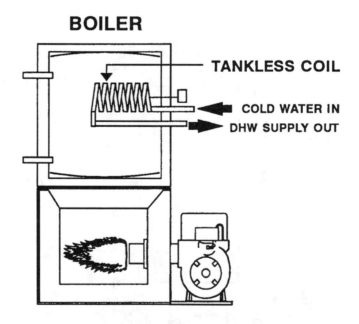

INTERNAL TANKLESS COIL

Figure 6-3

hot boiler water that surrounds the coil and the domestic water flows through the inside of the coil. A primary disadvantage of this configuration is increased heat losses form the added tank and piping, and the added cost for this equipment.

Tankless Coil With a Storage Tank. A tankless coil with a storage tank produces hot water in the same way as a conventional tankless coil (see Figure 6-5). This water is then stored in a separate hot water storage (booster) tank and the temperature of this water is maintained by a circulating pump controlled by an aquastat. This arrangement offers several advantages if it is installed and operated properly. The storage tank allows a smaller tankless coil to be installed because some of the peak water demand is met by the stored water. Also, in some cases, the firing rate of the burner can be reduced slightly, which can improve system efficiency.

However, the firing must be carefully selected and the boiler controls must be modified to prevent burner opera-

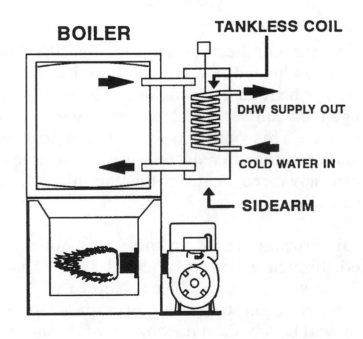

EXTERNAL TANKLESS COIL (SIDEARM)

Figure 6-4

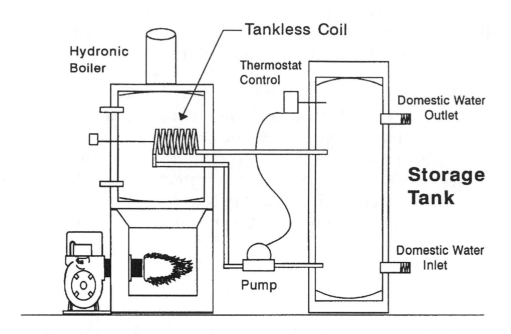

TANKLESS COIL WITH STORAGE TANK

Figure 6-5

tion during the non-heating season after the hot water storage tank is heated. Otherwise, boiler off-cycle heat losses will not be reduced, and the added heat losses from the storage tank can actually lower the overall efficiency of the system. This option is best suited for low-mass boilers that operate with reduced off-cycle heat losses and incorporate advanced controls that permit efficient hot water generation.

Hot-Coil Storage Tank. In this case, boiler water is circulated through a hot coil located at the base of the domestic hot water storage tank as shown in Figure 6-6. This is similar to the tankless coil with a storage tank, except the coil is located at the bottom of the storage tank. Several manufacturers produce this type of indirect water heater. This option provides a large reserve of stored hot water ready for use in the house. It overcomes the disadvantage of the tankless coils which can not produce more

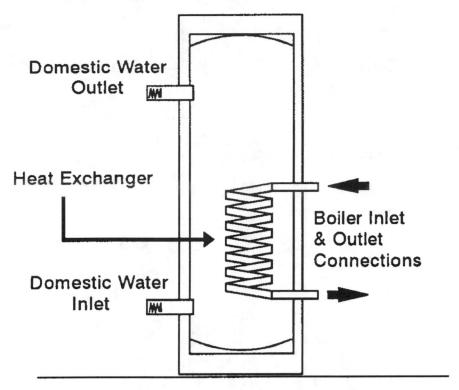

Hot Coil Storage Tank

Figure 6-6

hot water than their rated gallon-per-minute capacity because they have no reserve volume. Disadvantages include slightly increased heat losses from the insulated storage tank (compared to internal tankless coils without tanks), higher equipment costs, and increased floor area needed for the storage tank.

Cold-Coil Storage Tank. This is similar to the hot-coil case, except the boiler water in contained in the tank and the cold domestic water flows through the inside of the coil located in the storage tank (see Figure 6-7). This configuration is less popular than the hot—coil system. A major disadvantage is increased jacket heat losses from the hot boiler water contained in the tank. This arrangement is similar to the external tankless coil (sidearm water heaters) described earlier.

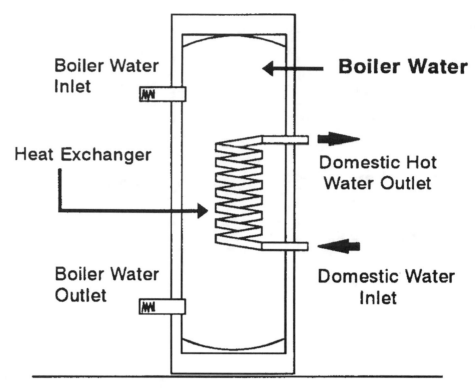

Boiler Water Inlet

Heat Exchanger

Boiler Water Outlet

Boiler Water

Domestic Hot Water Outlet

Domestic Water Inlet

Cold Coil Storage Tank

Figure 6-7

Double-Tank Water Heaters. Another indirect water heater configuration is the double-tank system, which can be described as a tank within a tank (see Figure 6-8). In one type of double-tank system, the inner tank contains the domestic water, and boiler water is circulated between the inner and outer tank. Adequate thermal insulation must be used to avoid excessive jacket heat loss from the heated boiler water. A second configuration has the boiler water flowing through a center pipe in the middle of the domestic storage tank. This is similar to a center flue direct-fired water heater except boiler water flows through the center pipe instead of flue gases.

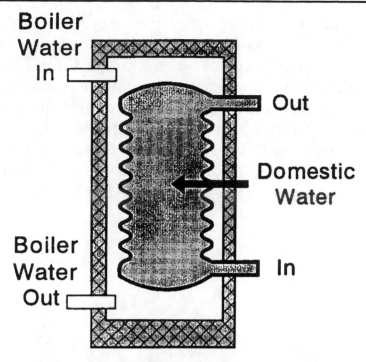

DOUBLE TANK WATER HEATER

Figure 6-8

Integrated Heating and Water Heating Systems

A new innovation in the oil heat industry is the integrated heating **system** that efficiently produces both space heat and domestic hot water. This uses a low-mass boiler that operates with very low off-cycle losses and high annual heating system efficiency. A very efficient plate-coil heat exchanger is used to transfer heat from the boiler water to the domestic hot water which is stored in an insulated tank. A microprocessor control operates the burner only when needed for space heating or when domestic hot water use pulls the storage tank temperature below the set point. After a burner on-cycle the controller purges the heat stored in the boiler mass to either the last heating zone that called for heat or the domestic hot water storage tank, depending on which triggered the burner on-cycle. In the non-heating season the heat is always purged to the domestic hot water storage tank. This minimizes boiler off-cycle flue and jacket heat losses. When new rating systems for combined water and space heating appliances are implemented, it is expected that this new **energy system** will be rated one of the most efficient methods now available for producing domestic hot water.

6.2 Heat Losses and Efficiency of Domestic Hot Water Generation

Heat losses occur during the operation of direct-fired and indirect domestic water heaters that lower their overall efficiency. Direct-fired systems sustain heat losses (see Figure 6-9) that include:

> - On-cycle Flue Heat Loss while the burner is firing;
> - Off-cycle Flue heat loss when the burner is not operating;
> - Jacket heat losses during the on-cycle and during the off-cycle from the hot water stored in the tank.

These are similar to the heat losses discussed earlier for oil boilers. In fact, indirect water heaters that use boiler water as their heat source sustain the same on-cycle and off-cycle losses as discussed in Chapter 3. The size of these heat losses and the system efficiencies produced for each of these domestic hot water systems will be outlined. When available, efficiency ratings and test data will be presented so that domestic water heater efficiencies can be compared.

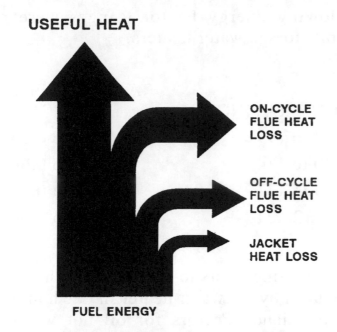

USEFUL HEAT

ON-CYCLE FLUE HEAT LOSS

OFF-CYCLE FLUE HEAT LOSS

JACKET HEAT LOSS

FUEL ENERGY

HEAT LOSSES FROM DOMESTIC WATER HEATERS

Figure 6-9

Direct-Fired Water Heaters

U.S. Department of Energy Test Procedures for Water Heaters apply to direct-fired oil storage water heaters. These test procedures determine an **Energy Factor** (EF), which is a measure of the overall efficiency of a water heater. It is determined by comparing the energy supplied in heated water to the total daily fuel consumption of the water heater. This Energy Factor takes on-cycle and off-cycle (standby) heat losses into account and can be used to compare the efficiency of different water heaters. The Energy Factors for oil, gas and electric-powered water heaters are published twice a year in the "Consumers' Directory of Certified Efficiency Ratings For Residential Heating and Water Heating Equipment" by the Gas Appliance Manufacturers Association (see Chapter 3 for availability).

The following Energy Factor Ranges were recently listed for oil storage water heaters.

1st HOUR RATING	RANGE OF ENERGY FACTORS
87 to 99	0.55 to 0.55
100 to 114	0.53 to 0.64
115 to 131	0.54 to 0.65
OVER 131	0.64 to 0.64

The first hour rating refers to the gallons of hot water that can be produced by the water heater in one hour of operation. The Efficiency Factors for oil hot water heaters range from 0.53 to 0.65 with an average value of approximately 0.60. This means that only 60 percent of the energy contained in the fuel oil is converted to hot water used in the home, while 40 percent goes to on-cycle and off-cycle heat losses from the water heater. Always recommend oil water heaters with the highest EF to minimize these heat losses.

Indirect Water Heaters

Many types of indirect water heaters are available, but they all have something in common. The domestic hot water is heated by boiler water and not by a separate oil burner. Therefore, the overall efficiency of this system depends primarily on the efficiency of the boiler and secondarily on how the heat is transferred and stored by the water heater. The efficiency of internal tankless coils will be discussed in detail, and then the efficiency of other indirect water heater configurations will be briefly reviewed. The U.S. Department of Energy efficiency rating program does not apply to indirect water heaters, so another measure of efficiency performance will be used.

Tankless Coils. Brookhaven National Laboratory and the National Institute of Standards and Technology have conducted extensive efficiency testing for residential oil boilers to determine their efficiency during steady-state and cyclic operation. They then used these data to calculate system efficiency for space heating and domestic hot water production. The test data have been used to evaluate the efficiency of tankless coils (and other indirect water heaters) so that they can be compared to other sources of domestic hot water.

The efficiency determination for tankless coils is complicated because it depends on many factors:

- Boiler design and heat losses;
- Burner design and adjustment;
- Size of boiler relative to space heating and domestic hot water demand;
- Burner firing rate;
- Daily volume of domestic hot water consumed;
- Geographic location;
- Other adjustment and operating variables.

The important fact about tankless coils is that while their efficiency is low during the summer months (on the order of 40%), they are much more efficient during the heating season (on the order of 80%) because the boiler is already heated to meet the space heating load. The overall efficiency of tankless coils over twelve months is expected to be in the 65% to 70% range for a modern oil boiler equipped with a flame-retention head burner.

Other Indirect Water Heaters. The efficiency calculations for tankless coils also apply to other indirect water heaters that rely on a boiler as their primary heat source. Therefore, efficiencies of 65% to 70% are generally expected for well designed indirect water-heater systems. Some of these heaters may have lower efficiencies than internal tankless coils for the following reasons.

- External Tankless—Added tank surface area and piping heat losses can lower the efficiency compared to tankless coils.
- Internal Tankless with a Storage Tank—Added surface area and piping can lower efficiency if the boiler controls are not adjusted to prevent boiler operation during the non-space-heating months after the storage tank is heated.
- Hot-Coil Storage Tank—Insulation is needed to avoid increased heat losses and lower efficiency compared to tankless coils.
- Cold-Coil Storage Tank—The large surface area of the tank that contains the hot boiler water can increase heat losses significantly and lower efficiency, when compared to storage tanks that contain lower temperature domestic hot water.
- Double-Tank Water Heaters—The increased surface area can reduce efficiency, especially when the hot boiler water is contained in the outer tank if not properly insulated.

Integrated Space-Heating and Water-Heating Systems

No standardized efficiency testing and rating program is required for these new highly efficient systems, but available test data can be used to estimate their performance. A review of efficiency tests for one low-mass boiler system with storage tank and electronic controls is useful for estimating the potential domestic hot water efficiency of this new type of oil heating equipment.

The low-mass boiler (about two gallons of boiler water) is combined with a water storage tank. This system operates with very low off-cycle heat losses. The efficiency tests completed by Brookhaven demonstrated the effectiveness of this low-mass design in lowering off-cycle losses. This has an important impact on domestic hot water generation during the non-space-heating months. The boiler operates only when needed to supply domestic hot water and all residual heat is sent to the insulated storage tank. This lowers the boiler off-cycle heat losses (the tank does not have a flue) and increases the efficiency of domestic hot water generation compared to both separate storage hot water heaters and internal tankless coils.

The annual heating efficiency of this space heating and water heating **system** is above 80 percent, and only a slight decrease is expected during the non-heating-season for production of domestic hot water because of the low-mass boiler and separate storage tank. Therefore, the expected efficiency for domestic hot water generation over a twelve-month period is in the range of 75% to 80%. This is among the highest domestic hot water efficiencies now available from any oil system.

Comparison of Domestic Hot Water Generation Efficiencies

This section summarizes the foregoing information on efficiency.

Direct-fired oil water heaters with storage tanks have efficiencies (Efficiency Factors) that range from 53% to 65%, for an average of about 60%.

Domestic hot water generation efficiencies by tankless coils in modern oil hot-water boilers have been found to be in the range of 65 to 70 percent.

A similar conclusion is reached by the American Council for an Energy Efficient Economy in their book **Consumers' Guide to Home Energy Savings** which shows that an indirect water heater with an efficient oil boiler has the lowest lifecycle cost of all domestic hot water sources.

Other indirect water heaters are expected to produce efficiencies somewhat lower than internal tankless coils because of somewhat higher system heat losses.

Integrated space and water heating systems that feature low mass boilers and thermal storage tanks can produce domestic hot water efficiencies in the 75% to 80% range.

The Table below collects this information:

	AVERAGE DOMESTIC HOT WATER EFFICIENCY (%)
Direct-Fired Storage Heater	60
Tankless Coil	65–70
Other Indirect Heaters	somewhat less than 65–70
Integrated System with Low-Mass Boiler	75–80

6.3 Energy Conservation Options

A number of important conservation options are available to reduce excessive fuel use by both new and existing domestic water heaters that use oil. These should be considered for all new oil heat installations, for all existing installations where equipment needs to be replaced, and for some existing installations where improvements can be implemented during normally scheduled maintenance service calls.

Use High-Efficiency Oil Hot-Water Equipment

Always recommend and install high-efficiency domestic hot-water equipment as follows:

- High-efficiency integrated heating and hot water systems;
- Internal tankless coils with high AFUE oil boilers;
- Other indirect water heaters with high AFUE oil boilers;
- Separate oil hot water heaters with the highest energy factors (EFs)

Install High AFUE Oil Boilers

All indirect water heaters depend on the oil boiler as the primary source of heat. High AFUE boilers not only increase space heating efficiency, but also increase the efficiency of domestic hot water production.

Consider Solar Water Heaters with Oil Back-up

Solar water heaters can be supplemented by an efficient oil water heater to produce the highest system efficiency and reliability that is now available. Solar energy can be used whenever available, and an efficient oil tankless coil can supply an instantaneous back-up as needed. This combination offers improved efficiency and reduced fuel use, without a loss in convenience when the sun doesn't shine.

Replace Electric Water Heaters with High-Efficiency Oil Heaters

The electric hot water heater is very costly to operate. The Energy Factors for electric heaters with first-hour rating comparable to oil heaters are high (0.77 to 0.95), but the overall efficiency is low because of heat losses at the electric power plant heat losses. The efficiency of electricity generation to the home is only about 29%.

So even though the average Energy Factor is 86%, based on electricity use in he home, if we were to define an overall Energy Factor based on fuel use at the power plant, it would be only

$$0.86 \times 0.29 = 0.25$$

In other words, only about 25% of the fuel energy burned in the power plant is converted to useful hot water in the house. This is much lower than even the separate direct-fired oil water heater with an average Energy Factor of 60%.

This low efficiency is reflected in the higher cost for heating water with an electric heater as published in the **Consumers' Directory of Certified Efficiency Ratings for Residential Heating and Water Heating Equipment**. The average annual water heating cost is $424 for electric heaters and $237 for oil heaters with comparable water delivery rates.

The Table below summarizes efficiency and energy-cost information from the directory of efficiency ratings.

First Hour Rating (Gallons of Water)	Average Efficiency Factor		Average Energy Cost ($/Yr)	
	Electric*	Oil	Electric	Oil
87 to 99	0.26	0.55	$403	$196
100 to 114	0.25	0.58	$428	$186
115 to 131	0.24	0.60	$442	$183
Over 131	NA	0.64	NA	$169
	0.25	0.59	$424	$184

*Includes electric power generation and distribution efficiency of 29%.
Based on electricity prices of $0.0824 per kilowatt-hour.
Based on fuel oil prices of $1.00 per gallon.

The average direct-fired oil storage hot water heater (EF of 60%) is more than twice as efficient in terms of fuel consumption as a comparably sized electric water heater (overall EF of 25%). This is reflected in the annual operating costs where replacing the average electric water heater with an average oil water heater can save homeowners $240 a year. This is a 56% reduction in water heating costs. Even larger savings are possible if an existing electric water heater is replaced by a high-efficiency integrated oil heating system, a tankless coil with a high-AFUE oil boiler, or another type of indirect oil water heater with a high-AFUE boiler.

Reduce Temperature of Hot-Water Storage

The jacket or casing heat losses for all water heaters and the off-cycle flue heat losses from direct fired water heaters can be reduced by lowering the temperature of the water stored in the tank. A tank of very hot water loses heat faster than one that is only moderately hot. Always set the water temperature at the minimum level needed to satisfy the uses in the home, and instruct homeowners to avoid increasing the storage temperature. This is especially important for boilers with indirect water heaters. The aquastat temperature should be lowered during the summer months to lower off-cycle heat loss as long as adequate hot water is supplied. Tests with older oil boilers found that boiler losses could be reduced as much as 8% by lowering the boiler temperature from 210°F to 140°F. The boiler-water temperature can then be increased before the peak heating months so that adequate space heat is provided.

Insulate Hot Water Storage Tanks

The standby heat loss from the casing of a hot-water storage tank can be lowered by adding additional thermal insulation. This can be installed on older, poorly insulated tanks and even on newer storage tanks to help lower heat loss. Electric utilities have been doing this for several years, and the cost of the jacket is usually reasonable. Fuel savings of 4 to 9 percent are typical. Check with the manufacturer of direct-fired heating equipment to be sure that added insulation is recommended, and be sure not to block the combustion air supply to the burner.

Insulate Hot Water Pipes

Thermal insulation should be added to bare domestic hot water pipes for two reasons. First, it reduces pipe heat loss and lowers annual fuel use. Second, it improves convenience because the water in the pipes remains hotter, and less time is required after a faucet is opened for hot water to be delivered. For example, an uninsulated 3/4 inch domestic hot water pipe at 130°F has a heat loss of approximately 30 BTU per hour per linear foot. This calculation assumes that the bare pipe stays at 130°F all the time. Actually it cools down between draws. If we assume the heat loss actually occurs 25% of the time over an entire year (8760 hours), the heat loss from 50 feet of bare pipe is equivalent to 24 gallons of fuel oil. If the water heater is operating with an efficiency of 59%, and the water pipe remains hot all year, this represents an increase in fuel use of 40 gallons per year. This could double the amount of fuel consumed for water heating. Therefore, complete insulation of hot water piping is an important energy conservation measure.

Install Heat Traps

Heat traps are devices installed in the water piping at the inlet and outlet of the water heater to prevent off-cycle flow that can increase heat losses. These should be installed with new water heaters whenever available. Also, it is a good idea to insulate the cold water piping near the water heater connection to reduce losses from any heat that conducts to this pipe.

Reduce Pipe Runs

Another way to lower piping heat loss is to minimize the length of pipe runs to faucets and appliances in the house. If possible locate the water heater in a central location to reduce the amount of piping needed, and the heat losses that are produced.

Add a Storage Tank for Older Boilers with Tankless Coils

In some cases adding a hot-water storage tank can improve system efficiency. The separate tank may make it possible to reduce the size of the burner fuel nozzle and lower the temperature of the boiler water, in cases where these options would not be practical otherwise. Reduced-size fuel nozzles can improve boiler efficiency by lowering both on-cycle and off-cycle heat losses from the older boilers. Lower boiler-water temperature can reduce off-cycle boiler heat losses. These options are discussed in more detail in Chapter 7. These changes are much more important for older low-efficiency oil boilers that operate with higher off-cycle heat losses than the new high—efficiency oil boilers that are now being installed. The on-cycle and off-cycle heat losses with new high AFUE boilers are low, and the additional heat losses from the storage tank system (if not properly designed) can actually increase fuel use in some cases.

Hot Water Conservation Program

Another important energy conservation opportunity is to educate homeowners about ways to reduce their daily domestic hot water use. This includes options such as reduced flow-rate shower heads (2-1/2 gallons per minute or less), low-flow faucet aerators (less than 1 gpm), cold-water rinse cycles for washing machines, and many other hot-water saving measures. Also, all leaking hot-water faucets should be repaired immediately. These important energy conservation measures are low in cost and can generally be installed by homeowners.

Summary

These energy conservation options, ranging from equipment replacement to simple adjustments, can improve the domestic hot water production efficiency of oil heat systems, and make oil heat one of the most efficient and cost-effective ways to generate hot water in homes. Oil heat service technicians have an important opportunity to educate homeowners about the efficiency advantages offered by oil heating equipment for producing domestic hot water.

QUESTIONS

6-1. What are five (5) ways to heat domestic hot water using home heating oil?

6-2. What is the difference between direct-fired and indirect fired water heaters?

6-3. What are the primary heat losses associated with direct-fired water heaters?

6-4. What are the advantages of indirect water heaters?

6-5. In direct-fired water heaters, most of the heat transfer occurs in the combustion chamber. True or false?

6-6. Which of the following is *not* an indirect type water heater
   1. Cold coil storage tank
   2. Hot coil storage tank
   3. Tankless coil
   4. Oil-fired water heater

6-7. On and off cycle flue heat loss and jacket heat loss occur only in direct-fired water heaters. True or false?

6-8. Domestic hot water is heated by a separate oil burner in indirect water heaters. True or false?

6-9. Radiation is heat transfer without direct contact. True or false?

Chapter 7—Adjustment of Oil Heating Equipment for Maximum Efficiency

Installation and adjustment of oil heating equipment for peak efficiency is as important as equipment design. Even the most efficient oil heating unit can waste fuel if it is not installed and adjusted carefully by a well trained service technician. For example, a modern flame-retention head oil burner installed in a furnace or boiler will result in a combustion efficiency of 85% or higher. If the burner nozzle is too large, and if the burner air shutter is open too wide, then the combustion efficiency can be lowered by 10 to 15 efficiency points. Therefore, it is extremely important that every person that installs and adjusts oil heating equipment understands the importance of good adjustment procedures.

The oil heat service technician must be an **energy expert** so that the customer gets the best possible performance from each heating system. Oil heat is an efficient, economical, and safe home energy heating fuel that produces as little air pollution as other clean fuels. Careful equipment adjustment and service is vital to assure that these advantages continue for oil heat.

This Chapter and the next one will give you a step-by-step method for giving your customer the best service possible. Chapter 7 will focus on the adjustment and upgrading of oil heating equipment for maximum efficiency. It discusses the following topics:

- Combustion Efficiency Testing Procedures
- Understanding Combustion Efficiency Test Information
- Adjustment of Oil Burners for High Efficiency
- Reduced Fuel Nozzle Size
- Boiler Water temperature Reduction
- Pipe and Duct Insulation.
- Automatic/Manual Thermostat Set-Back

Chapter 8 will emphasize the more major investments your customer may want to consider. Burner replacement is in between the low-cost and major-investment area, yet it is often the most cost-effective upgrade. For this reason it is an integral part of the both Chapter 7 and Chapter 8.

7.1 Combustion Efficiency Testing Procedures

The following is a simple 10 step method for measuring combustion efficiency using combustion testing equipment.

STEP 1. Drill two 1/4 inch holes in the flue pipe. These sample holes should be located between the outlet of the heating unit and the barometric draft damper. One hole is used for the stack thermometer and the other is for measuring draft, carbon dioxide (or oxygen), and smoke number (see Figure 7-1). If electronic combustion test equipment is used, only one sample hole is needed.

STEP 2. Insert the Stack Thermometer (see Figure 7-2) into one sample hole and leave it for reading the temperature after all other measurements are completed. The tip of the thermometer must be located in the center of the flue pipe. If electronic combustion test equipment is used that has a built-in temperature probe, this step is not needed.

STEP 3. Operate the burner and measure the flue draft. Wait 3 to 5 minutes after burner start-up to take the readings. Place the draft gauge on a level surface and adjust its zero if required (see Figure 7-3). Insert the sampling end of the draft instrument into the second sampling hole in the flue pipe and measure the draft. The draft varies slightly, so the average values should be noted. If wide fluctuations are observed, this could indicate a chim-

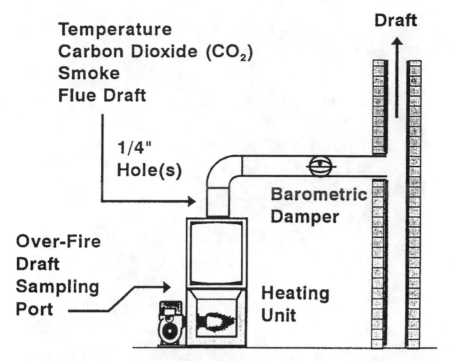

Temperature
Carbon Dioxide (CO_2)
Smoke
Flue Draft

Draft

1/4"
Hole(s)

Barometric
Damper

Over-Fire
Draft
Sampling
Port

Heating
Unit

Combustion Efficiency Measurements

Figure 7-1

Stack Thermometer

Figure 7-2

Draft Gauge
Figure 7-3

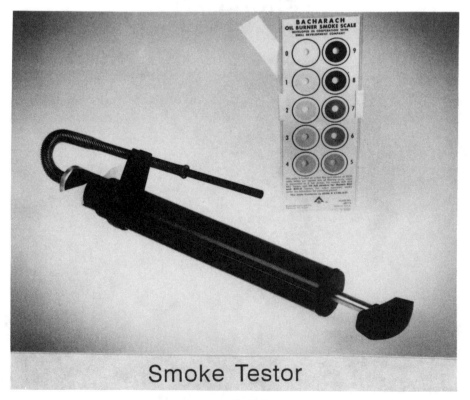

Smoke Testor
Figure 7-4

ney or vent system problem. Refer to Chapter 4 for more information. Record the flue draft reading.

STEP 4. Measure the overfire draft by inserting the sampling end of the draft gauge through a small opening into the combustion chamber above the fire. In some cases the flame inspection port can be opened slightly so that the draft reading can be taken. Record the overfire draft reading and seal the sample hole after the tests are completed.

STEP 5. Prepare the smoke tester (see Figure 7-4) by inserting a strip of smoke filter paper into the slot provided. Be sure that the paper is clean.

STEP 6. Measure smoke number by inserting the sampling end of the smoke tester into the hole in the flue pipe, and slowly pump the handle of the tester ten complete strokes to draw a sample of flue gas through the filter paper. Sample as close to the center line of the flue pipe as possible. Remove the filter paper and compare the smoke spot to the standard Bacharach Smoke Scale included in the combustion test kit. Record the smoke number from the standard smoke scale (see Figure 7-5) that most closely matches the smoke spot measured.

STEP 7. Prepare the carbon dioxide tester. First, hold the tester upright and depress the plugger valve and then release. Invert the tester to allow all of the fluid to flow to the top chamber. Turn the tester upright and allow the fluid to return to the bottom chamber. Hold the tester upright for an additional five seconds before reading the scale. If necessary, adjust the movable scale on the side of the instrument so that the fluid level is at the zero mark (see Figure 7-6). If electronic carbon dioxide or oxygen testers are used, this step is not needed. Calibrate any electronic test equipment periodically as required in the manufacturer's instructions.

STEP 8. Pump a sample of flue gas from the center of the flue pipe into the carbon dioxide instrument. Insert the sample end (metal end) of the flue gas aspirator into the flue pipe and press the rubber cap end firmly over the

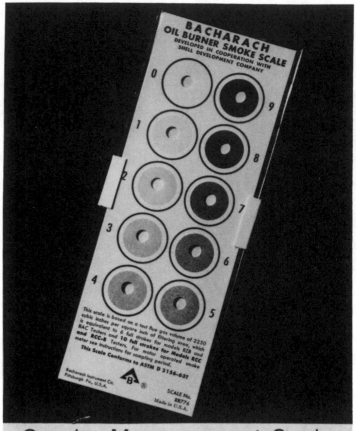

Smoke Measurement Scale

Figure 7-5

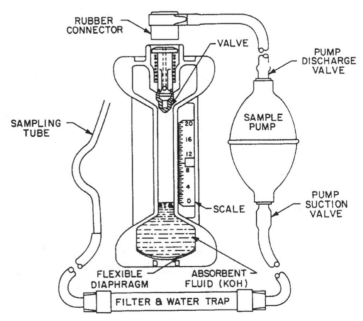

Carbon Dioxide Analyzer

Figure 7-6

plunger valve on the tester. This will depress the valve and permit a sample of the flue gas to be pumped into the test instrument. Pump the rubber bulb on the aspirator 18 times to transfer a sample of flue gas into the tester. After the last pump, release the plunger valve on the carbon dioxide tester before releasing the rubber bulb on the aspirator. If electronic instruments are used, a sampling tube is simply inserted into the flue pipe and a flue gas is automatically drawn by an electric pump within the tester.

STEP 9. Read the carbon dioxide level in the flue gas. Immediately after the sample is pumped into the tester, turn the instrument over and allow the fluid to bubble to the top chamber. Turn the tester over again and allow all the fluid to return to the original chamber. Repeat these steps once more. Hold the tester upright and wait about 5 seconds before reading the carbon dioxide percent from the scale on along the center tube of the test instrument. Record this reading. If electronic instruments are used, the carbon dioxide or oxygen levels are simply read from the output display.

Note: Check the fluid strength periodically by inverting the tester a third time. If the carbon dioxide reading changes when the tester is turned over more than twice, replace the fluid. Be sure to follow all the safety precautions from the manufacturer.

STEP 10. Read the flue-gas temperature and calculate combustion efficiency. Read and record the flue-gas temperature after it reaches a steady value. The temperature must be read while the thermometer is in the stack. Then use the slide rule (see Figure 7-7) or efficiency tables included with the test kit to calculate the combustion efficiency. The percent carbon dioxide (or oxygen) in the flue gas, and the net flue gas temperature (flue gas temperature minus room temperature) are used to determine combustion efficiency. Some electronic test kits automatically calculate and display the efficiency. Record the stack temperature and combustion efficiency.

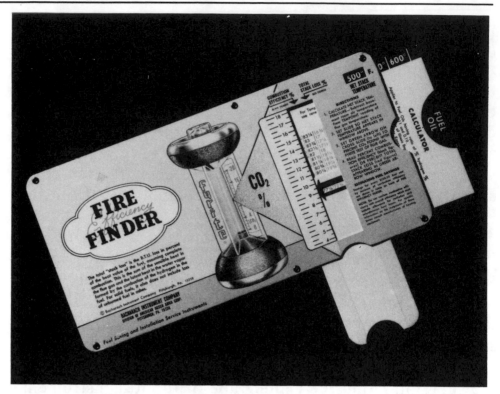

Record Efficiency Determined By Slide Calculator

Figure 7-7

Important Note: All combustion test equipment, both manual and electronic, must be kept in good working condition and calibrated frequently so that reliable results are obtained. Combustion testing supplies very important information on the operating condition of the equipment and helps to diagnose system problems. Be sure that accurate combustion efficiency tests are always performed.

7.2 Understanding Combustion Efficiency Test Results

Combustion efficiency testing not only indicates the efficiency of the heating unit, but it provides important information about operating problems and how to improve performance. This section summarizes how to use the information supplied by combustion efficiency testing to

diagnose combustion problems. For **causes and solutions** to combustion-related problems, see Chapter 2.

Carbon Dioxide Content of Flue Gas

The carbon dioxide percent of the flue gas indicates the amount of excess combustion air that is supplied by the burner and by secondary air leakage.High CO_2 readings are desired for high combustion efficiency (indicating minimum amounts of excess combustion air). Flame-retention oil burners should produce carbon dioxide levels between 11% and 13-1/2% when properly adjusted. Lower CO_2 readings contribute to reduced combustion efficiency and corrective action is recommended.

Some common causes of low carbon dioxide levels are:

- **High Overfire Draft**—if the chimney draft is too high it can produce a draft over the fire that is too strong. This increases the amount of excess combustion air passing through the burner, and it increases the amount of secondary air entering through air leaks in the heating unit. Both of these conditions lower combustion efficiency (see Figure 7-8). If over-fire draft is excessive, adjust or repair the barometric damper for lower overfire draft. (See Section 7.2.4 for information on what is excessive.)
- **Excess combustion air**—Opening the burner air shutter too wide—readjust the air shutter and retest Carbon Dioxide, Smoke, and Flue Gas Temperature (see Figure 7-9).
- **Secondary air leaks** around burner or heating unit—seal all air leaks with furnace cement and readjust burner air setting (see Figure 7-10).

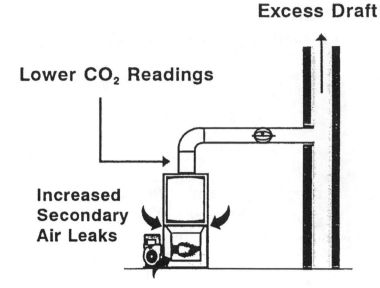

Excess Draft

Lower CO_2 Readings

Increased Secondary Air Leaks

High Draft Can Cause Low CO_2 Readings

Figure 7-8

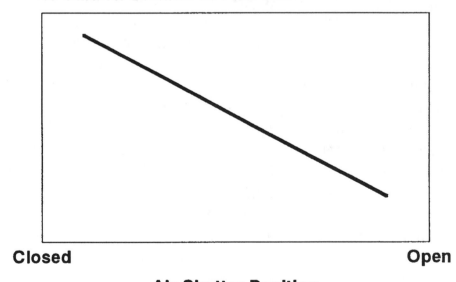

% Carbon Dioxide In Flue Gas

Closed   **Open**

Air Shutter Position

Burner Air Shutter Open Too Wide Can Cause Low CO_2 Reading

Figure 7-9

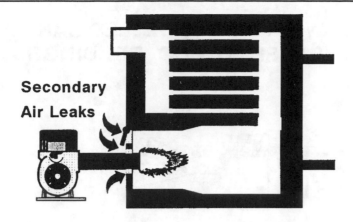

Secondary Air Leaks Can Cause Low CO_2 Readings

Figure 7-10

- **Worn or plugged fuel nozzle**—produces imbalanced fuel spray causing poor fuel-air mixing, or produces large fuel droplets that are difficult to vaporize and burn (see Figure 7-11). This requires more excess combustion air to produce clean burning. Replace worn nozzles and be sure that fuel spray pattern matches the burner air flow.
- **Cold oil**—can produce large fuel droplets that require more excess combustion air for clean burning (see Figure 7-12). Avoid above-ground outdoor fuel tanks or use fuel-line pre-heaters.
- **Low Oil Pressure**—can produce large fuel droplets that require more excess combustion air for clean burning (see Figure 7-13). Check the oil pressure and adjust the pump as recommended by the burner manufacturer (usually 100 to 140 pounds per square inch).
- **Oil Nozzle Spray Pattern Does Not match Burner Air Flow**—and more excess combustion air is needed for clean burning (see Figure 7-14). Use the nozzle spray angle and pattern (solid, semi-solid, or hollow) recommended by the equipment manufacturer. Also be sure that the nozzle assembly is centered within the burner air tube.

WORN FUEL NOZZLES CAN CAUSE LOW CO_2 READINGS

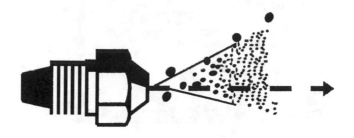

WORN FUEL NOZZLE PRODUCES:

* Larger Fuel Drops That Need More Air For Clean Fire

* Imbalanced Fuel Sprays That Require More Air

Figure 7-11

COLD OIL CAN CAUSE LOWER CO_2 READINGS

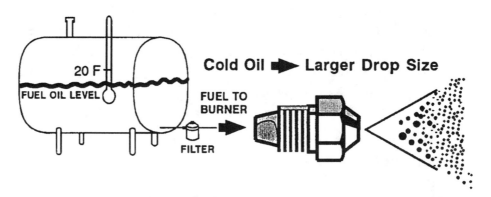

Cold Oil Produces Larger Fuel Droplets That

Need More Combustion Air For A Clean Fire

Figure 7-12

LOW OIL PRESSURE CAN CAUSE LOW CO_2 READINGS

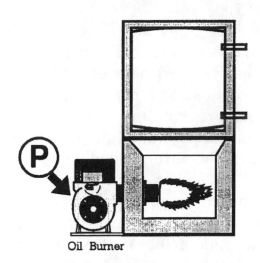

Oil Burner

Low Pressure Oil Produces Larger Fuel Droplets That Need More Air For A Clean Fire

Figure 7-13

WRONG FUEL SPRAY PATTERN CAN CAUSE LOW CO_2 READINGS

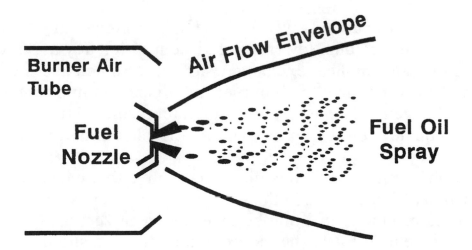

Air Flow Envelope

Burner Air Tube

Fuel Nozzle

Fuel Oil Spray

Air Flow Too Wide For Oil Spray Pattern

Figure 7-14

- **Problems with Burner Air Handling Parts**—can reduce the effectiveness of fuel-air mixing and more excess combustion air is needed for clean burning (see Figure 7-15).
  - Incorrect burner end cone—some burner end cones are sized for the fuel firing rate. If the wrong end cone is used, less effective mixing of the fuel and combustion air will occur. Be sure the correct end cone is installed.
  - Improper burner head adjustment—some burners have an adjustable burner head that is varied to accommodate different burner firing rates. Be sure that the burner head is properly adjusted.
  - Worn or dirty air handling parts—replace or clean all burner parts that affect fuel-air mixing including: the retention head, air turbulators, air blower wheel, and other components.
- **Outdated Oil Burners**—cannot mix the air and fuel as completely as flame-retention burners. They produce lower carbon dioxide levels and lower combustion efficiency. Replace these outdated burners with new flame-retention models (see Figure 7-16).

Smoke in Flue Gas

Smoke production by oil burners is **unnecessary** and can cause a gradual lowering of system efficiency as soot accumulates on heat exchanger surfaces. Some causes of smoke formation with oil burners are discussed in Chapter 2. The general causes are insufficient combustion air, inadequate fuel-air mixing, and low flame temperature.

Many of the conditions discussed above that cause low carbon dioxide levels in the flue gas can also cause excess smoke production. A smoke level between zero and 1 is recommended for all heating equipment. This should assure clean operation and no loss in combustion efficiency over an entire heating season. Adjust oil burners for zero to a trace of smoke (less than number 1). If this cannot be done without reducing the carbon dioxide level (and effi-

PROBLEMS WITH BURNER AIR HANDLING PARTS CAN LOWER CO_2 READINGS

- Dirt or Soot Accumulation
- Burned or Brooken End Cone
- Dirty Air Blower Wheel
- Wrong Burner Head
- Improper Burner Head Adjustment

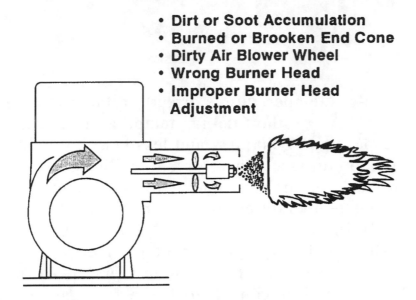

Figure 7-15

OUTDATED OIL BURNERS CAN CAUSE LOWER CO_2 READINGS

Conventional Burner

Flame Retention Burner

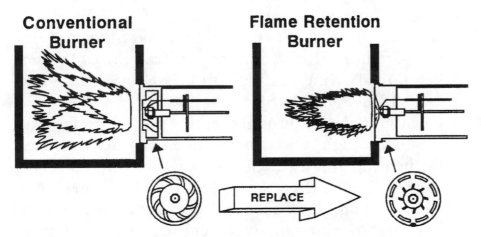

REPLACE

Outdated Oil Burner - Replace With Modern Flame Retention Oil Burner

Figure 7-16

ciency) to an unacceptably low level, the burner is probably an outdated model that should be replaced with a new flame-retention model.

Flue-Gas Temperature

The flue-gas temperature is directly related to combustion efficiency. As the flue-gas temperature rises, more heat escapes up the chimney and less heat is retained by the boiler or furnace. Therefore, low flue-gas temperatures produce the highest combustion efficiencies. Typical flue-gas temperatures for modern oil heating equipment fall in the range of 350°F to 500°F. Some **condensing** oil heating equipment produce even lower flue temperatures, and the manufacturers' performance guidelines should be consulted. If the flue-gas temperature is too high, check for the following conditions and take corrective actions as needed.

> - **Soot accumulation** on heat transfer surfaces—If present, vacuum clean these surfaces. This problem can be minimized by proper burner adjustment or burner replacement as described in this chapter.
> - **Fuel nozzle size** that is **too large** for the boiler or furnace—If the fuel firing rate is too high, the flue temperature will rise as a smaller fraction of the heat is retained by the heating unit. See Section 7.4—**Reduced Fuel Nozzle Size**.
> - **Excessive draft** through heating unit—If the draft is set too high, excessive amounts of air can enter the heating unit through the burner or though secondary air leaks. (See Section 7.2.4 for discussion of what is too high.) These leaks lower the combustion temperature and thereby lower the rate of heat transfer in the boiler or furnace. This **increases** the temperature of the flue gases and lowers efficiency. Be sure that the barometric damper is properly adjusted and secondary air leaks are eliminated.

- **Outdated heating units**—Some older boilers and furnaces cannot effectively transfer the heat from the combustion gases to the boiler water or forced warm air. These units can produce higher flue gas temperature and reduced efficiency. Note that this is a "double whammy." Outdated equipment can give both low carbon dioxide <u>and</u> high flue-gas temperature, with devastating impact on efficiency. Replace outdated oil heating units with new highly efficient models that operate with lower flue-gas temperatures and higher Annual Fuel Utilization Efficiencies (see Chapter 3).

Draft

Proper draft conditions are required to exhaust the flue gases from the heating unit safely away from the house. Typical values for draft are as follows:

Overfire: -0.01 TO -0.02 inches water column

Flue Draft: -0.04 TO -0.06 inches water column

Refer to the equipment manufacturer recommendations to determine the optimum draft settings for a particular system. If the flue draft is high, and the overfire draft is low, inspect the heat transfer passages in the boiler or furnace for soot accumulation or blockage. Refer to Chapter 4 for more information on chimney draft and draft—related issues.

7.3 Oil Burner Efficiency Guidelines, Installation, and Adjustment

Clean and efficient burner operation requires careful attention to every detail during burner installation and adjustment. Chapter 2 describes many factors that affect burner performance including: fuel oil temperature, fuel pressure, proper fuel nozzle size, fuel nozzle spray angle, spray pattern type, combustion chamber design, chimney draft, and burner excess air setting. Each of these must be considered when a burner is installed or adjusted to assure continued customer satisfaction with oil heat. For example, if the burner air is adjusted without the aid of combustion testing equipment, then the ideal air setting cannot be determined. The cleanest and most efficient oil flame cannot be assured. Too much burner air lowers efficiency and not enough air increases the frequency of cleaning calls for the heating unit. **Combustion testing equipment must be used to accurately adjust the burner air setting**. All professions rely on specialized equipment to do the best job possible. Oil heating equipment adjustment is no different. Use the tools that are available to you.

The installation and adjustment of oil burners requires that the four steps listed below be carefully followed. There is only one way to properly install and adjust oil burners, but many incorrect ways. Good burner installation and adjustment requires a **standardized** plan of attack that is used for all installations. This plan should follow these four steps in sequence.

Step 1.   Clean and Service the Existing Burner or Install a New Oil Burner

Step 2.   Adjust the Burner Air Supply For Low Smoke and High Efficiency

Step 3.   Measure Combustion Efficiency and Diagnose and Correct Problems Indicated by Test Efficiency Results

Step 4.   Perform Final Checks—Document Service Call and Test Results

The first decision that must be made is whether or not to replace the existing burner. Sometimes the decision is obvious. If the existing burner is an outdated non-flame retention model that has been giving trouble, then either the burner or the entire boiler or furnace will need to be replaced with a modern, high-efficiency unit. Even if an outdated burner is running well, replacement is probably warranted if the boiler or furnace has at least 5 years of life remaining. On the other hand, if the burner is a flame-retention model, and the heating plant appears to be performing adequately, there is probably no reason to replace it.

See Chapter 8 for more information on how to make this decision.

Once the decision whether or not to replace the burner has been made, go either to Step 1—NEW or Step 1—EXISTING, as appropriate.

STEP 1. Installation for NEW Burners

1-1 (New) Inspect the existing boiler or furnace and be sure that the heating unit has at least five more years of useful life before proceeding. If not, recommend replacement of the entire boiler or furnace with a high-efficiency model that includes a flame-retention oil burner. Remember, the new burner produces a hotter flame that is not suitable for some older units. The condition of the combustion chamber is a critical part of the inspection. If the combustion chamber is in poor condition, replace it or repair it. Do not install a flame-retention head burner if the chamber is not in good condition. Be especially careful of older dry-base boilers and furnaces that may not tolerate the hotter combustion gases.

1-2 (New) Check source of combustion air to be sure adequate air is available for the burner and draft regulator.

1-3 (New) Check the fuel oil supply to determine if low fuel temperatures are expected in the colder months (an above-ground outdoor fuel tank, for example). Consider fuel-line or nozzle preheaters, or other actions to prevent excessively low-temperature oil that can cause smoke and efficiency loss. Also, tighten all fuel—line fittings to prevent air from entering the fuel line. This will help to reduce nozzle after-drip problems.

1-4 (New) Inspect the combustion chamber and determine if it can handle the higher flame temperatures produced by the new oil burner. Typically the flame temperature can increase by as much as 600 degrees F. Replace the older chamber or install a low-mass, high-temperature rated refractory liner.

1-5 (New) Carefully follow the instructions of the burner manufacturer for assembly, installation, and preliminary adjustment of the burner. Each burner model has specific installation requirements that must be followed. Read and follow these instructions and do it right the first time.

1-6 (New) Seal all air leaks around the burner flange and other parts of the combustion chamber to reduce unneeded air from entering the heating unit. This reduces **secondary air** (leaks) that cools the flame and lowers efficiency. It also lowers off-cycle air flow through the boiler or furnace and allows the new burner to better reduce off-cycle heat losses for improved savings.

1-7 (New) Use the smallest fuel nozzle that can satisfy the heating demand of the boiler or furnace. Many burners have nozzles that are oversized for the heating load, which lowers efficiency. Usually, the firing rate can be reduced by one nozzle size (from 0.85 to 0.75 gallon per hour, for example) when a flame-retention burner is installed because of the higher combustion efficiency. Never install a nozzle that is larger than the boiler or furnace design firing rate, or above the rating of the burner. A fuel nozzle selection procedure is included later in this chapter.

1-8 (New) Consult the equipment manufacturer for recommended fuel nozzle spray pattern and angle. This information is often included in the installation instructions. Be sure that this angle fits within the combustion chamber so that the flame does not touch any surfaces.

1-9 (New) Adjust or replace the burner head so that it matches the fuel nozzle size. On some burners, the nozzle assembly slides backwards and forwards to match the firing rate. Be sure it is set properly. Other burners have different burner heads (end cones) that match the fuel nozzle size. Be sure that the correct combustion head is installed for the nozzle size selected. Follow the recommendations of the burner manufacturer.

STEP 1. Clean and Service EXISTING Burners

1-1 (Existing) Clean all parts of the burner that can accumulate dirt and affect burner performance. Open the burner, remove the nozzle assembly and clean the air-blower wheel, burner-fan housing, burner air tube, burner end cone (retention head), and ignition electrodes and supports.

If the nozzle assembly position is adjustable, mark the burner housing before removing the assembly.

1-2 (Existing) Inspect the fuel nozzle and nozzle adapter. If the nozzle appears to be worn, plugged, or coated with deposits, it should be replaced immediately. Remember that good atomization is required for a clean and efficient oil flame (see Chapter 2). Always use the optimum nozzle size, spray angle and spray pattern. A nozzle size selection procedure is included in this chapter. If fuel is observed to be leaking from the nozzle adapter, replace it immediately.

1-3 (Existing) Inspect the condition of the ignition electrodes and insulators. Remove all deposits and replace if the insulators are cracked or damaged in any way. Adjust the electrode spacing, following the recommendations of the burner manufacturer. Rapid ignition is a key part of clean and efficient oil burning.

1-4 (Existing) Reinstall the nozzle assembly and close the burner. Be sure that the nozzle assembly is centered within the air tube (to avoid mismatching of the air and fuel spray) and check the position of the assembly (if adjustable).

1-5 (Existing) Open the flame inspection door and check condition of the combustion chamber. Badly worn, cracked or broken chambers should be replaced or relined to prevent damage to the base of the boiler or furnace. After inspection is completed, close the flame inspection port.

1-6 (Existing) Seal air leaks into the combustion chamber with furnace cement. Particular attention should be given to the area around the burner air tube, joints between cast iron sections, points where the combustion chamber joins the heat exchanger, and areas around loose-fitting inspection doors.

1-7 (Existing) Remove and inspect the fuel oil filter. Replace the filter periodically to prevent fuel nozzle plugging and efficiency loss. This is especially important for the smaller-sized fuel nozzles that operate at less than one gallon per hour. As the nozzle gets smaller, better filtration is required.

1-8 (Existing) Check and tighten all fuel-line fittings between the fuel tank and the burner to reduce air leakage into the fuel line. Air in the fuel line can increase fuel after-drip and cause unnecessary service calls.

1-9 (Existing) Open the bleed port on the fuel pump, operate the burner motor, and remove all trapped air from the fuel line.

1-10 (Exiting) Adjust the oil pressure to the setting recommended by the burner manufacturer. Install a pressure gage in the high pressure line that is connected to the burner nozzle line, and operate the burner momentarily. Adjust the pump pressure to the recommended level. Older burners and early flame-retention models often require 100 pounds per square inch (psig). Some of the newer burners operate better at higher pressures in the range of 125–140 psig. This produces improved atomization and smaller fuel droplets as discussed in Chapter 2.

1-11 (Existing) Again bleed all the air from the fuel line after removing the pressure gage.

STEP 2. Adjust the Burner Air for Low Smoke and High Efficiency

This procedure requires the use of the ten-step Combustion Efficiency Testing method described in Section 7.1.

2-1 Complete **Step 1, Step 2,** and **Step 3** of the Combustion Efficiency Testing Procedure.

2-2 Adjust the burner air shutter for a good flame by visual inspection. Fine tune with combustion test equipment.

2-3 Measure the Overfire draft. **Step 4** of Combustion Efficiency Testing Procedure.

2-4 Adjust Overfire Draft by varying the draft control knob on the barometric damper to give an overfire draft reading as recommended by the heating unit manufacturer. Usually, a negative 0.01 to 0.02 inches of water column over the fire is adequate. If the overfire draft cannot be measured, a flue-draft reading of negative 0.04 to 0.06 inches of water column is often adequate (or as specified by the heating unit manufacturer).

2-5 Seal the overfire sample hole with a metal screw plug, or high—temperature furnace cement.

2-6 Measure the smoke content of the flue gas. **Steps 5 and 6** of Combustion Efficiency Testing Procedure.

2-7 Adjust the combustion air shutter on the burner to produce a smoke reading between zero and number one on the Bacharach Smoke Scale. Generally, if the smoke is higher than one, open the air shutter to allow more combustion air to enter the burner, and if the smoke is zero, close the air shutter until a trace of smoke is observed. Be careful because too much (excessive) combustion air can also cause the smoke number to increase (see Chapter 2). Remember that small changes in the air shutter can cause large changes the smoke reading (and combustion efficiency).

Important Note: Some oil burner manufacturers recommend adding a small amount of additional excess combustion air as a **safety factor** to prevent an increase in smoke production during the heating season. This reduces combustion efficiency by less than one percent and assures continued clean combustion. Refer to the installation instructions supplied with each burner for more details and recommended adjustment.

2-8 Lock the air shutter in place and again measure the smoke level to be sure that it at the correct level.

2-9 Measure the carbon dioxide or oxygen content of the flue gas using combustion test equipment. **(Step 7, Step 8 and Step 9** of the Combustion Test Procedure). CO_2 readings should be in the range of 11% to 13-1/2% for flame-retention oil burners. This verifies low excess-air levels and high combustion efficiency. If the CO_2 is too low (or oxygen reading is too high), identify and eliminate the source of the excess air.

2-10 Readjust the burner air setting, if needed, to reach the CO_2 and smoke levels recommended by the burner manufacturer. Be certain that the smoke number is still less than a number one on the Bacharach Smoke Scale, or as recommended by the burner manufacturer.

2-11 Read flue-gas temperature and calculate combustion efficiency. Follow **Step 10** of Combustion Test Procedure. The flue-gas temperature should be read while the thermometer is still inserted in the flue and after it reaches a steady value.

STEP 3. Review Combustion Efficiency Tests and Diagnose Problems

If the combustion efficiency or carbon dioxide readings produced by the burner are lower than expected (refer to manufacturer guidelines), take corrective action. See Section 7.2.

STEP 4. Perform Final Checks--Document Service Call and Test Results

4-1 Test flame cut-off at end of the burner cycle. The flame should extinguish immediately without smoke or fume production at the end of the burner firing cycle. Otherwise, check fuel pump shut-off and check for air trapped in the fuel line. Take action to eliminate smoke or fuel afterdrip at the end of the burner firing cycle to prevent a gradual loss of efficiency and possible homeowner complaints of bad odors.

4-2 Observe flame characteristics and take corrective action if needed. This includes the following checkpoints:

* Flame ignition—no delay should be observed on start-up.
* Flame color—should be yellow-orange. White flames indicate too much excess combustion air, while orange flames may indicate insufficient combustion air. Sparks or streaks may indicate atomization or nozzle problems.

- Flame shape—should be uniform. Non-uniform flames may indicate damaged air handling parts, defective fuel nozzle, off-center nozzle assembly, or an imbalance in fuel and air flow patterns, or other problems.
- Flame impingement—must not occur because it can produce soot and smoke, which can lower the combustion efficiency. Make sure the flame does not touch any surfaces within the combustion chamber or heating unit.
- Combustion odors—should not be present.
- Soot deposits—should not be seen, especially with flame retention oil burners. Investigate and correct the source of any soot or smoke before leaving the installation.

4-3 Check flame safety and operating controls to assure that the system is operating properly. Be sure that the furnace or boiler operating controls are set to avoid short-cycling of the burner.

4-4 Record results of Combustion Testing. A standard form should be used that includes:

- Homeowner and Address
- Identification of Service Technician and Company
- Date of Service
- Reason for Service
- Combustion Efficiency
- Carbon Dioxide (or Oxygen) Content of flue gas
- Smoke Number
- Flue Gas Temperature
- Boiler Room Temperature
- Draft Readings (overfire and flue)
- Fuel Nozzle size, angle, and spray pattern
- Oil Pressure (pounds per square inch)
- Problems that were observed and corrective actions
- Recommendations given to homeowners to maintain or upgrade high efficiency.

Be sure to leave a copy of the test results near the heating unit and with the homeowner. This will help with future burner service calls and will show the homeowner that you use up-to-date service methods.

4-5 Perform all other standard installation and safety checks that are part of normal service procedures followed by your company.

7.4
Reduced
Fuel Nozzle
Size—
Selection
Procedure

Introduction

Using a reduced-size fuel nozzle for oil heating equipment improves efficiency in two ways:

> • Combustion efficiency increases because the flue-gas temperature is lowered as the flame gets smaller. The heat exchanger in the boiler or furnace can extract a higher fraction of the energy released by the smaller flame.
> • Off-cycle heat losses are reduced as the length of the off-period is shortened.

Oil burners in homes do not operate continuously, but cycle on and off as the space-heating and hot-water demands change. On average the burner operates only about 15% or 20% of the time, and the rest of the time it is idle. Heat losses that occur during the burner off-cycle reduce system efficiency and increase annual fuel consumption. Reducing the size of the fuel nozzle is an important and low-cost method for reducing the off-cycle heat losses, improving efficiency, and reducing fuel use by up to 8 percent. This is especially useful for older heating equipment that may operate with somewhat higher off-cycle losses than modern efficient oil boilers and furnaces. Often these older systems used fuel nozzles that were oversized because of procedures that included many safety factors to assure adequate heat was available. New properly sized high-efficiency boilers and furnaces will not benefit from reducing the fuel nozzle size, because the off-cycle heat losses for these units are already very small.

The **optimum** fuel nozzle size is the **smallest** nozzle that will:

- Heat the house adequately on the coldest day of the year;
- Produce sufficient domestic hot water (a domestic hot water storage tank system may be needed);
- Produce a clean (smoke-free) flame with a combustion efficiency that is equal to or higher than the existing fuel nozzle.

Procedure

A simple and reliable method for selecting the optimum fuel nozzle size uses the Winter K-Factor. This K-Factor is used by many fuel oil dealers to schedule fuel deliveries and shows the number of degree-days per gallon of oil.

Degree-Days = 65F - Average Daily Temperature

For example, if the average outdoor temperature for the day is 40F, the degree-days for that day equals 25 (65 - 40 = 25). As the outdoor temperature drops, the degree-days increase. The K-FACTOR is the number of degree-days that requires one gallon of fuel oil to be consumed in a particular home.

A procedure for calculating the optimum size fuel nozzle for each home includes the following steps.

STEP 1.   Determine the minimum nozzle size (using k-factors)

STEP 2.   Tune-up burner and heating system

STEP 3.   Measure combustion efficiency of the heating unit

STEP 4.   Install reduced-size fuel nozzle and re-test combustion efficiency

STEP 5.   Try other nozzles if needed

STEP 6.   Record results

STEP 1. Determine Minimum Fuel Nozzle Size

1-1 Find Winter K-Factor for the most recent three or more months during the peak heating season (November to March) from company records if available. If not available from company records, the Winter K-Factor can be calculated as follows:

$$\text{Winter K-Factor} = \frac{\text{Total Heating Degree} - \text{Days}}{\text{Total gallons of fuel used}}$$

NOTE: Be sure not to add in the fuel gallonage at the starting date because this fuel filled the tank.

For example, calculate the Winter K-Factor for the fuel delivery record below:

DATE	GALLONS OF FUEL DELIVERED	DEGREE-DAYS BETWEEN DELIVERIES
11/25	FILLED TANK	
12/22	170	518
01/15	165	725
02/05	160	720
02/26	172	705
TOTAL	667	2,668

$$\text{Winter K-Factor} = \frac{2.668}{667} = 4.0$$

1-2 Determine the Local Outdoor Design Temperature for your geographic location. This value can be found in the **American Society of Heating Refrigerating and Air Conditioning Engineers Handbook—Fundamentals**, and from other sources. The Local Outdoor Design Temperature for several cities are shown below:

CITY	LOCAL OUTDOOR DESIGN TEMPERATURE (DEGREES F)
Augusta, ME	- 7
Boston, MA	6
Buffalo, NY	2
Chicago, IL	- 8
Columbus, OH	0
Des Moines, IA	-10
Minneapolis, MN	-16
New York, NY	11
Philadelphia, PA	10
Pittsburgh, PA	1
Portland, OR	17
Raleigh, NC	16
Spokane, WA	- 6
Washington, DC	14

1-3 Determine the Minimum Fuel Nozzle Size from the chart on the page that follows (see Figure 7-17).

> - Find the K-Factor along the bottom of the graph.
> - Move upward (parallel to the vertical lines) until the Design Temperature line for your area is reached.
> - Move to the left (parallel to the horizontal lines) and read the Minimum Nozzle Size from the chart.

For example, for a Winter K-factor of 4.0, and a Local Outdoor Design Temperature of 0 Degrees F, the Minimum Nozzle Size is 0.7 gallons per hour.

The equation below can be used instead of the chart to determine the Minimum Nozzle Size.

$$\text{Minimum Nozzle Size} = \frac{65 - \text{Local Outdoor Design Temperature}(^{\circ}F)}{(\text{Winter K–Factor}) \ (24)}$$

For example, for the same conditions described earlier, the Minimum Nozzle Size follows:

$$\text{Minimum Nozzle Size} = \frac{65 - 0}{(\text{K–Factor}) \ (24)} = 0.68$$

1-4 Determine the First Trial Nozzle Size—The Minimum Nozzle Size determined above is a starting point for selecting the optimum nozzle size, but it is a theoretical value. Some heating units cannot operate properly if the firing rate is reduced to this minimum value. These include:

- Outdated burners that may produce smoke at lower firing rates;
- Steam boilers that may not produce adequate steam;
- Boilers with tankless coils that may not supply adequate domestic hot water.

The first trial nozzle is selected based on the Minimum Nozzle Size as determined in Step 1-3 by considering the following limitations:

The reduced-size fuel nozzle must be:

- At least 0.5 gallons per hour, and added fuel filters may be needed for reliable burner operation below 0.65 gallons per hour.
- Smaller than the existing fuel oil nozzle.

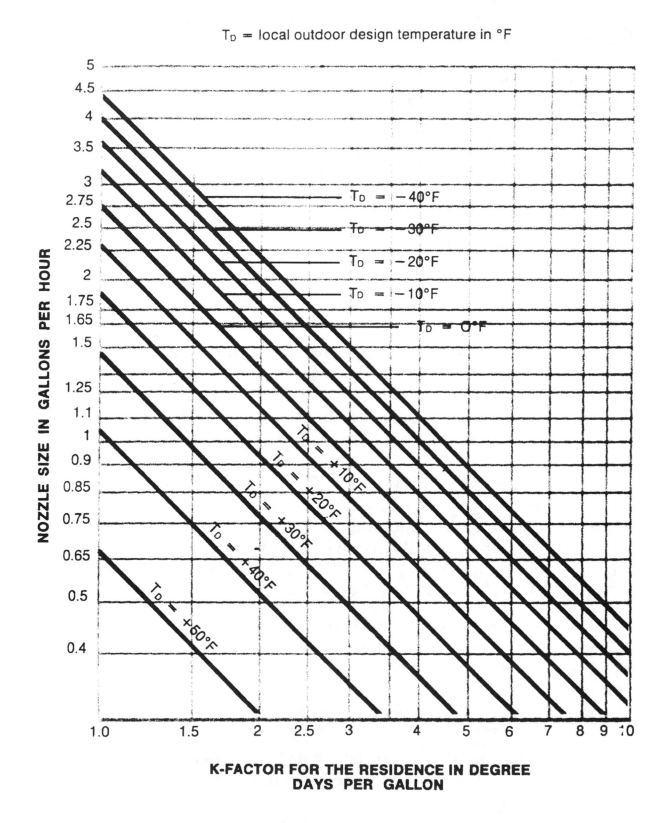

T_D = local outdoor design temperature in °F

Figure 7-17

- Within the rated firing range of the burner. Otherwise, some of the burner air handling parts (including the burner end cone or flame retention head) may need to be changed.
- At least 0.75 for boilers with tankless coils. Domestic hot water storage tanks may be needed if the new nozzle size is below 1.0 gph. Consult the boiler manufacturer for their recommendations.
- Within the input rating of the boiler or furnace. Inspect the heating unit to determine the maximum and minimum firing rates that are acceptable. Use a nozzle that produces at least 75% of the rated boiler or furnace input, or consult the manufacturer for guidance.

Select a first trial nozzle size based on this information.

STEP 2. Tune Up Burner and Heating System

Carefully check the heating equipment before performing combustion efficiency tests. Make all repairs necessary to reach peak efficiency.

- Seal air leaks into the heating unit.
- Vacuum clean heat exchanger surfaces (if needed).
- Adjust the burner for peak combustion efficiency.

STEP 3. Measure Existing Combustion Efficiency of the Heating Unit

Combustion efficiency tests are performed after the heating unit is tuned to peak efficiency with the existing fuel nozzle.

STEP 4. Install Reduced Size Fuel Nozzle, Readjust Burner, and Measure Combustion Efficiency

The first trial nozzle size determined in Step 1 should be installed and tested after the burner is readjusted as follows:

- Remove the burner nozzle assembly.
- Install a trial nozzle (see Step 1) with a spray angle and pattern similar to the original nozzle. Consult burner manufacturer recommendations, if needed.
- Replace the burner nozzle assembly and check the following:
  - Forward-backward position of the nozzle assembly within the housing;
  - Centering of the nozzle assembly;
  - Position of the ignition electrodes;
  - Size and condition of the combustion chamber (replace if needed).
  - Operate the burner and retune the burner for low smoke and high efficiency.
- Be sure that the flame fits within the combustion chamber and does not touch any inside surfaces of the chamber or the heat exchanger. If it does, try other spray angles and patterns. Also, check that pulsations or flame instabilities are not produced by the new fuel nozzle.

STEP 5. Try Other Fuel Nozzles If Needed

Compare the combustion efficiency of the heating unit with the new nozzle to the efficiency with the original nozzle after tune-up (Step 3). If the combustion efficiency with the new nozzle is less than the original efficiency, if the smoke is greater than number 1, or if the flue-gas temperature is less than 350°F, try other fuel nozzle spray angles, patterns. If needed, use a larger size fuel nozzle than the Minimum Nozzle Size (but never larger then the original fuel nozzle) and repeat Step 4. If the combustion efficiency with the reduced-size nozzle is equal to or greater than the original combustion efficiency, if the smoke number is less than one, and if the flue gas temperature is above 350°F, then the Optimum Nozzle Size is installed.

STEP 6. Perform Final Checks and Record Results

Perform final checks and be sure to record the final fuel nozzle size, spray angle and pattern, combustion efficiency, and all other important data for future reference. Attach a written service record to the equipment, give the homeowner a copy, and keep a copy for the service department files.

7.5 Boiler Water Temperature Reduction

The off-cycle heat losses from hot water boilers as described in Chapter 1 reduce system efficiency and cause annual fuel use to increase. This is especially important for older boilers with non-flame retention oil burners that operate with higher off-cycle heat losses. One low-cost option for lowering these off-cycle losses is to reduce the temperature of the boiler water.

Laboratory tests have shown that the rate of heat loss is directly related to the average temperature of the boiler water (see Figure 7-18). As the water temperature is lowered, heat is stored in the boiler at a lower temperature and off-cycle heat losses decrease. In many cases, fuel is saved without a loss of comfort. For example, if the water temperature is reduced from 200°F to 150°F (which is adequate for part of the heating season) off-cycle heat losses significantly. This can produce a fuel savings of up to 8 percent or more for some older heating boilers. Actual fuel savings will depend on several factors including:

- Off-cycle heat losses form the boiler;
- Present operating temperature of the boiler;
- The actual reduction in boiler water temperature.

High-efficiency oil boilers and low-mass boilers (that use a storage tank) are two examples of systems where boiler water temperature reduction will not reduce fuel use very much. New high-efficiency oil boilers use flame-retention head oil burners that have very low off-cycle air flows through the burner. Also, the air leaks around the burner are minimal, and the boiler jackets are usually well-insulated. This produces very low off-cycle heat losses (less than 3 or 4 percent) through the flue and jacket. Lowering the water temperature will not save much fuel with these boilers. The low-mass boilers that use a separate storage tank to purge the heat from the boiler during the off-cycle results in a near-zero off-cycle heat loss rate. Therefore, reducing the boiler water temperature will not have much affect their on off-cycle losses, which are already very small.

Various options are available for reducing boiler water temperature. These include both automatic and manual methods. Automatic equipment uses an Outdoor Air Temperature Sensor that controls the boiler water temperature (see Figure 7-19). As the outdoor temperature rises, the boiler water temperature is lowered to meet the reduced space heating demands. This lowers the off-cycle heat losses from the boiler for most of the heating season.

Another less expensive alternative is to manually reduce the temperature of hot water boilers whenever practical. Many boilers are set to operate with $200^{\circ}F$ to $210^{\circ}F$ water all year round and this wastes fuel. This high water temperature is needed only on the coldest days of the year so that the radiators can produce sufficient heat. In many homes the radiators will still deliver adequate heat, even on peak days, if the water temperature is reduced to $180^{\circ}F$ or lower (see Figure 7-20). In addition, for 99 percent of the heating season, the heating demand is below this peak level and lower boiler temperatures are sufficient. The best efficiency occurs if the boiler water temperature is adjusted several times a year. Use the highest temperature only during the peak heating period, lower the temperature for intermediate heating months, and lower the boiler temperature to the minimum practical setting during the summer months (for domestic hot water generation if a tankless coil is installed). One approach is to instruct

Higher Boiler Water Temperature Increases Off-Cycle Heat Losses

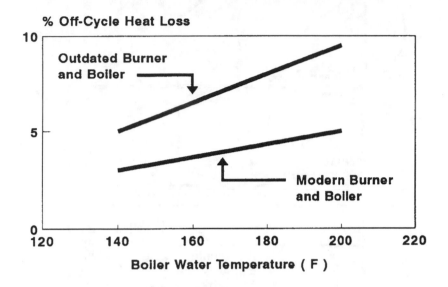

Figure 7-18

homeowners on how to adjust their boiler water temperature. The homeowner can reduce the boiler water temperature to the minimum setting that will produce adequate heat and hot water. Be sure to check with your service department concerning company policy and possible insurance restrictions before you instruct homeowners. Also, be sure to warn homeowners about the dangers of making any other adjustment. Because other kinds of adjustments may affect safe operation of the heating system, they must be performed by a trained professional.

Some heating system design guidebooks in the 1960's and early 1970's recommended sizing the baseboard radiation for $200°F$ to $210°F$ boiler water in order to minimize the initial cost of the heating system. This high water temperature produces maximum heat output for each foot of radiation. If the minimum radiation is installed, then the heat delivered to the house may be inadequate if the boiler water temperature is reduced too much. Check the amount of baseboard radiation and heat delivery rates at

Automatic Boiler Water Temperature Control

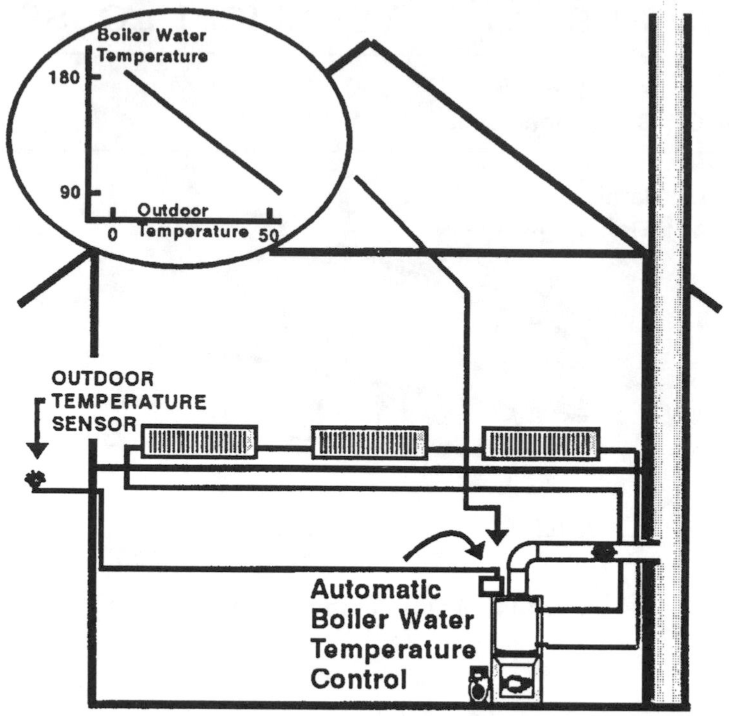

Figure 7-19

reduced temperature (from radiation rating books) before reducing the boiler water temperature.

For heating boilers that use a tankless coil for domestic hot water, it may sometimes be advantageous to add a hot water storage tank and revise the control system. Before doing that, though, check the tankless coil to see whether it is clogged with domestic water-side mineral deposits. If it is, clean or replace it so that more hot water can be produced at lower boiler temperatures. These changes can allow lower boiler water temperatures for improved space heating efficiency. It can also improve the efficiency of domestic hot water generation (see Chapter 6).

The efficiency of many hot water boilers (especially older models) improves as the boiler water temperature is reduced. Manual adjustment of boiler aquastats can be part of annual tune-ups and energy conservation procedures at low cost to homeowners. Homes and commercial

MANUAL ADJUSTMENT OF AQUASTAT TO CONTROL BOILER WATER TEMPERATURE

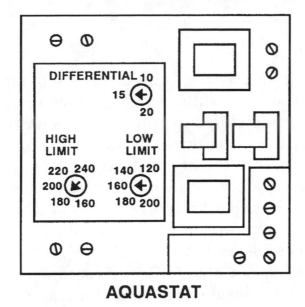

AQUASTAT

Winter	170 - 180
Spring / Fall	160 - 170
Summer	130 -140 (for DHW only)

Figure 7-20

buildings with older boilers and high annual fuel consumption may benefit from automatic controllers that sense outdoor air and vary the boiler temperature. These units may produce higher fuel savings with reasonable paybacks when the homeowner is unwilling to invest in a new high-efficiency boiler.

7.6 Pipe and Duct Insulation

Heat losses from hot-water pipes or warm-air ducts reduce the efficiency of the heating system and increase fuel use. This can be avoided by insulating all hot-water piping, and sealing and insulating all warm-air ducts. All hot-water piping, including domestic hot water, and warm-air ductwork must be adequately protected against heat loss.

Boiler Pipe Heat Losses

Heat loss from hot-water pipes can be separated into two parts; the heat loss while water is flowing and the heat loss from water stored in the pipe. Some of the heat produced by the boiler does not reach the home but is lost from the hot water flowing through the piping as it passes through the basement, crawl spaces, and other unheated or partially heated parts of the house. Additional fuel must be burned to replace this heat that does not reach the heated spaces in the house. The rate of heat loss from piping depends on a number of factors including the amount of pipe insulation, the temperature of the hot water in the pipe, the temperature of the air around the pipe, and the length and diameter of hot water piping.

For example, we can calculate the rate of heat loss for an uninsulated 150 foot run of 1 inch piping with water flowing at 180°F, with an average air temperature of 60°F. The piping heat loss rate for these conditions is 108 Btu per linear foot of pipe, or approximately 16,000 Btu per hour. If the peak heat demand of the house is 50,000 Btu per hour, this means that the piping heat loss at 16,000 Btu per hour represents 32% of the total. This represents an extreme case because all of the pipe is uninsulated and passes through unheated space. If only one-half of the piping goes through unheated spaces, this heat loss drops to about 16% of the heat produced by the boiler, which is still a significant fraction. By simply installing thermal insulation on the hot-water piping, this heat loss rate will decrease to less than 2% of the fuel use. All domestic hot water supply pipes should also be insulated to prevent unnecessary heat loss.

Another result from insulating hot pipes in unconditioned spaces must be considered. These spaces will get colder as the heating season goes on. They will not be gaining the heat normally lost by the piping system. The homeowner must be advised and understand that this will happen. This may not be acceptable to the homeowner, because the heat losses are providing some useful but uncontrolled tempering of the temperature within the unheated space. In this case the homeowner might wish to consider options to control these spaces by adding a proper building insulation (to code) and adding a new controlled hydronic zone to the heating system. The problem of unconditioned spaces getting colder must also be considered when cold—water pipes are present in the unconditioned spaces and the potential for temperatures to fall below freezing (32°F) exists. Do not allow this to happen. Particular attention to this problem must be given in colder climate zones.

Additional heat losses can occur from the hot-water piping during on-off cycling of the heating unit. Recall that off-cycle heat losses from the boiler reduce the overall efficiency and an Annual Fuel Utilization Efficiency must be determined to account for these off-cycle losses. Similarly, the hot-water piping continues to lose heat while it is in a standby mode, and this can add to the heat loss that occurred while the circulator was operating. The prior example is again used to estimate the **off-cycle** heat losses from the hot water piping. The total volume of water in 150 feet of one-inch pipe is about six gallons. If the water cools from 180°F to 80°F, about 5,000 Btu are lost. This represents the maximum added loss (each cycle) during the off-cycle from the hot water stored in the piping. The actual off-cycle piping loss will vary throughout the heating season, but it can add to the on-cycle heat loss calculated earlier. This off-cycle piping heat loss will be highest during the intermediate heating season when the burner-off periods are the longest. These losses could increase the total piping heat losses by more than a factor of two. As before, thermal insulation on the hot-water piping is the best way to lower these heat losses.

Ways to minimize these piping heat losses are to insulate all hot water piping, reduce the temperature of the hot water, not run piping in unheated spaces, and use reduced diameter piping and minimize the length of the piping runs.

Warm-Air Duct Heat Losses

Air ducts that distribute heated air from the furnace to the house can also lose heat in two ways: hot air can escape through leaks in the ducts before reaching the house, and heat can be lost through the walls of uninsulated ducts (see Figure 7-21). Research has found that these heat losses can account for up to 40% of the fuel that is consumed each year.

The heated air that escapes from the warm-air supply ducts is a direct heat loss because this air never reaches the heated space. Ducts that are poorly sealed, leaky duct connections, and joints between the furnace and house air registers all contribute to the loss of heated air. Additional fuel must be burned to replace the heat contained in the hot air that is lost. The size of this loss varies widely. It depends to a large degree on the attention to details during the construction and installation of the warm-air ducts.

Warm-air ducts frequently pass through unheated or partially heated spaces such as basements, crawl spaces, and attics. If this ductwork is not insulated, the hot air can lose some of its heat before reaching the air registers in the house. Although the warm-air temperature (typically in the range of 140°F) is less than for hot water systems, the surface area of air ducts is much larger than the surface area of hot-water piping. Therefore, the duct heat losses can also be a significant fraction of the fuel input.

The off-cycle heat losses from warm-air ducts may be smaller than from hot-water piping, because, pound-for-pound, sheet metal holds only a tenth as much heat as water. Nevertheless, an extensive duct system can contain a surprisingly large amount of sheet metal, so that off-cycle losses can mount up. Still, most of the heat loss in ductwork occurs during the furnace fan on-cycle. These losses can be reduced by inspecting warm-air ducts, sealing all air leaks, and adding thermal insulation to the outside surfaces of warm-air ducts.

Again, if duct losses provide a desired but uncontrolled tempering of the unconditioned spaces, consideration should be given to properly controlling the temperature of these spaces by adding ductwork, controls, etc. If not, consideration should still be given to unexpected problems such as cold-water pipes being exposed to sub-freezing temperatures when preventing heat losses from ducts in unconditioned spaces.

It is also important to emphasize that sealing ducts can change the pressure and air-flow balances between the various spaces of the home. In some cases, health and safety issues may arise. If you have a large number of warm-air systems in your service territory, you may want to consider getting trained in duct repair and making this part or your business.

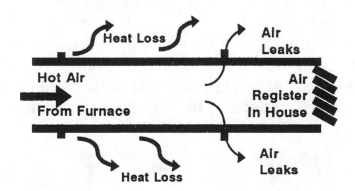

WARM AIR DUCT HEAT LOSSES

Figure 7-21

Recommendations

Heat losses from hot-water piping and warm-air ducts reduce system efficiency and increase annual fuel use. These losses are unnecessary and can be prevented by:

- Inspection of all piping and ductwork;
- Insulating all hot-water piping;
- Avoiding piping and ductwork runs in unheated spaces;
- Sealing all air-duct seams and connections;
- Insulating all warm-air ducts;
- Careful attention to details when ductwork and insulation are being installed.

Attention should always be given to existing situations that will be affected by the elimination of these heat losses. The temperature of unconditioned spaces will in almost all cases be colder as a result of eliminating the heat losses. Existing conditions, such as water pipes in unconditioned spaces must be considered. Water pipes are a major concern for obvious reasons, but attention must be paid to other things such as paint storage, children's play areas, and homeowner use of the unconditioned space as a laundry or for hobby activities. Northern climates that experience long periods of sub-freezing conditions are of particular concern. These problems can be resolved by adding new controlled heat zones (if desired by the homeowner), heat tracing cold water pipes, relocating pipes, etc. **And last, before getting into the duct-repair business, it is essential to get proper training to ensure that you leave duct systems at least as safe as you find them.**

7.7 Automatic/ Manual Thermostat Set-Back

The one control used with oil heating equipment that homeowners think they understand is the thermostat. Set it higher, the house gets warmer. Set it lower, the house gets colder. What many homeowners still don't recognize is that the thermostat is the single best control they have to control energy use and fuel bills. The problems with most homeowners have is first remembering to set the thermostat down when the house is to be unoccupied or at night, and second waiting for the house to warm back up to allow them to move about in comfort.

Every service technician knows that automatic set-back clock-thermostats are the answer. Many home owners just don't know how much they can save. A typical house using a 5 degree set-back over an eight hour period each day would save approximately 60 gallons of fuel each year ($60 at a dollar a gallon). The more hours each day or the more set-back in temperature, the larger the savings.

Thermostat set-back can be done to the extreme. Home-owners should be warned not to risk winter freeze-ups by deep set-backs during sub-freezing conditions. The home-owners should also be cautioned to consider the special problems of occupants that might suffer from temperature set-back. Young children, senior citizens, people who are ill all should be considered prior to turning down the thermostat. Strongly suggest that the homeowner check with a physician first to be sure of what is advisable for the homes individual occupants.

Turning down the thermostat is an option in every home. It is not an adjustment that will significantly affect any other oil heat energy savings option discussed in this manual. It can be highly recommened to every homeowner. The occupants of the house must determine the appropriate levels and times of set-back considering the factors mentioned above.

Thermostat set-back can be accomplished by manual adjustments by the occupants or automatically controlled by a clock-thermostat. Homeowners should also be informed of the option to zone the thermal distribution system in the house and that set-back clock-thermostats will enhance the effectiveness of this option as well. This will be discussed in Chapter 9 (see section 9-7).

QUESTIONS

7-1.   What is the most important procedure a well trained technician can know?

7-2.   What happens when off cycle heat losses are reduced?

7-3.   What does the percent of carbon dioxide in the flue gas indicate?

7-4.   What are some common causes of low carbon dioxide levels?

7-5.   On older boilers that don't have flame-retention burners off-cycle heat loss can be reduced by lowering water temperature. True or false?

7-6.   Air ducts that distribute heated air from the furnace to the house can lose heat in two ways. What are they?

7-7.   The thermostat is the single best control the homeowner has to control energy use and fuel bills. True or false?

Chapter 8—Selecting Efficiency Improvement Options

This chapter offers guidance for going beyond the routine adjustments and relatively low-cost options discussed in Chapter 7. It supplies oil heat service technicians with the information they need to help homeowners select the energy saving option or a combination of options best suited to their needs. It also offers recommendations on how to combine various conservation options to produce maximum energy savings.

Chapters 2 through 6 gave thorough descriptions of four major energy conservation options available for oil heating equipment. These included the following:

- **Flame-Retention Oil Burners** as replacements for older burners (Chapter 2).
- **High-Efficiency Oil Boilers and Furnaces** to replace outdated heating equipment (Chapter 3).
- **Chimney Repairs and Vent System Upgrades** if needed to improve system efficiency (Chapter 4 and 5).
  - Power Sidewall Venting especially for new high efficiency heating equipment and electric to oil heat conversions;
  - Chimney Relining and Insulation to permit the use of new high efficiency boilers and furnaces;
  - Vent Dampers for some older heating equipment.
- **Domestic Hot Water Efficiency Improvements** (Chapter 6).
  - New efficient boiler with tankless coil or indirect water heater storage tank;
  - Conversion of electric water heating to fuel oil;
  - Low-cost adjustments.

In Chapter 7, a step-by-step procedure for **efficiency tune-ups** is presented. In addition, several low-cost measures are described that should be considered whenever you service a system:

- **Reduced Fuel Nozzle Size** to reduce heat losses.
- **Lower Boiler Water Temperatures** to reduce off-cycle heat loss.
- **Pipe and Duct Insulation** for low distribution heat losses.
- **Setback Thermostats** to reduce the heating demand of the house.

8.1 Guidelines for Selecting Efficiency Improvements

Flame-Retention Oil Burners

The Flame-Retention Head burner produces more effective fuel-air mixing than outdated non-flame retention burner designs. This reduces the amount of excess combustion air required for clean burning, produces higher flame temperature, and increases boiler and furnace heat-transfer rates for lower heat losses and improved efficiency. Flame-retention oil burners also reduce off-cycle air flows through the boiler or furnace, which lowers off-cycle heat losses and improves the annual efficiency. New models of flame-retention oil burners are now available that operate with even higher static air pressure (about 3 inches water column) that increases flame stability and improves long-term efficiency in the field.

Advantages. The benefits to homeowners when older oil burners are replaced with flame-retention burners (especially high-static air pressure flame-retention burners) include the following:

- Efficiency Improvement—Average fuel savings of 15% to 18% when replacing older oil burners for an excellent payback in 2 to 3 years in most cases.
- Reduced smoke and soot emissions compared to outdated oil burners. Modern retention-head burners burn clean and, when properly adjusted, produce the same amount of particulate (soot) as residential gas burners.
- Improved burner stability (from the higher static air pressures) for less variation in burner air flow as the chimney draft changes during the heating season.
- Lower air pollution emissions due to more complete combustion and higher efficiency, which lowers fuel consumption.

Range of Fuel Savings. This section outlines a procedure for estimating fuel savings that can be used to encourage homeowners to install new flame-retention oil burners.

When older oil burners are replaced by new models, the average fuel oil savings are as follows:

	Average % Savings
Flame-retention burners	15
High-static air pressure flame retention burners	15 to 18

Laboratory and field tests over the past 15 years have demonstrated that installing flame-retention oil burners to replace older burners is one of the best investments for homeowners to reduce their heating costs. Figure 8-1 shows the typical breakdown of fuel oil savings that results from improved combustion efficiency (10%), reduced off-cycle heat losses (5%), and improved burner stability (3%) over the heating season.

Fuel Savings With New Oil Burners
Average Savings 15% To 18%

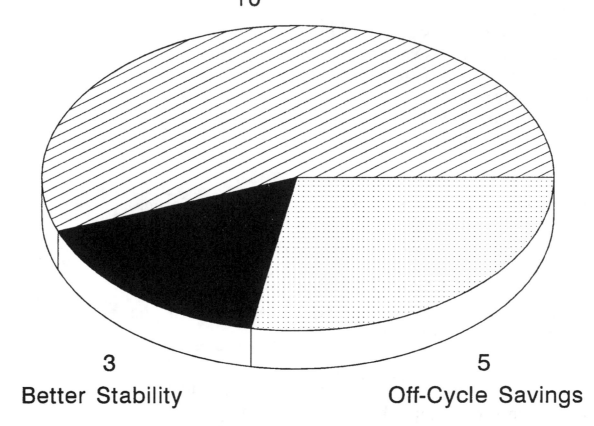

On-Cycle Savings

10

3
Better Stability

5
Off-Cycle Savings

Values Show % Savings

Figure 8-1

The actual fuel savings depends on many variables including:

- Combustion efficiency of the existing burner and heating unit;
- Off-cycle heat losses of the existing heating unit;
- Chimney design and draft control;
- Nozzle size (before and after burner replacement);
- Burner adjustment (before and after replacement).

The information that follows can be used to estimate the fuel savings produced by burner replacement for specific homes, based on the combustion efficiency of the existing non-flame retention oil burner.

$$\text{Fuel Savings (\%)} = \frac{\text{New Combustion Efficiency (\%)} - \text{Existing Combustion Efficiency (\%)}}{\text{New Combustion Efficiency (\%)}} \times 100 + 5\%$$

The 5% added on at the end is the typical fuel savings from reduced off-cycle heat losses with the new burner. This can be lower for furnaces, and for newer heating systems with low off-cycle heat losses. For older oil heat systems with higher off-cycle heat losses, this off-cycle savings can be higher than 5%.

An example of how this calculation works follows. If an existing oil heat system has a combustion efficiency of 74%, installing a new flame retention oil burner will produce the following savings:

Fuel Savings (%) = [(84 - 74) / 84 × 100] + 5 = 17%

Note: The Combustion Efficiency after the flame-retention burner is installed is assumed to be 84% based on a CO_2 reading of 12.5% and a net flue-gas temperature of 400°F. Estimated savings can be adjusted by using other Combustion Efficiencies in the equation above. Field experience with various boilers and furnaces can be used to determine the combustion efficiency after the new burner is installed for various types of boilers.

Figure 8-2 estimates fuel savings when upgrading to a flame retention oil burner, based on existing combustion efficiencies that range from 70% to 78%. The expected fuel savings range from 12% to more than 22%. Note the approximate adjustment factors at the bottom of Figure 8-2. This Table can be used to estimate the fuel savings for a specific oil heating system after the existing burner is tuned to maximum efficiency and the combustion efficiency is measured.

Estimating Cost Savings with New Oil Burners

The cost savings for a particular home heating system are estimated by multiplying the percent fuel savings from Figure 8-2 by the annual fuel use and the fuel price.

Estimated cost savings = (%) savings × fuel use × fuel price

where: (%) savings is estimated from FIGURE 8-2

Fuel Use is the average fuel used (gallons per year) over the past several years from company delivery records.

Fuel Price is the average price of fuel oil ($ per gallon) over the past year from company records.

For example, if a homeowner has an older oil burner with a measured combustion efficiency of 74 percent, with average fuel use of 900 gallons per year, and the fuel oil price is $1.00 per gallon, then the fuel cost savings is as follows:

Estimated Cost Savings = 17% × 900 × 1.00 / 100 = $153

Replacing an outdated oil burner with a flame retention model is one of the best options for homeowners to reduce their energy costs by investing in efficient oil heating equipment. The payback is determined by dividing the cost of the new burner by the annual savings. For example, if $153 is saved each year, and the burner cost is $450, then the payback is:

Payback = installed burner cost / annual fuel cost savings

Payback = $450 / $153 per year = 2.9 years

This means that the new burner pays for itself in less than three years and continues to reduce energy costs for many years after it pays back the initial cost. This is an excellent return (of more than 30%), which is a much better investment than putting money in the bank.

Estimated Fuel Savings By Replacing Older Oil Burners With Flame Retention Burners

Measured Combustion Efficiency Of Old Burner	Estimated Savings % With Flame Retention Burner
Below 70	More Than 22
70	22
71	20
72	19
73	18
74	17
75	16
76	14
77	13
78	12

Notes:

1. Based On Combustion Efficiency Of 84% For New Burner

2. Includes 5% Fuel Savings For Reduced Off-Cycle Losses

Adjustments: Subtract 5 Points For Furnaces
Add 5 Points For Old High-Mass Boilers
Add 2 Points If High-Static Air Pressure
Flame-Retention Burner Is Used

Figure 8-2

The actual energy savings (%), energy cost savings, and payback can be estimated for each homeowner after the combustion efficiency of the existing burner is measured.

When To Recommend Flame-Retention Oil Burners to Homeowners. All non-flame retention oil burners should be considered for replacement because of the many advantages offered by the new burners. This is especially important for outdated burners that have one or more of the following characteristics:

- Combustion efficiency of less than 78%;
- Steady-state smoke numbers of more than 2;
- History of smoke and soot production or reliability problems;
- Large open burner head designs;
- Heating systems with poor draft conditions;
- Burners whose firing rates cannot be reduced without smoke or loss of combustion efficiency.

If the boiler or furnace is outdated or inefficient in design, or its useful remaining life is expected to be less than five years, recommend the installation of a new high efficiency boiler or furnace with a flame-retention oil burner.

First measure the combustion efficiency of the existing burner. Then use Figure 8-2 to estimate fuel savings (%). Calculate fuel cost savings for the homeowner. Discuss cost savings with the homeowner (follow company policy). Discuss the other advantages of new flame—retention burners. Recommend burner replacement whenever a non-flame retention burner is operating with an efficiency below 78 percent, or smoke or soot are observed or burner stability problems are suspected. High-static air pressure burners are advisable for these cases.

After the homeowner has decided on a new burner, a standard installation procedure should always be used. Replacement burner installation and combustion efficiency testing procedures are described in detail in Chapter 7. Use them along with the manufacturer's instructions to produce the best results possible.

High-Efficiency Boilers and Furnaces

Over the past fifteen years, oil boiler and furnace design has continuously improved. The efficiencies (Annual Fuel Utilization Efficiency—AFUE) of new heating units are higher than most older equipment now in use. Therefore, homeowners can frequently lower their heating costs by replacing outdated oil boilers and furnaces with high-efficiency models. In addition, homes that are electrically heated can reduce their heating costs significantly by converting to efficient oil heating systems. The overall efficiency of electric heat is less than 30% compared to 85% or higher for new oil units.

Today's higher efficiencies are the result of several design improvements. Modern equipment designs incorporate larger, more effective heat exchangers to absorb more heat from the combustion gases passing through the unit. Additional casing insulation has been added to reduce jacket losses. The units are much tighter, improving efficiency by eliminating most sources of secondary air leakage into the systems. Many modern designs reflect low-thermal-mass concepts in order to reduce off-cycle losses. This is achieved by using lightweight combustion chambers, eliminating unnecessary material and weight in designing heat exchangers, and also in the case of boilers by designing systems with smaller water volumes.

The AFUE ratings that are based on U.S. DOE test procedures reflect these changes. The **average** efficiency of oil heating equipment has increased from 1978 to 1991. In 1978, the average AFUE was 76%, while in 1991 the average AFUE of all oil furnaces sold was 85%. This represents an efficiency increase and fuel use reduction of more than 10% for oil furnaces over the past 13 years.

Installing high-efficiency oil heating equipment is an important conservation option for oil heated homes.

Advantages. The benefits to homeowners when old and inefficient boilers and furnaces are replaced by high-efficiency models include the following:

- Efficiency Improvement—from the higher AFUE of the new heating equipment.
- Improved Reliability—produced when old furnaces, burners, controls and other components are replaced with the new boiler or furnace.
- Reduced Smoke, Soot and Air Pollution—emissions from flame-retention burners that are included with the new boilers and furnaces.
- Reduced Heating Costs—resulting from higher equipment efficiency.

Estimating Fuel Cost Savings. Average fuel savings resulting from the replacement of outdated boilers and furnaces with new high—efficiency models typically fall in the 20 to 30 percent range when AFUE and system efficiency factors are accounted for. The actual percent energy savings depends on many factors, of which the four most important are:

- The AFUE of the existing heating unit.
- The AFUE of the new model.
- Any reduction in jacket losses, which are not covered by AFUE.
- How the new heating unit is installed and adjusted.

To convert from percent savings to dollar savings you need to know the annual fuel use for the old system. This depends not only on the old system's AFUE, but also on the size, location, and thermal integrity of the home, as well as on system losses not accounted for by AFUE.

The AFUE testing procedures for boilers and furnaces were first published in 1978, and all heating units sold after that date have an AFUE rating. Unfortunately, some of the older boilers and furnaces that are now being replaced were manufactured before these efficiency ratings were available. Therefore, it is difficult to accurately determine the AFUE of the existing units. However, it is possible to estimate the AFUE based on the combustion efficiency and information that links AFUE with combustion test results. A U.S. Department of Energy Engineering Analysis found that the AFUE ratings for oil furnaces were 2.5 percentage points lower than the steady-state efficiency. The AFUE ratings for oil boilers were 4.5 percentage points lower than the steady-state efficiency. The combustion efficiency is approximately equal to the steady-state efficiency, and can be used to estimate the AFUE of older boilers and furnaces in the following ways for different example situations.

The AFUE for an older oil-fired boiler or furnace of typical design and construction is estimated by following a five-step procedure.

1. Clean heating unit and tune burner for peak efficiency using combustion testing equipment (see Chapter 7).

2. Measure the peak combustion efficiency after tune-up.

3. For boilers subtract 4.5 percentage points to estimate AFUE.

   For furnaces subtract 2.5 percentage points to estimate AFUE (see Figure 8-3).

4. For older boilers and furnaces with high thermal mass and high air leakage rates producing high off-cycle heat losses, Subtract 5 percentage points.

5. Record the combustion test data, combustion efficiency, and AFUE.

For example if the combustion testing on a boiler shows an efficiency of 78%, then the estimated AFUE is:

FIGURE 8-3. ESTIMATING "AFUE" FOR EXISTING BOILERS AND FURNACES

MEASURED COMB. EFF. (%)	BOILER		FURNACE	
	AVERAGE	HIGH MASS AND/OR AIR LEAKS	AVERAGE	HIGH MASS AND/OR AIR LEAKS
82	77.5	72.5	79.5	74.5
81	76.5	71.5	78.5	73.5
80	75.5	70.5	77.5	72.5
79	74.5	69.5	76.5	71.5
78	73.5	68.5	75.5	70.5
77	72.5	67.5	74.5	69.5
76	71.5	66.5	73.5	68.5
75	70.5	65.5	72.5	67.5
74	69.5	64.5	71.5	66.5
73	68.5	63.5	70.5	65.5
72	67.5	62.5	69.5	64.5
71	66.5	61.5	68.5	63.5
70	65.5	60.5	67.5	62.5

$$78\% - 4.5\% = 73.5\%$$

For an older, massive boiler with high off-cycle heat losses, the estimated AFUE is:

$$78\% - 4.5\% - 5\% = 68.5$$

If the combustion testing on a furnace shows an efficiency of 76%, then the estimated AFUE is:

$$76\% - 2.5\% = 73.5\%$$

For an older, massive furnace with high off-cycle heat losses, the estimated AFUE is:

$$76\% - 2.5\% - 5\% = 68.5\%$$

Remember that the AFUE rating refers only to the burner-boiler or burner-furnace under standard operating conditions, and does not include "system" heat losses such as pipe or duct heat loss and air infiltration into the house induced by the chimney. These factors are reviewed in Chapter 3, which shows how they affect overall efficiency and fuel use.

Chapter 3 discussed AFUE ratings for new oil heating equipment in detail. The AFUE rating of the new model can be compared to the estimated efficiency of the existing boiler or furnace, and the fuel savings can be estimated. A simple formula for estimating fuel savings can be used.

$$\textbf{Fuel Savings (\%)} = \frac{\textbf{New AFUE (\%) } - \textbf{ Old AFUE (\%)}}{\textbf{New AFUE (\%)}} \times \textbf{100}$$

For example if the estimated AFUE of an older oil boiler is 65% (based on combustion efficiency tests and AFUE corrections), and the AFUE of the new boiler is 87%, then the annual fuel savings is:

$$\textbf{Fuel Savings} = \frac{\textbf{87.0} - \textbf{65.0}}{\textbf{87.0}} = \textbf{25\%}$$

So far we have not considered the effect of any reduction in jacket losses. Since these are not covered by AFUE, this benefit will not be reflected in the above calculation. The amount of the benefit from reduced jacket losses will depend on the age and condition of the old furnace or boiler and on the location of the heating equipment within the house. If the equipment room is in a fully conditioned part of the house, the jacket losses are recovered as useful heat and there will be no benefit from reducing them. If the equipment is located in a totally unheated space such as a garage, any reduction in jacket losses will be reflected in improved heating system efficiency on a one-for-one basis. Probably the most usual case you will find is that the equipment is in a basement that is supposedly unheated but is located under an uninsulated house floor. In this case, expert opinion is that only part of the jacket losses are really lost, because they tend to warm up the basement and retard heat loss from above.

Dealing with jacket losses with complete accuracy would be very difficult and nor worth your time. What you need is a quick rule of thumb that will come close to the right answer. The following two-step process is suggested.

Step 1. Determine the percentage-point difference in jacket losses between the old boiler or furnace and the new one. If you have information from the manufacturer on these losses, use that. Otherwise, make an estimate according to the following schedule:

Age and Condition of Unit	Jacket Loss Estimate
More than 25 years old, poorly insulated	Furnace - 6% Boiler - 10%
Ten to 20 years old, moderate insulation level	Furnace - 4% Boiler - 6%
Modern, high-efficiency unit	Furnace - 2% Boiler - 2%

Example. An old boiler is an antiquated model from the "dark ages" and is to be replaced by a new, high-efficiency unit. The percentage-point improvement in jacket loss is estimated to be 10% - 2% or 8%.

Step 2. Multiply this percentage-point improvement by an appropriate factor based on the unit's location, to reflect the regain of jacket losses as discussed above:

Location of Equipment	Multiply By
Garage, crawl space, or other totally unheated space	1.0
Unheated basement under a well-insulated house floor	1.0
Unheated basement under an uninsulated house floor	0.5
In the living space or in a heated basement	0.0 (no benefit)

Example. The boiler described above is located in an unheated basement. The basement ceiling (house floor) is not insulated. Then the net increase in fuel savings is:

$$8\% \times 0.5 = 4\%$$

This 4% is added right on to the 25% found using AFUE's, for a total percentage fuel savings of 29%.

Annual cost savings and **payback period** can now be evaluated, based on past fuel use for the home.

Estimated Cost Savings = (%) Savings × Fuel Use × Fuel Price

where: (%) Savings is estimated from Figure 8-4 or using the equation above. Fuel Use is the average fuel used over the past several years from company delivery records. Fuel Price is the average price of fuel oil over the past year from company records.

FUEL SAVINGS (%) WITH NEW BOILER OR FURNACE

ESTIMATED AFUE OF EXISTING UNIT	AFUE OF NEW BOILER OR FURNACES								
	80	82	84	86	88	90	92	94	96
80	0	2	5	7	9	11	13	15	17
78	2	5	7	9	11	13	15	17	19
76	5	7	10	12	14	16	17	19	21
74	8	10	12	14	16	18	20	21	23
72	10	12	14	16	18	20	22	23	25
70	12	15	17	19	20	22	24	26	27
68	15	17	19	21	23	24	26	28	29
66	18	20	21	23	25	27	28	30	31
64	20	22	24	26	27	29	30	32	33
62	22	24	26	28	30	31	33	34	35
60	25	27	28	30	32	33	35	36	38

NOTE: DOES NOT INCLUDE IMPROVEMENT TO "SYSTEM" HEAT LOSSES - (e.g. Lower Jacket Heat Loss)

Figure 8-4

For example if the fuel savings is 30%, annual fuel savings use is 900 gallons per year, and the fuel price is $1.00 per gallon, the annual cost savings is:

Estimated Cost Savings = 30% × 900 × 1.00 / 100 = $270

Replacing an outdated oil boiler or furnace with an efficient model featuring a flame-retention model is one of the best options for homeowners to reduce their energy costs by investing in efficient oil heating equipment. The payback is determined by dividing the cost of the new equipment by the annual savings. For example, if $270 is saved each year, and the cost of the boiler or furnace is $2,500, then the payback is:

Payback = Installed Cost / Annual Fuel Cost Savings

Payback = $2,500 / $270 per year = 9.2 years

This means that the cost of the new heating system pays for itself in about nine years. While this is longer than for the flame—retention burner alone, it produces higher annual cost savings (30 percent compared to 15 or 18 percent). Over the 20-year lifetime of the new equipment, the cost saving with the new boiler is $5,400 assuming the fuel price is constant.

The actual energy savings (%), energy cost savings, and payback can be estimated for each homeowner after the burner combustion efficiency is measured, and the system heat losses are estimated.

How the Heating Equipment is Installed and Adjusted. Several steps should be included whenever a heating unit is replaced to assure high efficiency. These are:

- Use AFUE ratings to select a high-efficiency model.
- Size the boiler or furnace properly.
- Install the optimum fuel nozzle size.
- Look at other heating SYSTEM factors and minimize heat losses.
- Always use combustion test equipment to adjust the burner.

Chapter 3 describes how to use available AFUE directories to identify the efficiency of particular boilers and furnaces and compare them to other models. Advise homeowners to install high-efficiency models. They will produce the lowest costs over the lifetime of the heating unit. Every residential furnace or boiler rated at less than 300,000 Btu must be tested and assigned an AFUE rating. This is the key to selecting the best equipment. Use AFUE rating information in advising homeowners in the selection of a new heating unit.

Although the size of the new boiler or furnace can be selected by simply choosing the same output rating as the existing unit, this is not recommended. In many cases, the boiler or furnace that is now in place was oversized when it was installed. Also, any energy conservation efforts (such as new windows or attic insulation) that occurred after the unit was installed further aggravates the oversizing. A simple heat-loss calculation, such as the method recommended by the Hydronics Institute, should always be performed to determine the peak heating demand for the house. Avoid using oversizing factors such as piping losses and pick-up. These lead to boiler oversizing and are often unnecessary. If the piping losses are high, insulate the pipes to reduce this loss. Don't increase the output of the boiler. Also, pick-up factors are not always necessary for the lower-mass boilers now available that heat up rapidly. Try to accurately size the boiler or furnace for each application without adding unneeded excess capacity. Remember, the off-cycle heat losses increase and efficiency drops if the heating unit is oversized for the load.

If the boiler or furnace is correctly sized, the system efficiency will decrease if an oversized fuel nozzle is installed. This lowers efficiency in two ways. First, the steady state (combustion) efficiency is reduced because the flame is too large for the heat exchanger and more heat escapes up the chimney while the burner is firing. Second, the off-cycle heat losses can increase as the burner off-cycle increase. Both of these factors lower the efficiency of the heating unit. Chapter 7 gives information on optimum fuel nozzle sizing.

Always review each installation for "heating system factors" that can affect overall efficiency, as described in the earlier chapters. These include:

- Location of the heating unit (especially for dry-based heating units)
- Chimney draft
- Source of combustion air
- Burner design and static air pressure
- Zoning of distribution system
- Pipe or duct insulation (and air duct leakage)
- Source of domestic hot water.

Consider how the entire system is operating and make changes that minimize heat losses. For example, if a boiler is to be installed in an unheated basement, select a wet-base model with lower jacket heat losses. This will reduce these losses and improve the overall "system" efficiency.

Combustion test equipment must always be used when a new heating unit is installed or whenever a burner is adjusted. It is the only reliable way to reach the highest operating efficiency. Even a highly efficient boiler or furnace cannot operate at peak efficiency unless the burner is accurately adjusted. This requires combustion test equipment.

When To Recommend Replacement Boilers and Furnaces. All older boilers and furnaces should be considered for replacement with high—efficiency models, especially if one or more of the following **SYSTEM** conditions exist:

- The boiler or furnace is beyond repair—always recommend a high-AFUE replacement.
- An inefficient boiler or furnace with high jacket heat loss is in an unheated space (such as a dry-base boiler located in a basement or crawl space).
- High chimney draft is created by a tall chimney, which can increase off-cycle heat losses especially with a high-mass heating unit with air leakage.
- The heated space is the primary source of combustion air and draft-control air.

- High jacket and off-cycle heat loss is suspected from a boiler or furnace that is very large, contains a heavy combustion chamber, has excessive water storage, or has many secondary air leaks (such as inspection ports, cleanout door, or other openings that allow off-cycle air flow).

- Boilers and furnaces with high on-cycle heat loss (after cleaning and burner tune-up) is reflected in excessive flue—gas temperatures. This indicates poor heat transfer or inadequate area of heat-transfer surfaces.

- An outdated and inefficient boiler is used with a tankless coil to produce domestic hot water.

Steps to Follow before Recommending a New Boiler Or Furnace:

1. Clean the heating unit and adjust the burner for maximum efficiency.

2. Use Figure 8-4 to estimate fuel savings or use the equation provided earlier in this section.

3. Inspect the existing installation for SYSTEM heat losses that may not be reflected in AFUE comparisons.

4. Estimate fuel savings and annual cost savings.

5. Discuss cost savings and other benefits with the homeowner and encourage the use of the highest AFUE heating equipment.

6. If a new boiler or furnace is NOT selected, suggest a new flame-retention oil burner that can produce part of the savings at a lower initial cost.

Vent System Upgrades

Several venting modifications are available that can improve the energy efficiency of some oil heating systems. These are discussed in Chapter 5, and include vent dampers, power sidewall venting, chimney relining and insulation, and vent dampers. Two other options were more briefly described.

Power side-wall venting can replace conventional chimney venting and reduce the off-cycle heat losses and seasonal draft variations that are produced by chimneys. The sidewall vent system uses an electric powered fan to produce a steady induced draft to remove exhaust gas form the heating system. In electric heat to oil-heat conversions, sidewall venting can reduce the cost of conversion significantly.

Chimney relining and insulation can improve the performance of oversized chimneys, reduce chimney heat loss rates, and produce more stable chimney draft. This permits the higher efficiency boilers and furnaces to be installed without causing serious reductions in chimney draft, and reduces chimney damage.

Vent dampers can be useful in some oil heating systems that operate with high off-cycle heat losses produced by tall chimneys with high off-cycle chimney drafts, older boilers and furnaces with above-average air leakage rates, and steam systems. One example is old coal conversion boilers with large, poorly sealed clean-out doors with excessive air leakage rates. The vent damper closes during the off-cycle and reduces heat loss.

Outdoor installation eliminates many of the efficiency and safety concerns that exist with conventional chimney exhaust from units located inside of the house. In outdoor installations, the exhaust gases are vented directly outdoors and a chimney or power venter are not needed.

Some boiler manufacturers are now producing special outdoor installation components for their boilers.

Power
Sidewall
Venting

Advantages

- Lower off-cycle heat loss
- Reduced seasonal draft variation (improved combustion efficiency)
- Allows very high efficiency boilers and furnaces to be installed
- Reduced cost for new installations and electric-to-oil conversions.

Range of Fuel Savings. As with vent dampers, a wide range of savings is expected by replacing chimney venting with power sidewall venting. The fuel savings depends on many factors, such as the burner design and its off-cycle air flows, the boiler or furnace off-cycle heat losses, and the source of combustion and draft control air. If the sidewall vent is being compared to an existing chimney system, then chimney height, construction materials, diameter, and heat loss rate will affect the amount of savings expected from converting to the sidewall vent.

See Chapter 4 to see how chimneys affect efficiency in more details. It is difficult to accurately estimate the savings produced by power sidewall venting, which can range from 4% to more than 10% in some cases. In "average" cases, fuel savings on the order of 5% are possible. More important, sidewall venting allows ultra-high—efficiency heating units with very low flue-gas temperatures to be installed in houses where the existing chimney cannot supply adequate draft. Large-diameter chimneys with high heat-loss rates cannot operate effectively with the lower exhaust temperatures produced by high-efficiency boilers and furnaces. The power sidewall vent allows the new high-efficiency equipment to be installed, and also reduces vent-system heat losses for added savings above the savings predicted simply by comparing AFUE ratings. For example, if the AFUE increase for the new boiler or furnace is 20% and the vent system efficiency improvement is 5%, then the total fuel savings is approximately 25 percentage points.

For new installations, power sidewall venting can be a good choice because it reduces the cost of the installation compared to building a chimney. The installed cost is lower and energy costs are reduced. This is especially important for conversions from electricity to oil heat, where the payback period is reduced by using sidewall venting.

Estimating Cost Savings with Power Sidewall Venting. The cost savings for a particular home heating system are estimated by multiplying the percent fuel savings by the annual fuel use and the fuel price.

Estimated Cost Savings = (%) savings × fuel use × fuel price

where: (%) savings is an estimated value

Fuel use is the average fuel used over the past several years from company delivery records

Fuel price is the average price of fuel oil over the past year from company records.

For example, if a homeowner has an "average" heating system and the expected fuel savings is 5%, for an average fuel use of 900 gallons per year, and a fuel oil price is $1.00 per gallon, then the estimated fuel cost savings is

Estimated Cost Savings = 5% × 900 × 1.00 / 100 = $45

The payback is determined by dividing the cost of the sidewall venting by the annual savings. If the installed cost of the power sidewall vent is $550, this produces a payback of about 12 years:

Payback = Installed Burner Cost/Annual Fuel Cost Savings

Payback = $550 / $45 per year = 12.2 years

The annual fuel savings and payback can vary depending on the many chimney and heating system factors discusses earlier. If the fuel savings produced by the power sidewall vent is 20%, the annual savings are $180, giving a payback of only 3 years. No simple method now exists for estimating the heat losses produced by the present chimney venting system, so fuel savings generated by the power sidewall vent cannot be accurately determined. Research now underway may produce better fuel savings predictions in the future.

When to Recommend Power Sidewall Venting. Sidewall venting is not recommended as a retrofit option for existing heating equipment at this time. It is a better option for new construction, electric-to-oil conversions where there is no existing chimney, and when installing new high efficiency boilers or furnaces.

Chimney Relining and Insulation

Advantages

- Reduced flue-gas condensation and chimney damage
- Less combustion-gas spillage
- Reduced on-cycle and off-cycle heat loss for improved efficiency

Range of Fuel Savings. Fuel savings produced by vent system modifications depend on many factors as discussed before. The expected fuel savings by relining the chimney is difficult to estimate. Recent Canadian research involved a combination of options that included burner replacement with a high-static pressure flame—retention model, sealing the barometric draft control, and relining and insulating the chimney. Therefore it is difficult to determine the savings produced by chimney relining and insulation alone. However, if a new high-static air pressure oil burner is installed, the barometric damper is sealed, and the chimney is relined and insulated, then the overall savings are in the 20%-30% range. The savings for relining and insulating the chimney, however, are expected to be less than a power sidewall vent system.

When to Recommend Chimney Relining and Insulation. This option can be recommended when a new high-efficiency heating unit is being installed, and the existing chimney is not suited for the lower exhaust temperatures due to oversizing, high chimney heat losses, or deteriorated chimney condition, and power sidewall venting is not appropriate.

- It is recommended as part of a combined package of burner replacement (high static air pressure), and sealing of the barometric damper, if allowed by code.
- It is also recommended whenever the existing chimney condition has deteriorated or inspection reveals signs of significant flue-gas condensation or draft problems that can be corrected by relining and insulation.

Vent Dampers

Advantages

- Vent dampers will result in lower off-cycle air flows for reduced heat loss and higher efficiency.
- Vent dampers are a relatively low cost option with a good payback (for systems with very high off-cycle losses).

Range of Fuel Savings. Laboratory and field tests have shown that annual fuel savings produced by vent dampers installed on oil heating equipment can vary from 2% to more than 14% depending on several important factors including the burner design, chimney height and draft produced, and boiler or furnace air leaks (see Figure 8-5).

Flame-retention oil burners operate with lower off-cycle air flows, so that the fuel savings produced by vent dampers are much lower than for non-flame-retention models. A number of cases can be considered for both flame-retention and non-flame-retention oil burners for various chimney drafts and boiler or furnace air leakage rates.

Approximate estimates of fuel savings produced by vent dampers for various conditions are presented in Figure 8-6. However, inspection of the burner and boiler or furnace air leakage rates, and measurement of the chimney draft, can be used to estimate fuel savings based on Figure 8.6.

Estimating Cost Savings with Vent Dampers. As described earlier, the cost savings for a particular home heating system are estimated by multiplying the percent fuel savings from Figure 8-5 by the annual fuel use and the fuel price.

Estimated cost savings = (%) Savings × Fuel use × Fuel Price

where: (%) savings is estimated from Figure 8-6.

Fuel Use is the average fuel used over the past several years from company delivery records

Fuel Price is the average price of fuel oil over the past year from company records.

For example, if a homeowner has a flame-retention oil burner, average chimney draft (measured on the chimney side of the barometric damper), and average boiler or furnace air leaks, the expected fuel savings is about 4%.

SYSTEM FACTORS AFFECT VENT DAMPER SAVINGS

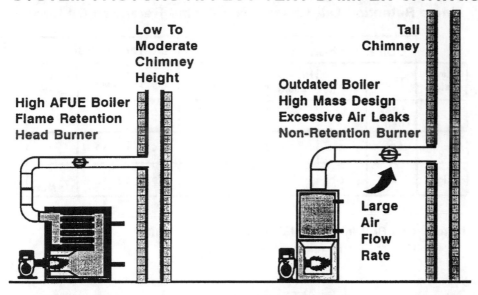

CASE: A
Typical Savings: 2%

CASE: B
Typical Savings: 10 - 20%

Figure 8-5

For an average fuel use of 900 gallons per year, and a fuel oil price is $1.00 per gallon, then the estimated fuel cost savings is

Estimated Cost Savings = 4% × 900 × 1.00 / 100 = $36

If the homeowner has a non-flame retention oil burner, high chimney draft, a boiler or furnace with many air leaks, and all the air for combustion and draft control is taken form the heated space, then the average fuel savings could be up to 14%. This would produce an annual cost savings of $126 for the conditions above.

The payback is determined by dividing the cost of the vent damper by the annual savings. For the two cases described above, the fuel savings were $36 and $126. If the installed cost of the vent damper is $350, this produces paybacks that range from about 10 years down to 3 years.

Approximate Savings (%) With Vent Dampers

Flame Retention Oil Burner

Chimney Height	Boiler Or Furnace		
	Tight	Average	High Air Leaks
Low	Less Than 2	2	4
Average	2	4	8
High	4	6	14 Or More

Non-Flame Retention Oil Burner

Chimney Height	Boiler Or Furnace		
	Tight	Average	High Air Leaks
Low	3	5	4
Average	6	10	12
High	9	12	14 Or More

Note: Can Be Higher If All Combustion And Draft Control Air Is Taken From Heated Space

Figure 8-6

Payback = Installed Burner Cost / Annual Fuel Cost Savings

Payback = $350 / $ 36 per year = 9.7 years

Payback = $350 / $126 per year = 2.8 years

It is important to estimate the fuel savings using Figure 8-6 or other similar references, because fuel savings can vary by more than a factor of 7. In some cases, however, vent dampers can be a good choice, with paybacks of under 3 years. Service technicians must use experience and judgment to identify cases where vent dampers are a good option.

Domestic Hot Water Efficiency Improvements

Several equipment modifications can improve the efficiency of domestic hot water generation. These include tankless coils installed with new high-efficiency oil boilers, conversion from electric to oil hot water heating, and low-cost adjustments.

Tankless Coils. Chapter 6 showed that new high-efficiency boilers with AFUE ratings in the 85%-89% range are the most efficient source of domestic hot water in oil heated homes. Whenever a new efficient oil boiler is installed, consider including a tankless coil to improve the overall efficiency of the heating and hot water system. The savings produced depends on the present source of domestic hot water, the AFUE of the new oil boiler, and the annual domestic hot water consumption.

Figure 8-7 shows approximate annual cost savings by replacing an existing hot water heater with a tankless coil in a high-efficiency (higher than 85% AFUE) oil boiler, for various daily hot water consumption rates. For example, if domestic hot water is now produced by a separate oil-fired water heater with an Energy Factor of 59%, and the hot water use is 60 gallons per day, then the estimated cost savings is $35 a year. This savings can reach $180 when the Energy Factor of the existing oil water heater is low, and the daily domestic hot water consumption is high. The en-

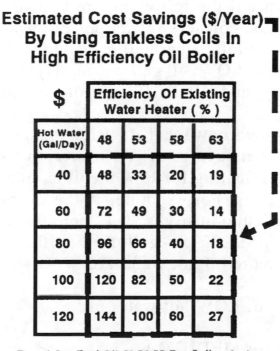

Estimated Cost Savings ($/Year) By Using Tankless Coils In High Efficiency Oil Boiler

$	Efficiency Of Existing Water Heater (%)			
Hot Water (Gal/Day)	48	53	58	63
40	48	33	20	19
60	72	49	30	14
80	96	66	40	18
100	120	82	50	22
120	144	100	60	27

Based On: Fuel Oil At $1.00 Per Gallon And Domestic Hot Water Efficiency Of 68% With Tankless Coil In High Efficiency Boiler

Figure 8-7

ergy savings from a new tankless coil can frequently offset the added cost. If the coil costs $250 installed and produces a savings of $50 per year, the payback is 5 years. In the case of new construction or conversion from electric to oil heat, the tankless coil costs less than a separate direct-fired oil hot water heater, and is the best option for lower initial costs and lower fuel costs.

Conversion from Electric to Oil Water Heating. Chapter 6 shows that conversion from electric water heating to oil can reduce annual heating costs. The average electric water heater costs about $420 a year to operate, while an oil-fired water heater costs only about $180. Therefore, replacing a typical electric water heater with an oil-powered unit can save about $240 a year based on U.S. Department of Energy calculations using average electricity and oil prices in the U.S. This conversion also reduces total energy use in the U.S. (oil is more than twice as efficient as electric water heating) and reduces air-pollutant emissions and environmental costs by more than a factor of ten. The annual cost savings can be estimated for each homeowner if the following are known: the cost of electricity to homeowners (cents per kilowatt-hour), the price of fuel oil (dollars per gallon), and the daily domestic hot water use (LOW: 40 gallons per day, MEDIUM: 80 gallons per day, and HIGH: 120 gallons per day).

Figure 8-8 shows how local electricity and fuel-oil costs affect annual fuel savings after conversion from electric to oil hot water heating for low, medium, and high water consumption rates. For example, if the average electric price for a particular utility is $0.12 per kilowatt hour, the fuel oil price is $1.00 per gallon, then the cost savings after conversion to oil hot water are:

$314 a year for LOW hot water use

$471 a year for MEDIUM hot water use, and

$628 a year for HIGH hot water use.

**Annual Cost Savings By Converting
From Electric To Oil Hot Water**

Electric (¢/kwh)	Fuel Oil Price ($/Gallon)				
	0.80	0.90	1.00	1.10	1.20
6	117	103	90	77	63
8	191	178	165	151	138
10	266	253	239	226	212
12	340	327	314	300	287
14	415	402	388	375	362
16	490	476	463	450	436
18	564	551	537	524	511

Notes:

The Values In This Table Are For Low Daily Water
Consumption (40 gpd). Multiply Savings By 1.5 For
Medium Hot Water Consumption (60 gpd). Multiply
Savings By 2 For High Daily Hot Water Consumption.

Figure 8-8

Conversion from electric to oil water heating can save homeowners hundreds of dollars each year, and pay off the cost of conversion in less than two years in many cases. Always use the actual electricity and fuel oil prices when estimating cost savings. Do not use state or national averages as these typically do not reflect reality in the local utility district.

Low-Cost Adjustments. Chapter 6 describes several low-cost adjustments to reduce energy use for domestic hot water production that should be considered for **all** oil hot water heating systems. The main ones are:

- Lowering the water domestic hot water (or boiler) temperature. This reduces stand-by heat losses and improves efficiency.
- Adding a hot-water storage tank and reducing the firing rate of older oil boilers
- Adding thermal insulation to hot-water storage tanks

> • Insulating all hot-water piping
> • Installation of heat traps on hot-water piping
> • Presenting information on hot-water conservation actions to homeowners.

Burner Tune-up for High Combustion Efficiency

Chapter 7 summarizes a procedure for improving the combustion efficiency of oil burners that is based on careful combustion efficiency testing. Annual fuel savings of up to 5% can be achieved by an active burner tune-up program. This is an important service offered to homeowners only by the oil heat industry, and it demonstrates the superior service offered to homeowners who heat with oil when compared to other home energy sources. Burner efficiency testing and adjustment should be included in **all** oil heat efficiency tune-up programs!

Be sure to follow a standard procedure, record the results of your work, and leave a report with the homeowner that shows the efficiency improvements you have provided.

Set-back Clock Thermostats

Automatic (or manual) set-back adjustment of the thermostat can always be suggested to homeowners that want a low-to-moderate cost option with excellent energy saving potential (if not already in use). Prior to selecting this option certain precautions should be reviewed by the occupants of the house regarding how much temperature set-back is used and the length of set-back period, see Chapter 7, Section 7.7.

The next section in this chapter will discuss combining energy efficiency improvement options. The set-back clock thermostat option **will not** be included in the discussion because it can be combined with any other equipment options or adjustments discussed in the manual. This is because the thermostat stands apart from the rest of the oil heating system in that it determines the load the heating system must match in its heat output to the house.

8.2 Combining Efficiency Improvement Options

Many equipment upgrades are available to improve the efficiency of oil heating systems. Each of these efficiency improvements affects one or more of the following heat losses as defined in Chapter 1.

- On-cycle Flue heat loss (while the burner is operating)
- Off-cycle Flue heat loss (while the burner is idle)
- Jacket or Casing heat loss from the boiler, furnace, or water heater
- Pipe and Duct losses while the heat is distributed to the house
- Air infiltration that increases the heating requirements of the house.

Figure 8-9 is a summary of efficiency options, showing the heat losses that are reduced by each efficiency option. For example, flame-retention oil burners primarily affect the on-cycle flue heat loss and the off-cycle flue heat loss, but do not affect the other types of heat loss in home heating systems.

Most of the energy options listed reduce one, two or three forms of heat loss, but none of them reduces all the main forms of heat loss. Therefore, in order to produce

Figure 8-9 SUMMARY OF EFFICIENCY OPTIONS AND HEAT LOSSES

		HEAT LOSSES THAT ARE REDUCED					
		ON CYCLE FLUE LOSS	OFF-CYCLE FLUE LOSS	JACKET LOSS	PIPE & DUCT LOSSES	AIR INFILTRAT. LOSS	ELECTRIC GEN. & DIST. LOSS
HEATING UNIT	FLAME RETENTION OIL BURNER	X	X				
	NEW HIGH EFF. BOILER OR FURNACE	X	X	X			
	VENT DAMPER		X			X	
VENT SYSTEM	POWER SIDEWALL VENTING		X			X	
	CHIMNEY RELINING AND INSULATION	X				X	
DOMESTIC HOT WATER	TANKLESS COILS FOR DHW		X	X			
	CONVERT FROM ELEC. TO OIL DHW						X
LOW COST ADJUSTMENTS	LOW COST ALT.	X	X	X	X		
	REDUCED FUEL NOZZLE SIZE		X				
	LOWER BOILER WATER TEMP		X		X		
	PIPE & DUCT INSULATION				X		
	BURNER TUNE-UP	X					

maximum savings, combinations of energy saving options can be used for each heating system. The following discussion offer guidance on which combinations to recommend to produce the highest system efficiency at minimum cost to the homeowner. A review of Figure 8-9 shows that some options reduce the same heat losses and are not the best choices for use in the same house. For example, flame-retention oil burners and vent dampers both reduce off-cycle heat losses. If a flame retention burner is installed, a vent damper is usually not advisable because it produces minimum added fuel savings for its added cost. In a few cases, such as houses with very tall chimneys that produce high on-cycle and off-cycle air infiltration, a vent damper may be advisable in combination with a new flame retention oil burner. In contrast, low-cost options such as fuel nozzle size reduction and burner tune-up are advisable in combination with flame-retention burners because they can increase annual fuel savings with low added cost. Figure 8-10 summarizes which combinations of energy saving options for oil heating systems are often advisable. The primary equipment option is listed in the left-hand column, and all combinations are shown in the other columns to the right. The general recommendations are offered for each combination as:

R—Recommended

NR—Not Recommended in most cases, and

S—Sometimes Recommended.

The notes included with Figure 8-10 explain reasons for the general recommendations that are presented concerning the flame-retention burner as a primary option (1st row).

8.3 Summary— Putting It All Together for the Homeowners

The following steps can be followed to use the information in this chapter to help homeowners select the best efficiency improvement options.

STEP 1. **Measure the Combustion Efficiency** (after heating system tune-up) See Chapter 7 and develop standard testing procedures.

STEP 2. **Inspect the Heating System** to determine condition of the existing equipment and sources of heat loss such as tall chimneys, excessive air leakage, uninsulated pipes and ducts, and massive outdated heating equipment.

STEP 3. **Determine and Evaluate Primary Equipment Upgrades** based on the procedures outlined in Chapter 7 and 8 (flame—retention burners, high-efficiency boilers and furnaces, and other equipment upgrades).

STEP 4. **Recommend Secondary Energy-Saving Options** using the information in Figure 8-10.

STEP 5. **Present Recommendations to Homeowners** and fully discuss all the options and the expected cost savings so that homeowners can make an informed decision. Assist homeowners to select an af-

COMBINING ENERGY SAVING OPTIONS
Figure 8-10

PRIMARY OPTION	A	B	C	D	E	F	G	H	I	J	K
	FLAME RETENTION BURNER	HIGH EFF. BOILER/ FURNACE	VENT DAMPER	POWER SIDEWALL VENT	CHIMNEY RELINING	TANKLESS COIL	CONV. TO OIL DHW	REDUCE FUEL NOZZLE SIZE	LOWER BOILER WATER TEMP.	PIPE & DUCT INSULA- TION	BURNER TUNE-UP
1 Flame Retention Oil Burner	---	---	NR	NR	NR	S	S	R	R	R	R
2 High Eff. Boiler or Furnace	Included	---	NR	S	S	R	R	R	S	R	R
3 Vent Damper	NR	NR	---	NR	NR	NR	NR	R	S	R	R
4 Power Sidewall Venting	NR	R	NR	---	NR	R	S	NR	NR	R	R
5 Chimney Relining & Insulation	R	R	NR	NR	---	R	R	R	R	R	R
6 Tankless Coils	R	R	S	NR	NR	---	R	R	R	R	R
7 Convert From Electric To Oil DHW	R	R	S	S	S	R	---	R	R	R	R

P - RECOMMENDED
NR - NOT RECOMMENDED
S - SOMETIMES RECOMMENDED

NOTES:
1C - Recommended only if excessive chimney draft exists.
1E - Chimney relining should not be needed.
1G - Recommended if AFUE with new burner is 75% or higher.
1I - Recommended Especially for older & larger boilers.
1K - Recommended to produce and maintain maximum combustion efficiency.

1D - PSV not recommended as retrofit for older systems.
1F - Tankless coils recommended if boiler off-cycle losses are low.
1H - Recommended because new burner produces higher efficiency.
1J - Always recommended.

fordable energy saving option or a combination of options that meets their needs.

Many homeowners will invest in oil heating equipment upgrades after they understand the cost savings and other benefits. Investing in equipment efficiency improvement is the best choice for reducing energy costs. The Consumer Energy Council of America, an independent consumer energy organization, has said that investing in high—efficiency oil heating equipment is a better choice for homeowners than switching to another fuel. Use this information to encourage homeowners to invest in modern, efficient oil heating equipment.

QUESTIONS

8-1.   When older burners are replaced with new flame-retention oil burners what are the average fuel oil savings?

8-2.   After installing a new flame-retention oil burner, the actual fuel savings depends on many variables. Name five.

8-3.   If the boiler or furnace is outdated or inefficient in design, or its useful remaining life is expected to be less than five years, recommend the installation of a new high efficiency boiler or furnace with a flame-retention oil burner. True or false?

8-4.   What steps should be taken whenever a heating unit is replaced to assure high efficiency?

8-5.   A new boiler or furnace should be sized using a heat-loss calculation, such as the method recommended by the hydronics institute. True or false?

8-6.   What are the advantages of chimney relining and insulation?

8-7.   Give at least two advantages to replace an old boiler or furnace with a new one.

8-8.   A good reason to recommend the replacement of a boiler or a furnace is if the equipment is beyond repair. True or false?

8-9.   It is time to recommend chimney relining and insulation when either flue gas condensation occurs or a high stack temperature is present. True or false?

Chapter 9—Guidelines for Efficient Oil Heat in New Construction

The previous chapters of this manual explain ways to improve efficiency by equipment upgrading and adjustment. This chapter will summarize the efficiency recommendations that are useful for new construction. In many ways, it is easier to produce high efficiency in new construction because the HEATING SYSTEM (each part and their interactions) can be designed for minimum heat loss.

A standardized HIGH-EFFICIENCY PACKAGE can be developed that uses the most efficient heating system parts (oil burners, boilers, venting equipment) arranged in the most efficient way. This package can offer home buyers the highest performance and lowest fuel costs at minimal added cost. Home builders, home buyers, and others in the home building industry must be informed of the many advantages of investing in new highly efficient oil heating equipment.

The recommendations for high efficiency will be presented for each part of the heating systems discussed in Chapters 1 through 8:

- Fuel storage
- Oil burners
- Boilers or furnaces
- Venting equipment
- Heat distribution system
- Domestic hot water equipment

In addition, heating system controls recommendations for high—efficiency oil heat in new construction will be presented for each of these parts of the heating system.

9.1 Fuel Storage

Outdoor above-ground oil tanks can produce cold oil, which can lower combustion efficiency by increasing the size of oil droplets and by increasing the oil flow rate delivered by the fuel nozzle.

Underground oil storage tanks have been used successfully for many years and supply oil at a constant temperature for an efficient and clean flame. However, recent concerns about potential tank leakage over the long lifetime of these tanks must be considered.

For these reasons two fuel storage methods are recommended at this time: oil storage tanks located in basement or garage, and outdoor above-ground tanks that are insulated (and heated) to maintain a constant temperature year round (see Figure 9-1).

Basement storage tanks keep the oil at a nearly constant temperature, which produces high combustion efficiency all year regardless of the outdoor air temperature. Also, the installation costs can be lower than for below-ground tanks because excavation and backfilling is avoided. Another advantage is these tanks can be more easily cleaned or replaced. New fuel oil tanks are now available that are narrow and tall that do not require as much basement floor space as some older tank designs.

Insulated enclosures for outdoor above-ground fuel storage tanks are another good option. The insulated enclosure protects the oil tank from the low outdoor air temperatures and can reduce most cold oil problems. In some cases, a small heat source may be useful within the insulated enclosure. The tank enclosures are also more attractive than bare oil tanks located on the outside wall of the house. Fuel oil tank enclosures are now produced by some oil equipment manufacturers.

Recommended Locations For
Residential Fuel Oil Tank

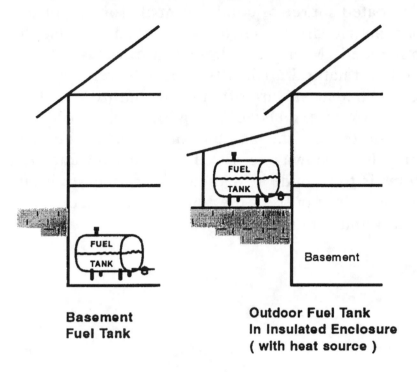

**Basement
Fuel Tank**

**Outdoor Fuel Tank
In Insulated Enclosure
(with heat source)**

Basement

Figure 9-1

9.2 Oil
Burners

The flame-retention oil burner is an important equipment advance that improves the efficiency and lowers air emissions by oil heating systems. A flame-retention burner should always be included with each new oil heating unit that is installed.

Newer flame-retention oil burner models that operate with high static air pressure are now available from most manufacturers. These burners produce very stable flames that are less sensitive to draft changes for higher combustion efficiency and clean operation over the entire heating season. They can also produce lower off-cycle heat loss for improved efficiency. These high-static air pressure burners are highly recommended for use with high-efficiency equipment and also whenever draft conditions are marginal.

A dedicated source of combustion air for the burner and the barometric draft controller (if used) is also highly recommended. Many new homes are very tightly constructed and natural air infiltration is lower than in older houses. Exhaust fans are often used (bathrooms, kitchen, grill-top power exhaust cooking ranges, whole house). These can reduce the amount of air available for the burner. The best way to avoid combustion and venting problems is to provide a "dedicated" source of air such as an outdoor air supply in the boiler or furnace room (see Chapter 4 and Figure 9-2).

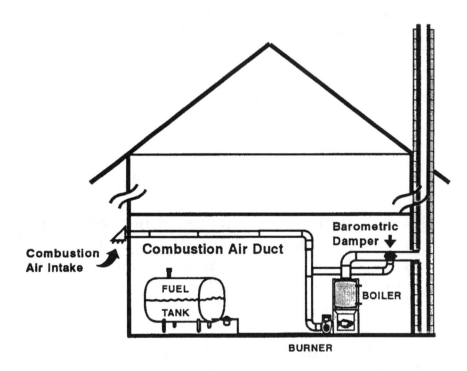

Outside Air For Combustion

Figure 9-2

9.3 Boilers and Furnaces

The Annual Fuel Utilization Efficiency (AFUE) rating for boilers and furnaces is based on U.S Department of Energy Efficiency testing procedures.

In new construction always select equipment with high AFUE ratings. The difference in costs between high—and medium-AFUE equipment is relatively small when compared to the labor to install either system. The benefits of using the high-efficiency system will last the lifetime of the equipment and will over time pay back the homeowner again and again. If the house is mortgaged (as most are) the small difference in the monthly payment will be almost insignificant. In recent years, "energy-efficient mortgages" have become more common. These new mortgages allow the homeowner to qualify for a larger home because the mortgage company understands the fuel bills will be more manageable for the homeowner if he elects to install high-efficiency features and equipment like high-AFUE heating units. The high AFUE systems will also enhance the resale value of the home.

The boiler and furnace AFUE rating program is an important resource for comparing and selecting efficient heating units. This rating is based on a set of **standard** operating conditions which may vary for a particular house. It is important to understand how these **system** factors affect the actual operating efficiency. A summary of some of the important system factors discussed in Chapter 3 follows.

Location of the Heating Equipment in the House

Boilers with very low jacket heat losses (such as wet-base models) are advisable when the boiler is located in the basement or any other unheated part of the house (see Figure 9-3). The AFUE test procedure assumes that jacket losses produce useful heating in the house, which is not

Boiler Locations Where Low Jacket Heat Losses Are Important

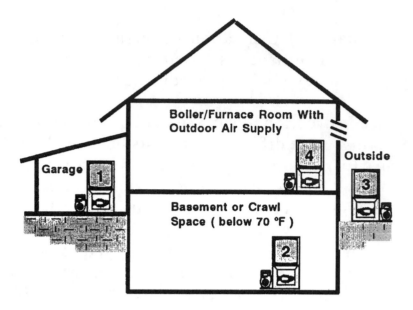

Figure 9-3

always true. The models with low jacket loss will produce higher efficiency in these installations.

Boiler or Furnace Sizing

Oversizing of a boiler or furnace can lower actual operating efficiency by increasing the off-cycle heat losses (see Figure 9-4). Be sure to accurately size the heating equipment using an accepted heat loss calculation method to avoid a loss in efficiency. Refer to Section 7.4 for detailed instructions, which are just as valid for sizing new equipment as for upgrading existing units.

9.4 Venting Equipment

The method used to vent heating equipment can affect efficiency of operation and annual fuel use. Three of the methods now available for new construction are: chimney

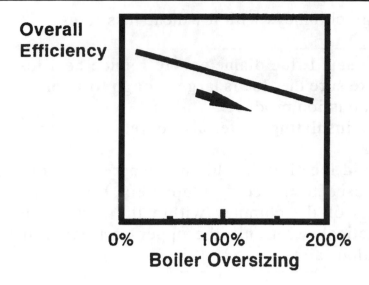

Figure 9-4

venting, power sidewall venting, and outdoor boiler (or furnace) installation.

Chimney Venting

Chimney venting is still the most common method used today. Review Chapter 4 for general information on this topic. Some things to keep in mind especially for new construction are:

Avoid excessive chimney height—the chimney must be high enough to create adequate draft for venting the boiler or furnace, but not too high. Excessive chimney height can cause a number of problems:

- Too much excess combustion air and lower combustion efficiency;
- High off-cycle heat loss from the boiler or furnace;
- High rates of cold-air infiltration into the house to replace the air vented by the chimney;
- Possible flue-gas condensation because of excessive heat loss.

Design chimneys with low heat-loss rates:

> • Use small flue diameters (to reduce heat loss), but make sure the flue is large enough to safely vent the combustion products.
> • Use insulating materials to reduce chimney heat loss.
> • Avoid locating the chimney where it is completely exposed to the cold outdoor air. Locate the lower parts of the chimney within the house, whenever practical, with only the upper part exposed to the outdoor air.

Reduce heat losses from the flue connector by using double-walled flue pipe or adding thermal insulation. This is especially important with high-efficiency boilers and furnaces, which produce lower flue—gas temperatures.

Avoid excessive air dilution by the barometric damper, which can cool the exhaust gases too much. Consider elimination of the barometric damper for new high-efficiency equipment that includes a high-static air pressure flame retention oil burner. First check with local building codes and the heating equipment manufacturer.

Avoid condensation of flue gases within the chimney to prevent chimney damage, corrosion of the flue pipe or heating unit, and chimney freeze-ups in extremely cold climates. If necessary, increase the fuel nozzle size of high-efficiency heating equipment to produce flue-gas temperatures that prevent condensation.

Build a tight chimney with no air leakage, blockages, off-sets or other features that can negatively impact chimney draft.

Power Sidewall Venting

Power venting through the wall (without a chimney) is a new method that costs less than conventional chimneys in new construction and has some energy saving potential, depending on the design. Review Chapter 5 for more information. Sidewall venting may become the preferred method of the future because it is better suited to high-efficiency equipment that operates with exhaust temperatures that are too low for chimney venting.

Some important operating features that all power sidewall vents should have are worth repeating here:

- Complete removal of all combustion product gases even with heating units that produce very low flue-gas temperatures;
- Draft that does not vary with changes in outdoor air temperature and wind speed or direction;
- Resistance to condensate attack;
- Controls to prevent burner operation if the power vent is not functioning properly.

It is important to be aware of potential problems and advantages of these new venting systems. Consider power sidewall venting in combination with high-efficiency boilers and furnaces for new houses.

Outdoor Boiler Installation

Section 5.5 described another alternative to chimney venting, namely installing the boiler outdoors so that a venting system is not needed. This is being offered by some boiler manufacturers and has both advantages and disadvantages. One advantage for new construction is that it can be designed into the system from the start. More research and field experience is needed in order for the merits of this approach to be fully evaluated.

9.5 Heat Distribution

Heat losses from the warm-air ducts or pipes that distribute heat to the house can also reduce the overall efficiency of the heating system. Several important steps can be taken in new construction to lower these heat losses.

Warm-Air Systems

Reduce the heat loss from duct surfaces and air leakage between the furnace and the air supply registers in the house.

- Use seamless duct materials whenever possible.
- Design the ductwork for minimum distance between the furnace and the air registers to reduce the number of connections and total surface area of the ductwork.
- Avoid running ducts through unheated areas of the house such as crawl spaces, unheated basements and attics. Always insulate ducts passing through these parts of the house.
- Be sure that all duct seams and joints are completely air tight to prevent the loss of heated air before it reaches the air registers.
- Whenever possible run the duct within the heated space so that duct heat losses are captured.
- Carefully size ducts to reduce the heat loss, minimum surface area when possible.

Hot-Water Systems

- Insulate all hot-water pipes.
- Design the piping for minimum distances from the boiler to the house radiators.

- Avoid running pipes through unheated areas of the house such as crawl spaces, unheated basements and attics.
- Carefully size the pipes for minimum diameter to reduce the amount of hot water stored in them. During on-off operation the heat loss from hot water stored in these pipes can be significant. Doubling the pipe size increases heat storage by a factor of 4.
- Install sufficient baseboard radiation within the house so that a boiler water temperature can be operated at 180°F or less. This lowers boiler heat loss and hot-water pipe heat loss.

Zoning of Heat Distribution

If multiple heating zones are used, annual fuel use can be reduced significantly (see Figures 9-5 and 9-6). The heating of each part of the house should be controlled by clock thermostats. Heat is supplied only when needed and

WARM AIR FURNACE WITH SEPARATE HEATING ZONES

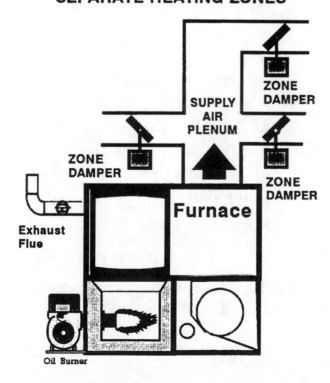

Figure 9-5

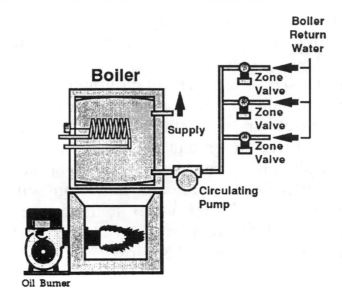

**Hot Water System With
Separate Heating Zones**

Figure 9-6

house heat loss and fuel use are lowered. This is an important energy conservation feature for new homes.

9.6 Domestic Hot Water Source

Chapter 6 reviews the heat losses and efficiencies of various sources of domestic hot water and recommends the following systems listed from highest to lowest efficiency.

	EFFICIENCY (AVG.)
Integrated high-efficiency boiler with insulated storage tank	75%–80%
Tankless coil with high-AFUE boiler	65%–70%
Direct-fired oil water heater	60%

The integrated high-efficiency boiler with a separate insulated storage tank is the best option for efficient production of domestic hot water because it operates with the lowest off-cycle (standby) heat losses. The next highest efficiency is produced by a high-efficiency (high AFUE) oil boiler with a tankless coil. In addition to high efficiency, these hot-water generators are less costly than separate direct-fired water heaters. The direct-fired water heater has the next highest efficiency, and if this option is chosen a unit with the highest Energy Factor (EF) rating should be selected. See the rating books for boiler, furnace, water heaters referenced in Chapter 3. Electric water heaters are **not recommended** for new construction because they operate with the lowest overall efficiency (about 25%) when you consider the fuel burned by the electric utility.

If the peak domestic hot water demand is much higher than the peak space heating load, a separate (insulated) hot water storage tank should be considered. This will allow the lowest fuel nozzle size to be used and can improve overall system efficiency.

Some other domestic hot water efficiency improvements should also be considered for new construction. These include:

- Solar hot water heater with an efficient oil back-up system;
- Reduced boiler or water-heater temperatures to minimize standby heat loss;
- Thermal insulation for all hot-water storage tanks;
- Thermal insulation for all domestic hot-water pipes;
- Reduced pipe sizes (both length and diameter) to reduce pipe heat loss.

9.7 Heating System Controls

In new construction an important energy-saving feature is the use of zone controls for warm-air or hydronic heating systems that heat parts of the house only when occupied. Hydronic systems are zoned by breaking up the hot water piping into several loops each with a separate circulator or zone valve controlled by its own zone thermostat. Warm-air systems can also be zoned by installing motorized dampers in some of the distribution ducts so that only part of the house will be heated. Zone thermostats can control the operation of these air dampers. Care must be given in designing a well engineered system when zoning warm-air systems to achieve proper balancing of the air flows.

A clock thermostat controls the heat delivery to each house zone so that heat is delivered only when needed to the two, three, four, or more heating zones. The thermostat can be programmed to deliver heat only during certain hours. For example, if the house is unoccupied during the day, the temperature of all the zones can be lowered. Heat can be delivered only to the main living level in the afternoon and evening, and to the bedrooms in the evening followed by night set-back after midnight. Homeowners can adjust these settings as needed to meet their changing needs. The savings by this type of multiple zone temperature control with night set-back can be as high as 30%.

Another advance in heating-system controls is a microprocessor—based control that enables optimum operation of space heating and hot water heating. One of the low-mass boilers now available uses this type of control to operate the boiler only when needed and to use the last zone calling for heat or the domestic hot-water storage tank to produce the highest system efficiency.

These efficient control systems should all be considered for new construction to produce the highest efficiency for the entire heating system.

QUESTIONS

9-1.   If there are no other locations for a fuel tank but outside, what can be done to keep the heating oil warm?

9-2.   The best way to avoid combustion and venting problems in new homes is to provide a "dedicated" source of air such as an outdoor air supply in the boiler or furnace room. True or false?

9-3.   In new construction, avoid excessive chimney heights and design chimneys with low heat-loss rates. True or false?

9-4.   Sidewall venting may become the preferred method of the future because it is better suited to high-efficiency equipment that operates with exhaust temperatures that are too low for chimney venting. True or false?

9-5.   Several important steps can be taken in new construction to lower heat-losses from warm air ducts. What are they?

9-6.   If multiple heating zones are used, annual fuel use can be reduced significantly. True or false?

9-7.   The integrated high efficiency boiler with a separate insulated storage tank is the best option for efficient production of domestic hot water because it operates with the lowest off-cycle heat losses. True or false?

Chapter 10—New Technology Research and Development—The Future of Oil-Heat

There is a bright future for the residential and light-commercial oil-heating industry in the United States. New and emerging oil-heat technologies will be discussed in this chapter to provide the reader with knowledge of recent innovations and a vision of the industry's future. Heating oil is an essential resources for ten million homes and businesses in the Northeast and Mid-Atlantic regions alone. Heating oil is the principal fuel in over 40% of the homes in these states and the most commonly chosen fuel for new custom-built homes. New technology is continually being developed to provide the heating oil consumer with the best value for his dollar in terms of heating comfort and efficiency. At the same time, technical advancements will result in environmentally cleaner systems than those available today. With today's efficient modern oil-heating technology already as clean as any competitive heating fuel, the industry should have no problem promoting fuel oil as the home heating fuel of the future.

Advances in controls and automatic monitoring are leading the way to the future for the oil-heat industry. New concepts in burner design will allow the development of innovative, compact, high-efficiency appliances for the home. They may also open up alternative oil-heat-comfort market areas such as recreational vehicles, boating, and tractor-truck cab heating. Progress in oil-heat technology development will also allow the oil-heat industry to continue to be part of the "Intelligent House" upscale home construction market.

10.1
Advanced
Control
Systems

Multi-Purpose Remote Monitoring Systems

One development in the last five years has been the advent of multi-purpose remote monitoring systems that link the customer's home to the fuel oil company computer via telephone line. Two systems are currently marketed in the U.S. and Canada. These systems provide for remote monitoring of fuel-tank levels, low-temperature conditions in the home (freeze-up alert), and burner lock-out conditions requiring remedial action by the oil-heat service department. If any of these conditions are detected by the monitoring system, it will automatically call to a modem—equipped computer at the oil company (see Figure 10-1). The system in the house "talks" electronically with the computer at the oil company and communicates the customer's name and location, and identifies the specific sensor that triggered the automated call. The computer logs the information and alerts the office staff to respond with appropriate action. This type of system can also be used to send messages to a personal paging device and a separate telephone service in addition to the company computer to provide 24-hour information to "on call" service personnel.

These systems have obvious benefits in detecting equipment related problems early-on and allowing solutions to be provided in a timely manner. This can dramatically reduce the potential for an uncomfortable and unhappy oil-heat customer sitting in a house already cold because the heating system failed many hours ago. They can provide for more efficient and productive fuel delivery, taking the guesswork and worry out of conventional delivery scheduling based on degree-day systems. All of these

Remote Monitoring Using Flame Quality indicator

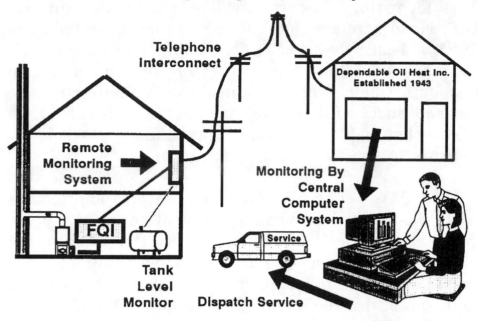

Figure 10-1

benefits add up to an even more important result, a warm comfortable satisfied customer with the peace of mind that someone is keeping a close eye on his or her heating system so they don't have to worry about it. The only real problem with these systems is that they are costly to install, and this currently limits there widespread use. It is anticipated that the cost of such systems will become more reasonable as more and more are installed. In the future these systems will surely be designed to allow more sensors to be added and to interconnect with other home automation systems such as security systems, home computers, and other advanced control features.

Flame Quality Indicator (FQI) Monitor

An emerging patented technology developed by the United States Department of Energy at Brookhaven National Laboratory is the Flame Quality Indicator (FQI). This technology is currently licensed by two different U.S. manufacturers and will be test marketed during the 1993/94 heating season. The two companies have individual plans for field testing units (100 per company) in this test marketing phase. Assuming these marketing trials are deemed successful by the manufacturers involved, the FQI technology will be widely available to the oil-heat industry by the 1994/95 heating season.

The FQI is a simple device that monitors the brightness of an oil-burner flame using a control circuit and a conventional CAD cell (cadmium sulfide) flame sensor (see Figure 10-2). When the flame brightness falls outside a preset range, the flame quality or excess air has changed to the point that the oil heating appliance should be serviced. The FQI can output this information directly in the form of indicator lights mounted on the unit or can trigger a signal to an automated multi-purpose monitor system as described earlier. A green light condition indicates "Condition Normal" with the flame quality about the same as

Flame Quality Indicator Schematic

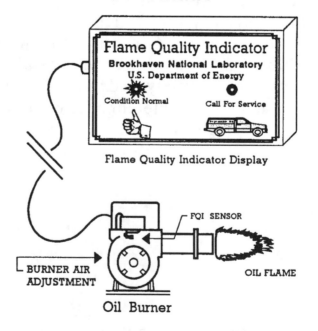

Figure 10-2

when last adjusted by a service technician and within the established range of acceptable performance. Red indicates a "Call for Service" is in order. The manufacturers planning to market this device will control the limits of the acceptable performance range by the final circuit designs used in their product lines. Successful designs will eliminate any concern of an overly sensitive device flagging false indications.

The FQI also depends on a knowledgeable service technician to properly adjust the burner to establish the best possible conditions (clean and efficient) using combustion test equipment prior to adjusting the FQI set-point. This establishes a starting point. The unit then detects any changes that occur. If the unit exceeds the pre-determined performance range limits, it will signal a red-light condition. This can be due to fuel—rich or fuel-lean conditions, or other changes that affect the flame quality. In the future the service technician can then service the burner using the FQI as a diagnostic tool indicating when the best conditions are re-established without lengthy retesting.

The device can be used in many different ways. It can be designed to be used directly by the homeowner with an indicator light mounted in the living space. This would be much like a warning light on a car to check the engine when service is required. It could be designed to be used without the customer being aware of it if connected to an automatic monitor system as mentioned above. It can be used as an on-board diagnostic tool for use by the service technician. Original equipment manufacturers could use the FQI to pre-set systems at the factory to simplify the installation of heating systems in the field.

The device is a low-cost option and is currently expected to be installed for less than $150. If a major control manufacturer were to combine this concept with a microprocessor-based primary flame safety control, the added cost would be about $10, less than a tenth of a stand-alone device. The installation can be very simple. One FQI manufacturer has already designed simple mountings for the majority of oil-burner designs currently marketed by working directly with the burner manufacturers.

There are several technical performance benefits associated with the FQI. It provides an immediate indication that the oil burner needs to be serviced. Currently the homeowner calls for service when there is no heat or when oil combustion odors are present in the home. The FQI can signal that something is going wrong long before these problems get to the point that the consumer is inconvenienced. The FQI will provide early detection allowing a service call to be scheduled at a time convenient to both the homeowner and the service technician and not in the middle of a cold winter night. Once properly installed, the FQI will in the future reduce the time to service the burner as compared to conventional procedures. Efficiency can be improved by setting the burner at its optimum adjustment point without concern. If conditions change and soot starts to form it can be detected early on before the heat exchanger becomes fouled to the point that efficiency drops off and extensive cleaning is required. When modern clean-burning oil heating systems are installed, the FQI will allow for longer intervals between tune-ups, which could be supplied on an as-needed basis only.

10.2 New Oil Burner Advances

New oil burners are under development that use air-atomizing fuel nozzles instead of conventional pressure atomizers. This technology can dramatically improve oil burner performance. Two of these burners will be discussed. The first was developed by Babington Engineering Inc. and is available in Europe as a residential oil burner with a firing range of 0.2–0.6 gph. The second is under development by the U.S. Department of Energy at Brookhaven National Laboratory and will also have a low-firing-rate capacity coupled with an extremely clean emissions profile. The unit will produce less than half of the nitrous oxides of flame-retention head burners, and also less particulates, and it will be capable of firing in various types of appliances.

The availability of new oil-burner technologies will result in even more environmentally friendly, efficient oil heating systems properly sized for the energy-efficient homes being built today and those that will be built in the future. The unit will allow for compact system designs with extremely high efficiency ratings. These systems will be able to fire at any point in the firing range without changing the atomizing nozzle. The systems have the potential for modulating firing rate automatically.

Current oil-burner designs have a practical lower limit of 0.5 gph (70,000 Btuh) due to the limits of the pressure-atomizing nozzles. Nozzle manufacturers have attempted to market 0.4 and 0.3 gph nozzles over the last 15 years with no success. The physical environment and the fuel quality that the high-pressure atomizing fuel nozzle must tolerate usually results in nozzle performance problems within a few weeks at these extremely low firing rates. This is not acceptable. The air-atomizing fuel nozzle concepts being developed do not exhibit these problems.

Babington Burner Technology

The Babington atomizer is simple in concept and has been the subject of a great deal of product research and development effort over the last 15 years. The atomizer is successfully used in the medical field and has a proven record in prototype combustion systems as well. One European oil-burner manufacturer uses the Babington atomizer in a residential burner design capable of firing in the range of 0.2–0.6 gph. It has also been used in designing oil burners in different sizes (firing ranges) intended for devices used by the U.S. military for cooking, tent heating, lighting, and absorption refrigeration. It has not yet been manufactured for the U.S. oil-burner marketplace. Understanding this new oil burning technology is important, however, because it illustrates the wide range of future applications that are already possible and that can be considered when fuel oil is burned cleanly and efficiently. All of the appliance concepts presented in the photographs in this section are full-scale working prototype models and have been fired and tested with standard highway diesel fuel and or No. 2 heating fuel.

Although the burner has many technical advantages that will be discussed, a large problem is that it would initially cost about 2 to 3 times more to manufacture than conventional flame-retention head oil burners. Moreover, it is a major departure from current oil—burner designs. These two factors have kept it out of the current U.S. market. However, the technology and its unique characteristics make it a strong candidate for use by the U.S. military, which has been directed to use a single logistical fuel, diesel fuel, for future use in troop-support applications in the field, worldwide. The military appliances require fuel firing rates well below 0.5 gph, which are not practical for pressure atomizing oil burners for the reasons already mentioned. This new technology is being developed for its military applications. It also is expected that at some point in the future it will also be available for secondary markets including residential oil-fired heating appliances. By then, with military production underway, production start-up expenses will not factor into the costs of entering the residential market.

A schematic, Figure 10-3, shows how the European burner designed to use the Babington atomizer works. Low-pressure (10–12 psi) air, supplied by a small air compressor designed as part of the burner's power package, flows to the inside of the hollow fuel-atomizing hemisphere and leaves the atomizer through a small slit. Fuel oil (at atmospheric pressure) flows over the outside of the atomizer and forms a thin film. As this oil film passes over the atomizer, air is ejected outward through the small slit. This causes a mist of fuel-oil droplets to be formed. This air atomizer produces a very fine mist of uniform fuel droplets that burn with small amounts of excess combustion air, producing excellent combustion

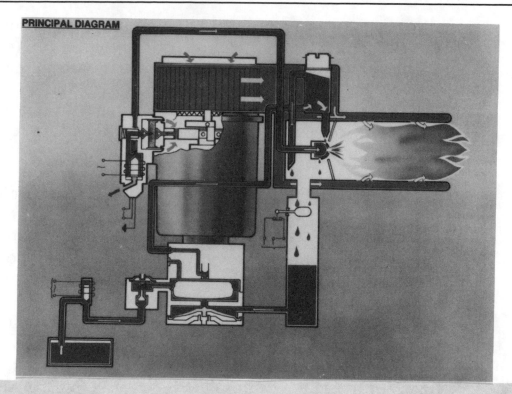

PRINCIPAL DIAGRAM

Schematic: European Burner Using Babington Atomizer
Figure 10-3

efficiency. The uniform array of small fuel droplets (an improvement over high-pressure atomizing nozzles) can also produce extremely low levels of smoke and soot. The burner can start, run, and stop virtually smoke-free, eliminating the start-up and shut-down transient particulate emissions associated with conventional oil burners.

Fuel oil that is not atomized after passing over the sphere is returned to the burner fuel supply. This flow of oil on the outside surface of the atomizer allows the burner to use fuels that contains impurities without "nozzle plugging" problems that are often encountered with low-input burners that use pressure—atomizing nozzles with very small oil passages. After the fuel oil is atomized, it is mixed with combustion air that is supplied by an air blower.

These oil burners can fire at fuel-input rates as low as 0.004 gallons per hour (550 Btu per hour), but they can also fire up to more than 1.2 gallons per hour. This will allow for many new uses for heating oil in the home and in new market sectors such as in appliances for recreational vehicles and larger-sized boats. New applications include small space heaters, refrigerators, oil powered space cooling equipment, efficient domestic hot water generation, oil-powered ovens and cook tops, clothes drying, and oil lighting fixtures.

The reduced firing rates can be important efficiency advantage over conventional pressure atomizers. Chapter 7 discusses reduced fuel-nozzle size as one method for improving system efficiency. While conventional nozzles cannot reliably operate below 0.5 gallons per hour, the Babington atomizer can substantially lower the operating range of burners. This is especially important in new energy-efficient homes and condominiums that have low rates of heat loss. The burner input can be more accurately sized for the actual heating load.

Variable fuel firing rates are another advantage over conventional burners. The burner input can be easily selected to match the exact heating needs of boilers, furnaces, and water heaters. This can improve heating system efficiency and allow the firing rate to vary to meet the changing space heating and domestic hot water needs of the house.

The combination of reduced and variable firing rates can produce ultra-high efficiency oil heating equipment and continue oil heat's role as the most efficient energy source now available for home use.

Another important feature of the new air-atomizing burners is their ability to operate soot-free over a wide range of firing rates.

The burner performance is minimally affected by changes in fuel quality, and this is an important advantage over conventional pressure-atomizing burners, especially at the lower burner input rates. Pressure-atomizing nozzles typically require finer filtration to prevent nozzle clogging. The Babington burner, however, has the fuel oil

European Burner Using Babington Atomizer

Figure 10-4

flowing over the outside of the atomizer where particles in the fuel will not adversely affect the droplet spray. Fuel impurities simply flow over the atomizer without degrading its performance.

Several oil burners using the Babington atomizer have been developed that cover a wide range of firing rates. Three of these are presented here.

Figure 10-4 shows the oil burner using the Babington atomizer that is sold in Europe firing from about 0.2 to 0.6 gallons per hour, it could be used as a replacement burner for conventional boilers and furnaces. The flame size can easily be adjusted in the field with a screwdriver while the burner is operating. The firing rate can be varied until the desired flue—gas temperature is reached for maximum efficiency.

A mini-burner has also been developed that produces a smaller flame. This hand-held model is shown in Figure 10-5. This burner can allow designers to produce a new

Babington Mini-Burner

Figure 10-5

generation of small and highly efficient space heaters, water heaters, and other home appliances. The burner could be used to power advanced central heating appliances or local zone heaters powered by home heating oil.

Figure 10-6 shows a micro-burner that can use home heating oil to power absorption type refrigerators and other home appliances that require very low fuel firing

Babington Micro-Burner

Figure 10-6

Oil-Fired Compact Refrigerator (500 Btu per Hour)

Figure 10-7

rates. One example of such a device is the prototype oil-powered compact refrigerator shown in Figure 10-7. This appliance uses only 550 BTU per hour (about one gallon of fuel every 11 days) and operates without smoke or combustion odors. A larger commercial—sized prototype refrigerator using the same principle has also been developed for the U.S. Army. The same burner technology could be used in efficient space cooling equipment powered by home heating oil.

Other oil-powered equipment designs have been demonstrated using the Babington atomizer concept. One of these is a direct—fired instantaneous domestic hot water heater with an efficiency above 90%. The water is contained inside of coils that are directly fired by the Babington burner. In addition to high on-cycle efficiency, the off-cycle heat losses can be much less than conventional direct-fired storage heaters. This has the potential to become the most efficient domestic hot water heater available to homeowners.

The Babington burner has been applied to a specially designed convection oven that produces very uniform temperatures. The oil burner operates soot-free and without combustion odors. The prototype oil-powered oven,

Oil-Fired Convection Cooking Oven

Figure 10-8

developed for the U.S. Army, is shown in Figure 10-8. Larger-size ovens using the same principles are also possible.

The Babington burner was also developed to operate a cook top without smoke or combustion odors. This is a battery-powered unit that is well-suited for boats, recreational vehicles, and other outdoor uses. Its use could be expanded to residential cooking in the future. Figure 10-9 is again a working prototype built for the U.S. Army.

Babington burners have been used in tent heaters that operate automatically and cleanly using the smaller flames produced by the air-atomizing oil burners (see Figure 10-10). These heaters could be modified for residential use to produce highly efficient zone heaters powered by oil. Fuel oil supply could be safely distributed to reduced-size heaters located in various parts of the house. This type of oil heating unit would be an improvement over wood stoves and other low-cost "back-up" energy sources that are often used in electrically heated homes to offset the high heating costs. An alternative market would be do adapt these small space heaters for use in heating large highway tractor truck cab heating. Environmental regulations are beginning to be established in several states that will stop these trucks from idling for long time

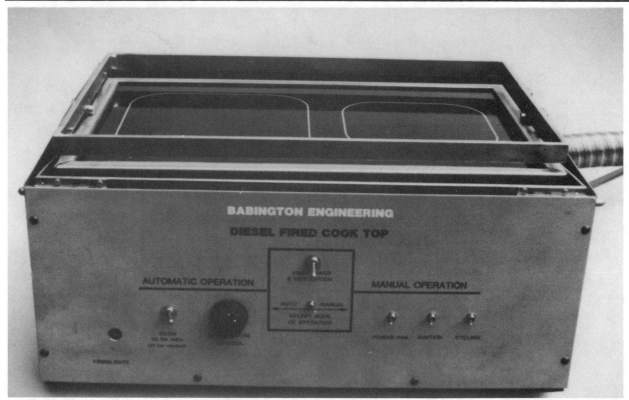

Prototype Oil Fired Cook Top

Figure 10-9

Prototype Oil Fired U.S. Army Tent Heater

Figure 10-10

periods at highway rest stops to provide cab heat. This is potentially a very large market.

Lighting equipment using the Babington atomizer has also been developed. The atomizer was modified to generate very small fuel droplets that form an aerosol. This finely atomized fuel oil is burned on a mantle to produce a very intense source of light. This capability demonstrates the wide range of new applications for fuel oil that could be available in the future.

The Babington burners could also produce highly efficient and economical clothes drying equipment powered by home heating oil. This is better than electric drying because it produces higher efficiency, lower operating costs, and reduced air pollutant emissions, when all the emissions from the central power plant are considered.

The combination of the smaller and cleaner oil flame offered by the Babington atomizer produces many new opportunities for the efficient and economical use of home heating oil.

Most of the Babington oil burning equipment is in an advanced working prototype stage and is not now available to homeowners. The European oil burner is not available in the U.S. Many of the oil-powered equipment advances discussed here are being considered for use by the U.S. Armed Forces to meet their energy needs in field operations, where a single fuel, distillate fuel oil, is the fuel of choice. As these new oil-burner advances are developed for other markets, it is possible that their production may be expanded so that they will be available to homeowners.

Brookhaven National Laboratory (BNL) Fan-Atomized Oil Burner

Another air-atomizing oil burner is now under development by the United States Department of Energy at Brookhaven National Laboratory. The BNL oil burner also uses an air-atomizing nozzle to produce the following advances: fuel firing rates below 0.25 gallons per hour, low smoke and nitrogen oxides formation, and a simplified design that uses the same air blower for atomization and combustion. The goal is to develop a burner design that is small and compact, burns at very high efficiency, and can be built at a lower cost than conventional oil burner models.

This burner is based on many years of combustion research at BNL. Preliminary tests of the first prototypes of the new burner are very promising, with very low smoke production at start-up and shut-down. In addition, the nitrogen oxide levels are less than half of those achieved by for conventional oil burners.

All of the potential applications discussed with the Babington technology also apply to the BNL burner concept. Brookhaven has submitted a Patent Disclosure for the new burner, and the development and testing of the prototype continues.

10.3 Advanced Oil Heat Systems

The advanced oil burners that are being developed, when combined with new controls and exhaust-gas vents, will produce a new generation of highly efficient and clean burning oil heating **systems**. The word **system** is used because these units will not simply be burners, boilers, venting equipment, and other components that are joined together in the field. Instead, all the components will be engineered and packaged together for optimum interaction of the parts for maximum efficiency. These oil heat systems of the future will use the best technology ever available.

Advanced oil burners that feature low firing rates, ultra-high efficiency, and the lowest air emissions possible will convert fuel oil into heat energy. Highly efficient boilers and furnaces that will be redesigned to take advantage of the new low-input oil burners will absorb the heat energy from the hot combustion products and transfer the heat to the circulating warm air or hot water in the thermal distribution system. Advanced features will include reduced size, low-mass heat exchangers with rapid warm-up and reduced off-cycle heat losses, and highly efficient zoned distribution of the heat within the house. Small space heaters at several locations within the house may also be possible. These can reduce installation costs (less piping and duct-work) and improve comfort and efficiency with no distribution heat loss. Advanced exhaust methods such as power side-wall venting will reduce system costs, improves installation flexibility, and increase the overall efficiency of the heating **system**. New control devices such as the FQI will produce immediate attention in trouble-shooting equipment problems and allow scheduling service calls only as needed. This will lower service department costs. In addition, advanced thermostats and space heating controls will reduce equipment operating hours by applying available microprocessor technology to produce optimum operation of the space-heating, water-heating, and related equipment contained within the integrated heating, ventilating, and air-conditioning (HVAC) **system**.

Integrated **systems** can be developed that produce space heating, air conditioning, water heating, heat storage, exhaust venting, house ventilation, air filtration, and heat recovery all from a single central HVAC system. Figure

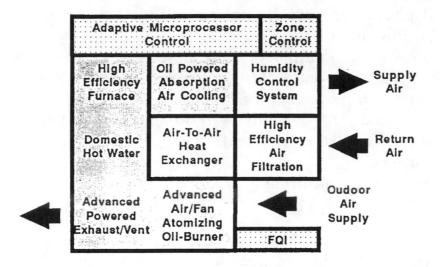

Schematic Of Integrated Oil HVAC System

Figure 10-11

10-11 is a schematic of one concept of an integrated HVAC system.

While these advanced oil heat systems are not available now, they will offer may advantages over conventional equipment designs in the future.

- Higher efficiency and lower operating costs.
- Improved reliability and lower service costs.
- Improved comfort.
- Lower air emissions.
- Lower installed costs
- Advanced controls for peak operating efficiency and improved reliability of the heating system.
- An improved image of oil heat as a modern energy source for homes.

Boilers and furnaces will be completely redesigned for the much smaller flames produced by the advanced oil burners. Prototype boilers have been demonstrated that are less than one-tenth the size of conventional boilers. This offers many efficiency and cost advantages:

- Higher efficiency through reduced jacket and distribution heat losses
- Lower-cost equipment (less materials are needed)
- Boiler rooms may not be needed and the heating units can be installed in the heated space. In some cases reduced-size units will replace a central heater and allow separate heating zones with separate burners.
- Improved comfort and improved economics.

Low-mass boilers are now available that can operate as a **system** with reduced heat losses (see Chapter 3). The future generation of oil heating equipment featuring mini-burners and micro-burners offer a drastic improvement over conventional heating system design. Figure 10-12 is one example of a mini-boiler that is fired by an air-atomizing oil burner at 0.25 gallons per hours. This can produce a peak heat output of 30,000 Btu per hour which can provide adequate space heat for most new energy-efficient houses.

Low Firing Rate Oil Fueled Mini-Boiler (0.25 gph)

Figure 10-12

Highly efficient mini-furnaces can also be designed that effectively use the smaller heat output produced by the new air—atomizing oil burners. The prototype oil-powered tent heater developed for military use could be adapted in the future for local space heating in homes.

Advanced exhaust methods including power side-wall venting are now being applied to oil heating equipment. These new venting designs can allow many new oil system designs. The exhaust temperatures will be much lower than today's boilers and furnaces and the exhaust gases will be safely vented from the house.

The FQI and other equipment control advances will be an important part of advanced oil heating equipment of the future. Side-wall venting requires that the burner operate very cleanly to avoid odors and smoke production. The FQI permits accurate burner adjustments and can produce a warning signal if the burner adjustment varies. This assures efficient and clean combustion that is important for the new generation of heating systems.

Integrated systems that supply all the heating, ventilating and air conditioning needs for the house offer many benefits. A single heat storage source can supply space and water heating, and efficiently use recovered heat from air conditioner operations and other heat generating sources such as solar collectors. Outdoor air for ventilation can be preheated by the HVAC module using air-to-air heat exchanges (with the warm exhaust air) and additional heat (if needed) from the heat storage device in the HVAC system. This allows the highest overall efficiency for the HVAC system by using all forms of heating produced in the house and recovered in the heat storage device.

10.4 When Will It Happen?

The equipment advances discussed in this section are in varying stages of development. Some are in the testing and demonstration stages. It is possible that some of these advances will be available to homeowners in the near future.

Advanced air-atomizing oil burners have been manufactured and tested over the past several years. Mini—and micro-oil—burners with very low firing rates have been successfully tested and are now being developed for military uses.

Venting system advances are taking place in oil-heated homes as power side-wall venting gains acceptance in new construction and in conversion of electric heated homes. Work at Brookhaven National Laboratory and other research institutes will help to establish guidelines for new venting methods in the near future. These are an important part of advanced oil heating equipment.

New control devices including the Flame Quality Indicator are in the process of field testing and will be available to homeowners in the near future. The FQI is now being field tested in 100 homes by a DOE-licensed manufacturer, and discussions with other manufacturers are ongoing. Other control advances, such a microprocessor controls for space and water heating, are now available with some oil heating equipment. As heating **system** designs become more popular, advanced computer controls will be used more frequently.

Integrated systems that supply all the heating, ventilating and air conditioning need from a single unit are not commercially available at the present time. The technology is available, however, to produce these **systems**, which may become more common in the next decade.

10.5 The Oil Heat House of the Future

We have seen that many heating-oil equipment advances are now available as prototypes and test models. These advanced technologies can be combined to produce an "OIL HEAT HOUSE OF THE FUTURE" that can demonstrate the many advantages of home heating oil and how it can be an important part of home energy use in the future. The oil equipment advances that could be included are:

- **Space Heating**—using air-atomizing oil burners in highly efficient advanced central boilers or furnaces or reduced size space heaters.
- **Hot Water Heating**—using the air-atomizing mini-oil burners in a highly efficient water heater (90%), or as part of an advanced efficiency space and water heating system.
- **Cooking**—using the air-atomizing oil burners to power ovens and cook tops with small clean-burning oil flames.
- **Refrigerators**—using air-atomizing micro-burners to power an absorption cycle unit.
- **Air Conditioning**—using the same technology applied to the oil-powered refrigerator to produce space cooling that can compete with electric—powered air conditioning equipment.
- **Outdoor Lighting**—using the air-atomizing burner principles.
- **Electric Power Generation**—using cogeneration a small oil-fired diesel engine produces the electricity for appliances used in the home. The system also produces heat, which can be used directly for space and water heating. The energy in the fuel oil is used in one form or another to satisfy all of the home's energy needs. A prototype cogeneration unit was tested at Brookhaven National Laboratory in 1991 (see Figure 10-13). The combined efficiency (electric and heat outputs both considered) was determined to be 92.6% (see Figure 10-14).

Applying the many oil heat technology advances to produce a highly efficient oil heat house of the future would be important for several reasons. It demonstrates important oil heat equipment advances that are now under development. It shows that home heating oil will continue to be a competitive, efficient, and clean home energy source in the future. It demonstrates that the role of home heating oil can increase in the future to include cooking, refrigeration, space cooling and other home energy needs by applying advanced technologies. It proves that oil heat is not outdated as new advances are constantly under development that can revolutionize the performance and efficiency of home heating equipment.

Intelligen Energy Systems 5kw Oil-Fired Cogenerator

Figure 10-13

Cogenerator Overall Efficiency Versus Load

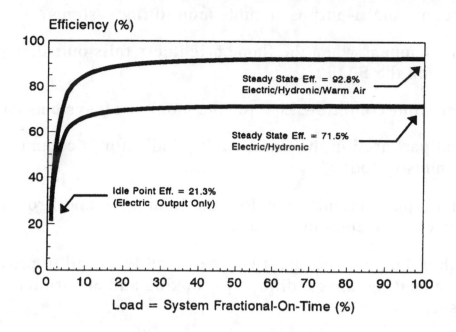

Figure 10-14

QUESTIONS

10-1.   What are multi-purpose remote monitoring systems?

10-2.   What happens when the flame brightness falls outside a preset range on the F Q I?

10-3.   Name four conditions that remote monitoring systems can detect.

10-4.   What part used in the flame quality indicator is common to the oil industry today?

10-5.   What type of atomization does the Babington and Brookhaven Labs experimental burner use?

10-6.   Within the next decade, it will be possibly for oil to provide home heating, air conditioning, cooking and electricity. True or false?

10-7.   The F Q I monitors the flame smoke number. True or false?

10-8.   In the future, a technician will be able to adjust the burner using a flame quality indicator. True or false?

Answers

CHAPTER 1

1-1.   1. Higher efficiencies.
        2. Clean operation
        3. Low pollution emissions
        4. Improved reliability

1-2.   No, you cannot see a #1 smoke by eye.

1-3.   1. Draft
        2. Smoke
        3. CO_2
        4. Stack temperature
        5. Calculate efficiency

1-4.   Not less than 3 ft. and must be 2 ft. above any permanent structure within 10 ft.

1-5.   When moisture starts to condense in the flue gas or about 350 degrees

1-6.   False. Cold oil increases the oil flow to the burner, also cold oil increases the size of fuel droplets produced by the nozzle. This requires additional excess air to burn cleanly.

1-7.   False. Too much chimney draft can lower system efficiency.

1-8.   1. On-cycle flue heat loss
        2. Off-cycle flue heat loss
        3. Jacket heat loss from boiler or furnace casing
        4. Distribution heat loss
        5. Infiltration heat loss from cold outdoor air flowing into the building

1-9.   True

1-10.   True

1-11.   True

1-12.   Annual fuel utilization efficiency. An estimate of on-cycle and off-cycle losses used to rate the overall efficiency of new heating equipment over an average heating season for "typical" operating conditions.

1-13.   True

1-14.   Removes the hot exhaust gases from the heating appliance safely

1-15.   True

1-16.   Installed or tuned up

1-17.   If the draft is set too high, too much combustion air can flow to the burner and the efficiency will be lower. Also, settings resulting in excess draft will increase off-cycle heat losses from the boiler.

CHAPTER 2

2-1.   True

2-2.   True

2.3   True

2-4.   True

2-5.   Fuel oil vapor and combustion air

2-6.   Hydrogen and carbon

2-7.   Soot and smoke

2-8.   True

2-9.   True

2-10.   True

2-11.   "2"

2-12.   "2"

2-13.   True

2-14.   "1"

2-15.   "2"

CHAPTER 3

3-1.   Convection, conduction, radiation

3-2.   Off cycle heat losses increase and efficiency drops

3-3.   1. Economical operation
       2. Improved reliability
       3. Cleaner operation
       4. Customer satisfaction and retention after their investment in new oil heat equipment

3-4.   True

3-5.   The A F U E value

CHAPTER 4

4-1.   Natural, forced, induced

4-2.   1. Burner on cycle flue heat loss
       2. Off cycle heat loss
       3. Air infiltration heat loss

4-3.   True

4-4.   True

4-5.   5

4-6.   True

4-7.   It helps to control the chimney draft to produce a nearly constant draft over the fire

4-8.   1. Loose-fitting clean-out door at base of chimney
       2. Unsealed cracks around the flue pipe where it enters the chimney
       3. Opening between adjacent flue passages in chimney
       4. Cracks or openings in chimney wall
       5. Other appliances or fireplaces connected to furnace flue
       6. Furnace flue not extended to base of chimney

4-9.   Forced draft is the air pressure created by the oil burner's air blower, which supplies combustion air and pushes the hot exhaust gases out of the boiler or furnace. Induced draft is accomplished by installing a draft booster fan in the breech and it pulls flue gases through the furnace or boiler and pushes gases up and out chimney or stack.

4-10.
1. Chimney
2. Flue collector
3. Draft control (barometric damper)

4-11. True

4-12. It can create a negative pressure in the building and diminish draft. Also, in the extreme, can cause back-drafting of combustion gases into the living spaces of the home. Creating unsafe conditions which must be avoided.

CHAPTER 5

5-1.
1. Safety switch that prevents the burner from firing until draft is proven
2. Post purge controller that operates the fan after the burner cycle ends to remove residual combustion fuel and cools the nozzle
3. Secondary safety switch (spill switch) that senses a backup of exhaust gases and shuts down the burner

5-2.
1. To always remove all combustion gases
2. To produce a nearly constant draft for stable burner operation
3. To operate under all outdoor air temperatures and conditions
4. To handle flue gases at temperatures up to 550 deg. F or manufacturer specifications.
5. All of the above answers are true

5-3.
1. Reduction in vent related heat losses for improved efficiency
2. Reduced installation cost compared to conventional chimneys
3. Reduced service calls relating to chimney draft problems
4. Lower smoke and air pollution emissions

5-4.
1. Chimney lining and removal of barometric dampers
2. Power side-wall venting
3. Vent dampers recommended for some installation as a last resort

5-5. Yes

5-6. 1. Always remove all combustion exhaust gases
2. Produce a nearly constant draft for stale burner air-flow rates
3. Operate under all outdoor air temperature conditions
4. Resist wind effects
5. Handle flue gases at temperatures up to 550 degrees F or meet manufacturer's specifications
6. Resist acid attach (from condensed flue gases)
7. Maintain flue-gas temperature above the dewpoint
8. Survive for many years with minimal maintenance

5-7. 1. Reduction in vent-related heat losses for improved efficiency
2. Reduced installation costs compared to chimneys
3. More constant draft that does not vary with outdoor air temperature
4. High-efficiency oil heating equipment can be installed
5. Reduced service calls because chimney draft problems are eliminated
6. Lower smoke and air pollution emissions

CHAPTER 6

6-1. 1. Direct fired
2. Indirect water heater
3. Internal tankless coil
4. External tankless coil
5. Tankless coil with a storage tank

6-2. Direct-fired water heaters use a separate oil burner to heat water that is contained in a storage tank. Indirect water heaters use a heat exchanger to transfer heat from hot water or steam produced by an oil-fired boiler to a storage tank.

6-3. 1. On-cycle losses
2. Off-cycle losses through the flue
3. Jacket (or casing) losses

6-4. 1. Elimination of exhaust flue (and reduced off-cycle heat losses)
2. A separate oil burner is not needed
3. Longer lifetimes than direct-fired equipment
4. Higher efficiency (when installed with an efficient oil boiler)

6-5. False

6-6.   "4"

6-7.   False

6-8.   False

6-9.   True

CHAPTER 7

7-1.   How to install and properly adjust systems by using combustion testing the equipment for highest efficiency possible

7-2.   System efficiency is higher and annual fuel consumption is decreased

7-3.   The amount of excess combustion air that is supplied by the burner and by secondary air leakage

7-4.   1. High over fire draft
        2. Excess combustion air (opening the burner air shutter too wide)
        3. Secondary air leaks
        4. Worn or plugged fuel nozzle
        5. Cold oil
        6. Low oil pressure
        7. Oil nozzle spray pattern does not match burner air flow
        8. Problems with burner air handling parts
            A. Incorrect burner end cone
            B. Improper burner head adjustment
            C. Worn or dirty air handling parts
        9. Outdated oil burners

7-5.   True

7-6.   1. Hot air can escape through leaks in the ducts before reaching the house
        2. Heat can be lost through the walls of uninsulated ducts

7-7.   True

CHAPTER 8

8-1.   15%

8-2.   1. Combustion efficiency of the existing burner and heating unit
       2. Off-cycle heat losses of the existing heating unit
       3. Chimney design and draft control
       4. Nozzle size (before and after burner replacement)
       5. Burner adjustment (before and after replacement)

8-3.   True

8-4.   1. Use A F U E ratings to select a high-efficiency model
       2. Size the boiler or furnace properly
       3. Install the optimum fuel nozzle size
       4. Look at other heating system factors and minimize heat losses
       5. Always use combustion test equipment to adjust the burner

8-5.   True

8-6.   1. Reduced flue-gas condensation and chimney damage
       2. Less combustion gas spillage
       3. Reduced on-cycle and off-cycle heat loss for improved efficiency

8-7.   1. Efficiency improvement - higher A.F.U.E. of new equipment
       2. Improved reliability
       3. Reduced smoke, soot and air pollution
       4. Reduced heating costs

8-8.   True

8-9.   False. Note: Excessive flue condensation may be an indicator of future chimney problems and may point towards recommending relining.

CHAPTER 9

9-1.   Tank can be installed in an insulated enclosure with heat if needed

9-2.   True

9-3.   True

9-4.   True

9-5.   1. Use seamless duct materials whenever possible
      2. Design the ductwork for minimum distance between the furnace and the air registers to reduce the number of connections and total surface area of the ductwork
      3. Avoid running ducts through unheated areas of the house. Always insulate ducts passing through these parts of the house
      4. Be sure that all duct seams and joints are completely air tight
      5. Whenever possible, run the duct within the heated space so that duct heat losses are captured
      6. Carefully size ducts to reduce the heat loss, minimum surface area when possible

9-6.   True

9-7.   True

CHAPTER 10

10-1.   These systems provide for remote monitoring of fuel-tank levels, low-temperature conditions in the home, and burner lockout conditions

10-2.   The flame quality or excess air has changed to the point that the oil heating appliance should be serviced

10-3.   1. Low fuel level
      2. Flame lockout
      3. Low temperature in the home
      4. Flame quality. Note: This can easily be used with a remote monitoring system like SCUL-TEL

10-4.   Cad cell eye

10-5.   Air

10-6.   True

10-7.   False

10-8.   True